The Roots of Participatory Democracy

Democratic Communists in South Africa and Kerala, India

Michelle Williams

First published in 2008 by
PALGRAVE MACMILLAN™
175 Fifth Avenue, New York, N.Y. 10010 and
Houndmills, Basingstoke, Hampshire, England RG21 6XS
Companies and representatives throughout the world.

PALGRAVE MACMILLAN is the global academic imprint of the Palgrave Macmillan division of St. Martin's Press, LLC and of Palgrave Macmillan Ltd. Macmillan® is a registered trademark in the United States, United Kingdom and other countries. Palgrave is a registered trademark in the European Union and other countries.

ISBN-13: 978–0–230–60640–1
ISBN-10: 0–230–60640–7

Library of Congress Cataloging-in-Publication Data

Williams, Michelle, 1969–
    The roots of participatory democracy : democratic communists in South Africa and Kerala, India / Michelle Williams.
        p. cm.
    Includes bibliographical references and index.
    ISBN 0–230–60640–7
        1. Communist Party of India (Marxist) 2. South African Communist Party.
    3. Communist parties—Case studies. 4. India—Politics and government—1977–
    5. South Africa—Politics and government—1994– I. Title.

JQ298.C62W56 2007
324.254'075—dc22   2007047141

A catalogue record for this book is available from the British Library.

Design by Newgen Imaging Systems (P) Ltd., Chennai, India.

First edition: June 2008

10   9   8   7   6   5   4   3   2   1

Printed in the United States of America.

For my parents, Barbara and Richard Williams

Contents

Tables

Terms and Acronyms

Kerala

AITUC	All-Indian Trade Union Congress (CPI-affiliated)
BJP	Bharatiya Janata Party
CDS	Center for Development Studies
CITU	Center of Indian Trade Unions (CPI(M)-affiliated)
Congress	Indian National Congress Party
CPI	Communist Party of India
CPI(M)	Communist Party of India (Marxist)
CPI(M-L)	Communist Party of India (Marxist-Leninist)
CSP	Congress Socialist Party
DCM	Documents of the Communist Movement of India
DS	Development Society
GOI	Government of India
GOK	Government of Kerala
INTUC	Indian National Trade Union Congress (Congress-affiliated)
IRTC	Integrated Rural Technology Center
KSKTU	Kerala State Karshaka Thozhilali Union (CPI(M)-affiliated agricultural union)
KSSP	Kerala Sastra Sahitya Parishad (People's Science Movement)
LDF	Left Democratic Front (CPI(M)-led coalition)
UDF	United Democratic Front (Congress-led coalition)
Crore	10 million
Grama Sabhas	People's assemblies or village councils
Panchayats	Rural municipalities

South Africa

ANC	African National Congress
Alliance	ANC, SACP, COSATU, and SANCO
PB	SACP's Polit Bureau
CC	SACP's Central Committee
CNETU	Council of Non-European Trade Unions

COSATU	Congress of South African Trade Unions
CPSA	Communist Party of South Africa
CST	Colonialism of a Special Type
DP	Democratic Party
FOSATU	Federation of South African Trade Unions
GEAR	Growth, Employment, and Redistribution Strategy
GNU	Government of National Unity
ICA	Industrial Conciliation Act (1924)
ICU	Industrial and Commercial Workers Union
IFP	Inkatha Freedom Party
LRA	Labor Relations Act
MDM	Mass Democratic Movement
MK	Umkhonto we Sizwe (Spear of the Nation)
NACTU	National Council of Trade Unions
NCASA	National Cooperative Alliance of South Africa
NEC	ANC's National Executive Committee
NEDLAC	National Economic Development and Labor Council
NEUM	Non-European Unity Movement
NFA	National Framework Agreement
PAC	Pan Africanist Congress
PEC	SACP's Provincial Executive Committee
PWC	SACP's Provincial Working Committee
RDP	Reconstruction and Development Program
SACP	South African Communist Party
SACPO	South African Coloured Peoples Organization
SACTU	South African Congress of Trade Unions
SADF	South African Defense Force
SAFTU	South African Federation of Trade Unions
SAHRC	South African Human Rights Commission
SAIC	South African Indian Congress
SANCO	South African National Civics Organization
SAP	South African Police
SATUC	South African Trade Union Council
TLC	Trades and Labor Council
TUCSA	Trade Union Council of South Africa
UDF	United Democratic Front (1980s mass formation in South Africa)

General

PB	Polit Bureau
CC	Central Committee (of Communist Parties)
COMINTERN	Communist International (Third International)
CPC	Communist Party of China
CPGB	Communist Party of Great Britain
CPSU	Communist Party of Soviet Union
HDI	Human Development Index

IMF   International Monetary Fund
ILO   International Labor Organization
NGO   Non-Governmental Organization
WB   World Bank
WTO   World Trade Organization

Preface

It is 8 A.M. and the streets of Alexandra Township[1] are alive with the rhythm of thousands of marchers moving to the sounds of liberation-era songs such as "I am a communist...." Warmed by the rising sun on the chilly winter morning, township residents come out of their tidy but overcrowded dwellings to join in the boisterous singing of the passing marchers. The atmosphere is jubilant. The buzz in the air makes one feel like something significant, something good, is happening. The General Secretary of the South African Communist Party (SACP) is leading the march, flanked by provincial leaders and Central Committee members. The jubilant atmosphere is befitting such a high-level delegation. The march winds its way through the narrow, maze-like streets of the bustling township, announcing to everyone that the "leadership" has arrived.

After two hours of parading through the streets, the marchers congregate at the Community Center for a public forum. In the packed hall the leaders give speeches popularizing the Financial Sector Reform Campaign, which this event is launching. The speeches are followed by the event everyone has been waiting for: the residents get a chance to tell their leaders personally about their problems and complaints. The jubilant mood of the street has now become heavy with discontent. The dissatisfaction of residents is palpable and they have no problems expressing their unhappiness to their leaders, demanding that the government—which the SACP is indirectly part of—deliver on the promises of a better future for all. After an hour of taking scathing comments from the audience, the general secretary closes the proceedings with a promise that the complaints have been noted and will ultimately inform their final report. The meeting closes with more singing and dancing, bringing the event full circle.

After this mass event, the national campaign to reform the financial sector shifts gears and primarily focuses on high-level negotiations and government forums. The mass event was organized from above to encourage and demonstrate support for a state-led transformation process that would—it was promised—trickle down to the residents.

Five thousand miles away, and in stark contrast to the leader-led mass event in South Africa, the Communist Party in Kerala is also busying itself with community residents. At 2 p.m. in the hot, sweltering heat of the mid-day sun in the lush region of Mararikulam, Kerala, 19 women congregate for their weekly meeting

under the shade of the jackfruit trees in the empty field next to their homes.[2] Next to the meeting in the open space children play, taking a break from the stifling heat every now and again by venturing into the shade to sit next to their mother or grandmother for a few minutes before they return to their play. The rhythm of the meeting is one of familiarity, of regularity. The mood seems to say that there is nothing exceptional going on at this meeting. The business of the day is to discuss with local Communist Party of India (Marxist) (CPI(M)) activists the progress of the group's economic activities and the need for more training. The group had formed two years earlier, when a group of women with the support of Communist Party activists decided to form a women's neighborhood group. In the beginning their primary activity was savings and loans. The group quickly became more ambitious and began a micro-production unit harvesting vegetables. The women explain how the Communist Party activists provided training and linkages with the local government institutions and helped the group initiate proper bookkeeping methods and records of meetings and accounts. The activists also encouraged the women to talk about problems in their villages from social, political, and economic issues to environmental concerns. The women proudly tell how these weekly discussions helped them become a very vocal and successful force in their village assemblies. One of their achievements was the construction of a road in their village.

The purpose of this meeting is to enlist party activists' help in setting up local markets to sell their vegetables. After an hour and a half of discussions the meeting adjourns and everyone disappears back to their daily routines. After the meeting the party activists and local officials managed to get the local government to set up a temporary produce market for the micro-production units sprouting up in the area.

These vignettes from my fieldwork in South Africa and Kerala capture the deep involvement of both the SACP and CPI(M) in the lives of ordinary citizens. In both South Africa and Kerala the centrality of the Communist Parties in the political arena has helped shape the degree to which subordinate classes engage the state and demonstrates the crucial role political parties play in organizing civil society. The vignettes also capture crucial differences in the parties' political projects. Instead of documenting similar efforts at implementing a common vision of radical, democratic, egalitarian politics, my field notes tell a story of divergent political practices. After discovering that these two parties share a similar understanding of "socialist democracy" grounded in participatory democracy, I expected to find convergence in their efforts to realize their vision. Their extraordinary ideological renewal, after all, showed that these two parties did not accept the inevitability of neoliberal triumphalism prescribing flexible labor markets, privatizing state assets, and deregulating markets nor were they abandoning radical alternatives as a response to the Soviet Union's failures. Having traversed the difficult road of ideological renewal, I, therefore, expected to find similar efforts at operationalizing their visions. Much to my surprise I did not find a convergence in their practices. The SACP has tended to emphasize state-led development that enlists mass actions and high-profile events, while the CPI(M) has given much emphasis to society-led development enlisting local-level capacity building and empowerment.

Some might ask, given the failure of twentieth-century socialism, what is the significance of the political practices of two communist parties in the Global South? Studying the political trajectories of these two parties highlights the centrality of political parties in effecting economic and political development and, thus, provides insight into the possibilities of egalitarian, democratic alternatives in the twenty-first century. While political parties are crucial actors in the political arena, their role in development has been a secondary interest for many scholars of development, who have tended to focus on the role of the state (e.g., Evans, 1995; Kohli, 2005). States' goals and visions of development, however, are often defined by political parties representing a multitude of interests in society. Moreover, the Global South—from Venezuela to Brazil from Kerala to South Africa—is becoming the epicenter for creative challenges to the neoliberal development paradigm. These challenges are not uniform and tidy experiments, nor do they occur at a particular level of engagement. Rather they range from the national to the subnational, from the regional to the local and reflect the trials and tribulations thrown up from their particular societies. Indeed it is because of this variation and creativity that we have much to learn from these efforts.

Lying at the southern tips of two immense and vastly different continents, South Africa and Kerala, India have captured the imagination of peoples across the globe. Activists, academics, and politicians of every political hue the world over have found inspiration from these two remarkable societies. In the early 1990s South Africa ended a near-century-long liberation struggle through a peacefully negotiated settlement between the apartheid regime and the African National Congress-led (ANC) liberation struggle. Remarkably, and unlike many transitions from colonial rule to democratic governments, the erstwhile oppressors were not forced to leave, but rather were accepted as an integral part of the reconstruction of the new nation. Across the Indian Ocean, late twentieth-century Kerala defied Western development models by achieving indicators of physical quality of life and human development[3] that compare favorably with those of "developed" nations despite its low per capita income levels and slow economic growth. At the core of these remarkable achievements in both South Africa and Kerala have been indefatigable commitments to the merits and importance of democratic politics that seek to empower ordinary citizens to participate in the developments of their societies. What passes unnoticed by most admirers, however, is the fundamental roles played by the Communist Parties in these achievements.

With the collapse of the Soviet Union and the ascendance of capitalist globalization, democratic and socialist forces around the world have found it difficult to envision genuine alternatives that seek economic and social justice, environmental sustainability, and the empowerment of ordinary people. Many Left political parties were forced to engage in a process of ideological and practical reorientation, having to account for the failures of socialist visions around the world and the undemocratic nature of Soviet-style state socialism. The implications of the eclipse of Soviet socialism catalyzed communist parties to reexamine their dyed-in-the-wool ideologies and practices. For many parties, the challenge led to an accommodation with capitalism and a complete abandonment of socialist visions. For some parties,

however, the dramatic changes provided an opportunity for the rejuvenation of radically democratic socialist visions grounded in local conditions and practices.

The South African Communist Party and the Communist Party of India (Marxist) in Kerala are two parties that not only commanded strong and growing bases of support, but also met the challenges of the late twentieth century by creatively engaging their ideological foundations as well as their practices and methods of translating these aspirations into reality. Both parties envisioned *socialist*, not social, democracy, by which I mean a transcendent vision that goes beyond capitalism.[4] Indeed, they were navigating paths between Western social democracy and Soviet-style socialism that placed participatory democracy within representative institutions at the center of their socialist visions. Thus, the content of their new vision of socialist democracy represents a striking reversal of conventional wisdom that dismisses socialist experiments as anachronistic relics from a bygone era. Moreover, this challenge to conventional wisdom comes from two parties located in very different societies each with distinct paths to development, unique histories of political liberation, and divergent processes of class formation.

The SACP and CPI(M) are extraordinary not just for arriving at similar visions of socialist democracy, but are among the few communist parties that had growing numbers of supporters during the 1990s and access to state power (for the SACP access to state power is through its strategic alliance with the African National Congress[5]—the dominant political party in post-apartheid South Africa; for the CPI(M) state power is through Left electoral coalition governments in which the CPI(M) is the dominant political party). Moreover, both parties share long histories of political involvement dating back to the 1920s and were at the center of political developments in their respective societies for the second half of the twentieth century. These two parties thus pioneered novel visions of socialist democracy through their deep involvement in the politics of the times.

While both parties have understood socialist democracy in a broadly similar manner in which pluralistic, participatory democracy is placed at the center, they have tended to emphasize different practices in their efforts to realize this vision. In particular, the SACP has tended to emphasize state-led development, while the CPI(M) has focused on society-led development. There are thus two stories being told. One is a story of discovery—the shared vision of socialist democracy articulated by these two parties is both remarkable and unexpected. The other is a story of divergence—the CPI(M)'s and SACP's contrasting efforts to implement their visions allow us to compare two different attempts at building elements of socialist democracy.

What does this story of convergence and then divergence mean for transformative politics and political party initiatives in the twenty-first century? How does it enhance our understanding of political sociology, especially with regard to the role of political parties and social movements in societal transformation? More specifically, what does it tell us about the relation among civil society, the state, and the economy in transformative politics? The answers to these questions constitute the central concern of this book.

By this point some readers may have asked how it is that I can compare the CPI(M) in Kerala, a state within a nation, with the SACP at the national level. Of

course, any study comparing political parties at two different levels of analysis—one, the SACP, at the national level, and the other, the CPI(M), at the state level—must address the potential effects of the different structural positions in which the two parties are located. The CPI(M) is a dominant political party in a non-sovereign subnational unit, while the SACP is a subordinate alliance partner in a "sovereign" national state. Do these different locations set up varying constraints and possibilities for each party? At first glance, the different structural locations of national versus subnational seem to be paramount to any explanation of the different politics in the 1990s. However, a closer look at the actual structural conditions reveals that this seemingly enormous difference is of little consequence. While the government of Kerala certainly does not share the same power or face the same challenges as the government of South Africa given that it is a state government within India, India's federal structure devolves significant power, resources, and authority to the states. Moreover, the populations in the two places are roughly similar with South Africa registering approximately 44 million inhabitants and Kerala 32 million people, which is much closer than India's population of 1.2 billion inhabitants. More importantly, however, is the focus on Communist Parties—not the societies of South Africa and Kerala—which are quite comparable.

Reflecting the diversity of India, the organizational structure of the CPI(M) is largely a federal structure in which the state-level party has a great deal of autonomy. It is at the state level that practices and politics are played out. The CPI(M)'s Constitution specifically outlines the division of labor among the different tiers of the organization: the state-level structures are responsible for all developments within their respective states. This federal structure thus provides a great deal of autonomy to the state structures, allowing the Kerala CPI(M) the authority and power to respond to the conditions and demands of subaltern classes in Kerala. For the SACP the 1990s were marked by a high degree of unity, from top to bottom, as the SACP was rebuilding its structures. The SACP's unitary structure, which has become even more salient in the new millennium, thus makes a comparison between the SACP and the CPI(M) in Kerala feasible as the CPI(M)'s state structures have a similar distribution of powers as the national-level SACP. The CPI(M) in Kerala and the SACP at the national level are, therefore, comparable when looking at efforts to translate their ideological aspirations into reality.

I chose to study the SACP and CPI(M) for several related reasons. First, both parties survived the eclipse of Soviet communism and the ascendance of neoliberalism in the 1990s in remarkable and similar ways. Unlike many communist parties around the world, they did not abandon their commitments to socialism, but rather learned from the failures of the previous 80 years and sought to develop visions of socialist democracy. Second, both parties faced significant changes in their domestic conditions, which forced them to reimagine the way in which they conducted politics and related to their bases of support. Third, both parties share long histories of popular struggle, have strong links to robust mass-based civil societies and powerful labor movements, and have consistently remained at the center of politics for the second half of the twentieth century. Finally, both parties have been integrally involved in all the major political developments in their societies and have extensive written accounts chronicling their involvement. This commitment to written testimony has

left a great deal of primary data available for both parties, making it possible to piece together their histories and practices throughout the twentieth century.

This project was made possible by a range of funding sources. I received a two-year postdoctoral fellowship from the Mellon Foundation, which allowed me to revise the dissertation into a book manuscript. During graduate school I received funding at UC Berkeley from the Department of Sociology, the Graduate Division, the Dean's Office, the Center for African Studies, the Taussig Endowment Fund, and the Institute for International Studies. From beyond UC I received support from the American Institute of Indian Studies and the National Science Foundation. I am grateful to Luba Ostashevsky, my editor at Palgrave MacMillan Press, Joanna Mericle for her editorial support and advice, Sumitha Menon for her careful copy-editing, and Karin Pampallis for her comprehensive indexing.

My biggest intellectual debt of gratitude goes to Michael Burawoy, my dissertation chair. His intellectual imprint on this project will be clear to those familiar with his ideas. While his patience and encouragement helped carry me through this project, his intellectual rigor and commitment to teaching helped nurture my faith in the academic enterprise. Quite simply, I would not have had the courage or stamina to embark on or complete this project without his support. I also benefited immensely from the feedback from a number of other extraordinary academics at UC Berkeley: Kim Voss, Raka Ray, Peter Evans, Gillian Hart, and Michael Watts. The ways in which each of their ideas has shaped this study will also be clear to those familiar with their work. Each provided invaluable feedback on the entire manuscript at some stage. While Kim Voss has provided countless sessions of advice, one of the biggest rewards of working with her is the close friendship we have developed. Raka Ray, too, offered both immensely useful intellectual feedback and has become a friend. Peter Evans provided invaluable feedback and advice in the final stages of the project—his extraordinary capacity to think schematically challenged me to rework chapters that I had thought I had long completed.

For their advice and ideas I thank my three reading groups. One came at the beginning of the journey and helped clarify my thinking enough to send me into the field: thanks to Millie Thayer, Rachel Sherman, Teresa Gowan, Linus Huang, Bill Hayes, and Patricia Macias. The one that came at the end of the dissertation helped challenge me to clarify the way I expressed my ideas: thanks to Jenny Chun, Jeff Sallaz, Hua-Jen Liu, Ofer Sharone, Kerry Woodward, and Cinzia Solari. The one that came during my postdoctoral fellowship challenged me to refine my ideas in ways more appropriate for a book: thanks to Bridget Kenny, Shireen Ally, Irma du Plessis, and Kezia Lewins. I owe special thanks to Jenny Chun who has read more drafts than she or I care to remember and has been a constant support in the years during and after graduate school.

I would like to thank Neil Smelser for his encouragement, intellectual engagement, and personal friendship, which began long before I entered graduate school, Erik Olin Wright for feedback on the introduction, and Marcel Paret for helpful feedback and for the tables! Thanks to Geoff Gershenson, Jackie Cock, Patrick Heller, Sakhela Buhlungu, and Eddie Webster for their support at various stages.

Doing fieldwork in two foreign countries greatly expands the number of people to whom one owes a debt of thanks. I am indebted to the many people in the South

African Communist Party and Communist Party of India (Marxist) in Kerala who not only gave freely of their time, but also believed this project warranted access to their organizational structures and documents. In South Africa I owe special thanks to Vishwas Satgar, Mazibuko Jara, and the late Smiso Nkwayana. In Kerala I owe special thanks to K.N. Harilal, Jagjeevan, and M.P. Parameswaran. Without their generosity and trust, this project would not have been possible. I also thank the countless number of people on both continents who took time to meet with me, answer my incessant questions, and allowed me to interview them.

In South Africa I thank the Sociology of Work Unit at the University of the Witwatersrand in Johannesburg for providing me an institutional home during my fieldwork and Khayatt Fakier, Sarah Mosoetsa, Andries Bezuidenhout, and Shameen Govendar for making the institution a welcoming place. I have benefited from countless conversations with Vidhu Vedulankar, Devan Pillay, Langa Zita, Daryl Glaser, Ari Sitas, Saguna Gordhan, Zak and Anu Yacoob, and Karuna Mohan. Thanks to Sarah Ford and Paul James for providing me a home away from home and to Jim and Pat Robinson for acting as adoptive parents.

In Kerala I thank the Center for Development Studies and the American Institute for Indian Studies in Delhi for providing me institutional homes in India. I benefited from the many discussions with K.N Harilal, T.N. Seema, and Jagjeevan. I am grateful to Prema Nair for her friendship, extraordinary research assistance—my visits into communities were made possible thanks to Prema's assistance—and for her part in our failed attempt to make wine. Vanita and Chandan Mukherjee provided me both friendship and a sanctuary from the trials and tribulations of fieldwork in India.

While I am indebted to all the librarians and archivists I encountered in the archives I visited, I must specifically point out Padmanabhan of the CPI(M) Library in Thiruvananthapuram, Yasmin Mohamed of the Manuscripts and Archive department at the University of Cape Town, and Michelle Pickover of William Cullen Library at the University of the Witwatersrand for their generous assistance.

The process of writing was made much nicer thanks to the friendship of Annie Sugrue, Elsa Tranter, Janine Godfrey, Susana Wappenstein, Sarah Mosoetsa, Teresa Sharpe, and Lisa Ze Winters. Special thanks to Tanya Turneaure who has always provided a sanctuary of peace together with good friendship and hilarious laughs, to Lynnéa Stephen who taught me fundamental lessons about life and friendship, and to Elena Montoya who went well beyond her duties as a friend when she read the entire manuscript. I would also like to thank my sister, Tina, for being a rock on whom I often lean and my niece and nephews (Lexi, Tasso, Gavin, Cole, Conner, and Matthew) for constantly reminding me of the important things in life—laughter and play. Thanks also to Spyros, Steve, Lori, Ginger, Denny, and Meridee.

I owe special thanks to Vishwas Satgar for his indefatigable support and love during the last couple years of this project. He patiently listened to me while I figured out a story he knows well. His intellectual integrity and encouragement to tell it like I see it helped give me the tenacity to bring this project to completion. My greatest personal debt of gratitude is owed to my parents, Barbara and Richard Williams, who taught me to care about the world and nurtured my insatiable curiosity from an early age. It is their love and friendship in both my best and worst times that helped carry me through this long journey. It is to them that I dedicate this book.

Notes

1. Alexandra Township (or Alex as it is popularly called) is an apartheid-era township north of Johannesburg, which services the hyper-wealthy area of Sandton where some of South Africa's fantastically rich live and work. In contrast to the clean, tree-lined (and deserted) streets of Sandton, Alex is a bustling, densely populated township that is riddled with crime, high levels of poverty, and severe unemployment. The March was on July 21, 2001.
2. Women's Group Meeting, March 28, 2002.
3. Physical Quality of Life Index is a composite index of literacy, life expectancy, and infant mortality. Human Development Index is a composite of literacy, life expectancy, and income (George, 2005: 10).
4. For my understanding of social democracy I draw from Gustov Esping-Anderson's *Three Worlds of Welfare Capitalism* in which he emphasizes the role of parliamentary democracy to ameliorate conditions *within* capitalism.
5. After it returned to South Africa in 1990, the SACP formed a strategic alliance with the ANC and the Congress of South African Trade Unions (COSATU), which was later broadened to include the South African National Civic Organization (SANCO).

CHAPTER 1

Introduction: Hegemonic and Counter-Hegemonic Generative Politics

The late twentieth century was marked by an outpouring of scholarship hailing the arrival of a new politics that departed dramatically from the "old" political party model that characterized the twentieth century. The World Social Forum (WSF) in particular signified the culmination of a new era of political mobilizing that brought together activists and civil society organizations from the local to the global within one continuous, dynamic space (e.g., de Sousa Santos, 2006; Fisher and Ponniah, 2003; Mertes, 2004). This recent literature highlights the fact that under processes of neoliberal globalization, more and more people (especially the poor, disenfranchised, and landless) are exorcised from decision-making processes that directly affect the quality of their lives—from basic livelihood issues to the institutional allocation of resources. As a result, the literature has focused on social movement responses to the tremendous economic inequalities that divide the rich and the poor, the Global North from the Global South, tending to dismiss political parties as anachronistic relics from a bygone era. The focus on social movements, however, overlooks the continued importance of political parties in shaping the contours of political and economic development. This book, thus, looks at the role political parties play in fostering patterns of democratic, egalitarian development.

While perhaps not capturing the imagination of the global Left, political parties in many peripheral countries of Asia, Africa, and Latin America are important political actors, engaged in coordinating the panoply of voices into coherent political projects using many of the same practices as the celebrated global social movements. Unlike social movements, however, political parties do not focus their energy primarily on protest politics, but engage in generative politics in order to build new institutions and channels for mass participation. Thus, in the search for "another world" some political parties, and more surprisingly some communist parties, in the Global South have revisited their ideological foundations and developed

dramatically new understandings of party-civil society synergies that bridge participatory and representative democracy in both political and economic spheres. The activities of these parties are significant as they turn our attention from the level of global social movements to the level of local practice and reveal the vibrant role political parties can play in empowering people. The central question animating this study is why have some parties been more successful in engaging the state and civil society to initiate more equitable and democratic development?

The Communist Party of India (Marxist)'s (CPI(M)) and the South African Communist Party's (SACP) recent efforts in democratic transformation in Kerala and South Africa represent a challenge to the dominant wisdom permeating our thinking about twenty-first-century alternatives. Both parties have sought a politics that facilitates the capacity of ordinary citizens to participate in decision-making processes and have thus been at the forefront in pursuing a politics that engages the state in order to build new institutions and organizational strategies moored in participatory and representative democracy.[1] In Kerala the 1990s were marked by an extensive democratic decentralization campaign that included devolving significant financial and decision-making authority to lower tiers of government through participatory democratic institutions. In South Africa, the 1994 African National Congress (ANC) election victory ended the oldest liberation struggle on the continent and marked the beginning of the consolidation of a democratic South Africa that extended adult suffrage to the entire population and developed institutional mechanisms for participatory democratic politics.

In a global context in which political parties—and especially communist parties—are seen as anathema to dynamic social movements (e.g., de Sousa Santos, 2007; Holloway, 2002; Escobar, 1992; Klein, 2004), the efforts by the SACP and CPI(M) offer a powerful corrective to much of our scholarship on emancipatory politics. How do we understand political parties that are organizing and mobilizing in similar ways as global social movements? In this book, I undertake a comparative analysis that follows the CPI(M)'s and SACP's ideology and practices over the course of the 1990s. Drawing lessons from their experiences, I argue that democratic, emancipatory politics requires transforming the state and to do this requires political parties with deep roots in civil society.

Looking to two communist parties in the Global South might seem an unlikely place to find inspiration for theorizing the constituent elements of an egalitarian, democratic politics. Indeed, since the 1950s Western scholarship[2] on communism has painted a monolithic and devastating picture of the deleterious effects of communist parties, interested as it was in the Soviet Union's undemocratic and authoritarian control of the international communist movement (e.g., Claudin, 1975; Talmon, 1952; Selznick, 1952; Arendt, 1951; Marcuse, 1958). While the influence of this anticommunist genre of scholarship still bears its mark on academic literature, there have been studies interested in the implications of the collapse of the Soviet Union for socialist futures. For example, there have been studies on the causes and consequences of the demise of the Soviet Union (Miliband, 1991; Habermas, 1991; Hobsbawm, 1991), studies on the link between the fall of the Soviet Union and the expansion of neoliberalism (Eyal, 2002) as well as theoretical statements on the future possibilities of various

socialisms (Blackburn, 1991; Hobsbawm, 1991; Pierson, 1995; Panitch, 2001). There have also been studies locating the parties within broader studies of democratic transitions (e.g., Roberts, 1998), political party structures (e.g., Collier and Collier, 1991), and development initiatives (e.g., Sandbrook et al., 2007; Heller, 1999) as well as studies claiming a new type of politics that moves beyond the conventional structures of unions and parties (Holloway, 2002; Escobar, 1992; Klein, 2004).

Western scholarship that has looked at communist parties has focused on Soviet and European communist parties (e.g., Boggs and Plotke, 1980; Rabinowitch, 1978; Smith, 1983; Tarrow, 1967), largely ignoring communist parties in the Global South. In general, the rejuvenation of democratic socialist visions grounded in local conditions and democratic practices of actually existing communist parties have received little scholarly attention. Yet, it is these attempts to pursue democratic socialist alternatives in the Global South through synergies between political parties and civil society that is one of the most significant aspects of the contemporary political landscape.

The few accounts we do have from the Global South have often been penned by the participants themselves. Most books dealing with communist parties in the developing world are memoirs, written by participants, and, therefore, provide one-sided views, either sympathetic or hostile depending on which side of the political fence the author falls. There have been important contributions from both South Africa and Kerala on the politics of their societies and particular aspects of the Communist Parties' histories.[3] These studies have produced illuminating factual detail and important insights on aspects of the political conditions, historical events, and organizational histories. Despite these contributions there have been very few studies focusing exclusively, or even primarily, on the SACP's and CPI(M)'s historical trajectories. And there have not been any studies looking at communist parties that responded to the crises of twentieth-century socialism by returning to democratic visions of socialism and building party-civil society synergies. Yet, the efforts by the SACP and CPI(M) to construct democratic socialist alternatives in and through the current conditions provide tremendous opportunity to understand and theorize the role of political parties in the twenty-first century.

As an investigation of the role of political parties in social development in the Global South, this book addresses several interrelated scholarly debates. The first debate looks at the literature on political parties. This scholarship focuses on internal dynamics of political organization and allows us to clarify that organizations consist of competing factions of which there are three in this study: trade union, grassroots, and statist factions. This scholarship also focuses attention on the party's relation to its base of support and its practices of mass mobilizing and participatory organizing. The second more heated debate addresses scholarship on social movements where the tendency has been to dismiss political parties as inept and locate political action (i.e., oppositional politics) within the rubric of social movements. The literature on social movements does not help us understand how it is that some political parties organize and mobilize in similar ways to social movements. This scholarship, thus, turns our attention to the nature of politics (protest or generative politics). I address each literature in turn. I then conclude with an overview of the remaining chapters in the book.

Organizational Dynamics and Party Practices

A study focusing on political parties must deal first and foremost with the literature on the oligarchic nature of political organizations. The key point of departure is Robert Michels's *Political Parties* (1999 [1910]), which suggests that political parties, like most bureaucratic organizations, have an inherent, if unintentional, tendency to develop a growing divide between leaders and led to become increasingly conservative vis-à-vis goals and tactics and ultimately to become oligarchic (50, 79, 107, 335–38). Since Michels, there has been a vast literature posing the central question: why and when do organizations become oligarchic? Like Michels, this scholarship continues to see inherent laws governing the internal dynamics of the organization. For example, Alvin Gouldner (1955 and 1970) suggests that parties do not inevitably become oligarchic, but instead have inherent internal capacities to develop democratic visions. Similarly focusing on the internal dynamics, Piven and Cloward (1977) highlight the oligarchic nature and depoliticizing effects of formal political organizations. The problem with this literature is that it takes as its starting point inherent characteristics of political parties.

There have been important challenges to the focus on internal dynamics, which have argued that the historical genealogy and the broader social, political, and economic environments combine with the bureaucracy to determine the trajectory of an organization (e.g., Lipset, 1950; Lipset et al., 1956; Schorske, 1955). Drawing on Schorske's (1955) analysis of the importance of factions embedded in the larger political and economic contexts in the case of the German Social Democratic Party, this study argues that the balance of power among competing factions within parties directly affects their practices, and hence whether or not they become oligarchic. In this study, I pay particular attention to understanding how and why particular factions within the SACP and CPI(M) came to the fore at particular points in time.[4]

I have categorized the factions based on the particular understanding of who is the primary agent of change, which corresponds with a particular vision of societal development (e.g., modernization via industrialization or sustainable development via local-level initiatives). For example, in the SACP and CPI(M) there is a *trade union faction*, which sees the organized working class[5] as the crucial agent of change and holds a vision of national development through industrialization. A second faction, the *grassroots faction*, sees subaltern classes (unemployed, informal sector, *and* organized working class) as the primary agents of change and seeks development through local-level initiatives in economic and political fora in addition to a degree of industrial development. The grassroots faction questions the evolutionary growth path that ultimately leads to industrialization, and argues that not only is capitalism based on the continuation of inequality in the world system, but, and perhaps more importantly, the earth cannot sustain the consumption-based development model of the West. A third faction, the *statist faction* (mainly in the SACP[6]), sees state actors as the primary agents of change and, therefore, focuses its energy on using the state to create conditions for industrial development. The statist faction is most closely allied with political and economic elites and pursues state-led industrial development through synergistic relations between state actors and local capital.[7]

The political practices that link a party to its base of support can be grouped into two distinct types: mass mobilizing and participatory organizing. Mass mobilizing focuses on carefully orchestrated, high-profile, mass actions that attract the largest number of people possible, such as marches, demonstrations, and strikes. The populace is called on to demonstrate support for the leadership/party, who often make decisions on behalf of the citizenry. Leaders tend to have a hierarchical and instrumental relation to the base of support. This tradition gives much of the political process over to leaders and organizations who act on behalf of a citizenry, but is an effective practice for popularizing issues and gaining widespread visible support.

In contrast, participatory organizing reflects a more synergistic relationship between the party and the base of support and focuses on empowering the citizenry to meaningfully participate in political and economic arenas.[8] Here the emphasis is on educating and politicizing the citizenry through political education, party schools, seminars, workshops, and participation in local-level political and economic structures in an effort to empower subalterns to participate in social, political, and economic domains of social life. The primary emphasis is education and capacity building through concrete activity in political and economic fora. Participatory organizing is a long-term process, while mass mobilizing tends to be campaign based where leaders mobilize people for a specific outcome with participation ending when the campaign has achieved its goal. Participatory organizing seeks to institutionalize ongoing participation of the citizenry in the political and economic spheres and in their roles as consumers of public goods. While both forms of practices are utilized by political parties, trade unions, and civil society organizations, participatory organizing is especially important in promoting democratic politics.

While liberal political theorists argue that certain personality traits (i.e., "authoritarian" and "nondemocratic") have to be taken as given and the active participation of such people would be dangerous for the democratic political system (Pateman, 1999: 64), participatory organizing highlights that participation in a range of nongovernmental and governmental structures can foster the psychological qualities and a sense of political efficacy necessary for effective political participation. In this way, participatory organizing draws on a long tradition of theorists who argue that the experience of participation develops a "democratic personality" (e.g., Rousseau, John Stuart Mill, and G.D.H. Hall).[9] The liberal political tradition defines "participation" as voting for competing elites (e.g., Schumpeter, 1942), which contrasts markedly with a view of the individual evolving through participation in decision-making processes. In effect, participatory organizing reintroduces a fundamental precondition of participatory democracy: capable citizens who are able to effectively participate (i.e., ability to make decisions and implement them) in political and economic institutions that affect their lives.

The different practices of relating to the base are, then, used by the different factions in political parties. Political practices reflect ideas about the ways in which social organization can be changed and thus, either implicitly or explicitly, seek particular goals. For example, the trade union faction largely defines power in terms of numbers, leverage in terms of the working class's strategic location in the economy, and its *raison d'être* to secure the interests of the working class. It, thus, tends to emphasize practices that demonstrate its numerical support and ability to withdraw

labor and thus paralyze capital such as the strike and large public events. Because the trade union faction relies on working-class leverage, it tends to rarely see beyond protest politics enlisting mass mobilizing as it has been historically an effective means to secure working-class interests. This contrasts to the grassroots faction, which pursues sustainable local-level development and relies on the active participation of the citizenry in a variety of arenas.[10] It, therefore, tends to enlist participatory organizing by focusing on educating and building capacity for direct participation of subaltern classes—which include the unemployed, informal sector workers, and organized working class—in political and economic development. In contrast to the trade union faction, the grassroots faction cannot primarily rely on the leverage of popular classes—since they do not have the same leverage in the economy as the working class—but has to rely on the power subaltern classes can engender through joint participation and connection around alternative visions to the existing order— that is, by building counter-hegemony. The statist faction, by contrast, holds a state-led development vision, and, therefore, is interested in demobilizing both opposition and independent initiatives from subordinate classes. Rather, it seeks support from the citizenry for the state's development agenda and, therefore, tends to enlist mass mobilizing for propaganda purposes.

This focus on factions not only tells us a great deal about the internal dynamics of political parties, but also reminds us that political parties do not operate in a vacuum. Rather they are embedded in the political and economic milieu of their times and have concrete relations to different class actors. Indeed, one of the ways classes find their interests expressed in the political system is through political parties. Understanding the different factions within a political party, therefore, also reveals underlying party-class linkages. The trade union faction represents the interests of the working class, the grassroots faction is linked to subaltern classes, and the statist faction represents the state as a class actor and often has deep ties to local capital. Like Schorske, I, too, look to the broader social and political environment in which the SACP and CPI(M) operate and the particular organizational histories and characteristics of the parties to understand the balance of power among competing factions. I specifically draw attention to the varying party-class relations—and the balance of power among them—which helps account for the different politics of each party as the party-class nexus profoundly shapes the character of political projects. Like Barrington Moore's (1966) emphasis on the role of classes in the transformation into modern societies, I also look at the balance of power among dominant and subordinate classes, but shift the emphasis to include the paramount role of *party-class* linkages and show that different factions within parties reflect class interests. Understanding the internal dynamics and organizing practices of parties is paramount, but it is only part of the story. The way in which political parties relate to the state and civil society, and hence the nature of politics, is an equally important part of the story.

Generative Politics: Hegemonic and Counter-Hegemonic

Social movement scholarship has tended to (1) adopt a pessimistic view of political parties and (2) limit the scope of political action to "protest politics." On the first point,

the political process model of social movement scholarship has been strongly influenced by Michels's characterization of political parties' inherent tendency to become conservative and has, therefore, tended to dismiss all political parties as inept organizations that serve to demobilize popular energy. Perhaps the most influential exemplar of Michelsian scholarship in the social movements' literature is Piven and Cloward's *Poor People's Movements* (1977), which argues that formalized organizational structures depoliticize protest movements. Because windows of opportunity effecting tangible outcomes are short-lived, argue Piven and Cloward, protest movements are better served by spontaneous action than developed organizational structures. In other words, political action exists outside institutionalized political structures.

Also within the social movements' rubric has been a prolific literature contesting and challenging aspects of Michels's iron law (e.g., Gusfield, 1968; Garner and Zald, 1987), but not his pessimistic analysis of political parties. Most of this scholarship either looks at trade union or social movement organizations and not political parties (e.g., Jenkins, 1977; Voss and Sherman, 2000). The focus of these studies challenging Michels highlights the possibility for transformation after the entrenchment of oligarchy and conservatism, but none reintroduce the importance of political parties. This begs the question of how to explain the existence of *political parties* that have in certain instances defied Michels's pessimistic portrait and have remained at the center of transformative politics?

The roots of this pessimistic portrait of political parties, especially communist parties, can be traced back to the 1950s revelations of Stalin's atrocities, which seemed to only corroborate Michels's claims. At the 20th Congress of the CPSU in 1956 Kruschev revealed the magnitude of the horrors committed under Stalin. These revelations rocked the foundation for many people around the world, leaving profound doubt about the virtues of political parties. Moreover, in country after country were tales of failures by Left political parties in government who discovered the limitations of state power as pressures both from within and without restrained possibilities for transformation. State control, it was realized and eloquently articulated by Michel Foucault (1995 [1977]), was a major locus of power, but it was not the only site of power. Thus, while for much of the twentieth century political parties were seen to be a crucial actor in societal transformation, by the last quarter of the twentieth century the limitations (and dangers) of omnipotent political parties was patently clear.

As a response social movements exploded on the scene in the 1970s, and immediately began busying themselves with contesting the multiple spheres of power throughout society.[11] As a panoply of movements emerged, the notable characteristic of all of them was that each was organized around a specific theme or focus (e.g., community-level movements, ethnic, women's, ecology, antiwar), which tended to be local in orientation and specifically address issues germane to a particular constituency (Wallerstein, 1990: 52). The common thread across many movements was a shared rejection of the injustices of the global capitalist system and many responded by attempting to ameliorate the conditions in a particular area.[12] The movements also shared in the assumption that changes in advanced capitalism engendered new movement organizations, interpretive frames, and types of collective action (Touraine, 1981; Offe, 1985; Tarrow, 1990: 252).

While many Western social movements were successful at winning concessions in their particular areas of concern, they rarely posed direct challenges to the existing structure of economic and political power nor provided mechanisms to extend collective democratic control over the primary spheres of economic activity (Offe, 1990: 234–35, 245; Roberts, 1998: 33; Giddens, 1986: 13–16; Kitschelt, 1984). Rather, these movements were made of a multitude of subjects none of which served as a linchpin for an alternative social order or challenged entrenched structures of hierarchy and domination, a role traditionally assigned to socialist and communist parties. Moreover, political parties are the vehicle through which social actors can express their interests in the state. In general, however, social movement scholarship has failed to see these limitations. The fact that social movements can cohere into transforming society in conjunction with the efforts of political parties has been sorely overlooked by social movement scholars.[13] For example, much of the recent literature on the WSF celebrates the coming together of activists from across the globe to adumbrate the possibilities of "another world" (Fisher and Ponniah, 2003; de Sousa Santos, 2007; Mertes, 2004; Klein, 2004). Scholars, however, are quiet about the fact that the reason the WSF was first held in Porto Alegre was because the Brazilian Workers' Party (PT) governed both the city of Porto Alegre and the state of Rio Grande do Sul and thus created the ideal conditions for launching an alternative forum for movements to network and think together. The historical role of political parties to coordinate diverse interests into a transformative project and to express these interests in state institutions clearly continues to be as relevant today as it ever was.[14] Yet social movement theorists have tended to dismiss political parties as oligarchic and anachronistic forms of organizing.[15]

Ironically, as social movements continue to perceive political parties in a pessimistic light, some political parties have undertaken profound self-reflection and are seeking new ways of effecting societal transformation.[16] Unlike the 1960s and 1970s Italian experience in which political parties adapted to the challenge posed by social movements by co-optation and preemption (Tarrow, 1990: 251), in the 1990s certain political parties responded by linking up with and building on the strengths of organizations in civil society in an effort to renew a political project through party-civil society synergies. Social movement scholars' dismissal of political parties has blinded the field from recognizing important convergences between political parties and social movements and has narrowed the field's focus to oppositional politics.[17]

In addition to the pessimistic view of parties, social movement scholars have tended to reduce political action to oppositional politics and protest action.[18] While the field in general has tended to assume a protest politics orientation, in *Dynamics of Contention* (2001) McAdam, Tarrow, and Tilly have been the most systematic in theorizing and elaborating the mechanisms and processes that result in "contentious politics."[19] They define contentious politics to be fundamentally about claims made against a government and juxtapose contentious politics with the more common non-contentious politics (i.e., "ceremony, consultation, bureaucratic process, collecting of information, registration of events, and the like") (5). In general, social movement theorists locate efficacious political action in oppositional activities and cycles of contention.

While this focus on contentious politics is useful in understanding causal sequences of oppositional politics, it offers little insight into the dynamics of what

I call a generative politics that shifts from the defensive (or contentious) phase, and seeks to construct and develop new institutions and channels for mass participation.[20] I contrast generative politics to protest politics,[21] by which I mean a politics that aims to challenge or destroy an existing system of political and/or economic power.[22] Generative politics is neither inherently contentious nor is it simply institutionalized politics. Generative politics is about innovation in collective action that seeks to engender new political actors, organizations, and institutions. Like contentious politics it seeks to transform the social, political, and economic arenas. But unlike contentious politics' focus on claims against the state, generative politics primarily works through transforming the state and economy by developing new institutions. For this to happen, obviously, certain structural conditions must exist that allow for such changes. For one, generative politics assumes political parties have access to important sites of power that provide leverage to create new institutions. Most obviously, such sites ideally are located within state structures, but can also emerge in institutions of civil society. While NGOs, community-based organizations, and trade unions might also display generative qualities in that they too construct alternative institutions, I am specifically referring to the transformation of state power and thus define generative as a political concept that is linked to the use of state power.

Thus, protest and generative politics represent two distinct moments of political activity, each with its own logic, dynamics, and causal sequence. Protest politics tends to enlist mass mobilizing (e.g., high-profile, public events) as it primarily seeks to challenge existing systems of oppression and exploitation. Its goal is to win concession for specific demands. One of the unintended consequences of protest politics is that it creates robust institutions in civil society and a highly mobilized and politically minded citizenry. Thus, like generative politics, protest politics often results in new political formations. For protest politics, however, these formations are a secondary outcome of its primary goal of challenging the state around specific demands.

For generative politics the construction of new political actors, organizations, and institutions can take place in two ways. Generative politics can be either hegemonic or counter-hegemonic. By hegemonic generative politics I refer to the subordination of civil society by both the state and economy organized around particular class interests, invoking Gramsci's classic definition of hegemony[23] as the production of consent of the majority through institutions in civil society, which is underpinned by the state's coercive apparatus. Counter-hegemony, by contrast, attempts to establish alternative forms of social organization that break with the capitalist hegemonic forms and ultimately seek to subordinate the state and economy to civil society (Burawoy, 2003). Thus, hegemonic generative politics seeks to establish new institutions and practices that ultimately extend the role of the capitalist state—representing class interests—over the institutions in civil society, while counter-hegemonic generative politics attempts to establish new institutions and practices that extend the role of civil society over the state and economy (see table 1.1).

The concept of civil society is highly contentious and warrants clarification as it is often used to mean very different things (e.g., NGOs representing elite interests, conservative religious movements, and working-class organizations). While I

Table 1.1   Typology of politics

	Initiative from above (state)	Initiative from below (civil society)
Protest politics	State-led protest • Sanctioned by state. • Support state-led initiatives. • Demobilize civil society.	Civil society-led protest • Organized by mass- and class-based organizations. • Challenge the state. • Build civil society.
Generative politics	Hegemonic • Extend role of state. • Work with capitalist forms of social organization. • Seek arrangements for ameliorative solutions to the negative effects of capital accumulation.	Counter-Hegemonic • Extend role of civil society. • Seek to establish alternative forms of social organization. • Alternative logics of accumulation and political engagement.

recognize this limitation, for lack of a better term, I use civil society in this study in the following two distinct ways: (1) a domain of social organization that is analytically separate from, but connected to, the state and economy and (2) an arena of contestation in which different actors are organized into discrete social organizations. It is in the latter use of the term that the ambiguity arises. I refer to civil society as the arena of voluntary associational activity where a great deal of daily life is experienced. It is an arena of contestation by organizations with direct links to ordinary citizens with no primacy given to class associations. Rather it is an arena of collective associations rooted in interests and identities of all sorts. Thus, the empirical referents for civil society in this study are mass and class organizations, including, for example, student organizations, community-based and religious organizations, women's and ecology movements, and trade unions. In Kerala civil society also encompasses such things as neighborhood groups, women's groups, and village committees. In South Africa it includes such things as development forums, policing forums, and school committees. While civil society is not restricted to a particular class, the centrality of class is fundamental for counter-hegemonic generative politics. Indeed, it is around issues of class that the paramount role of political parties comes into sharp relief. Political parties, and especially communist parties, can infuse civic associations with a class project, organizing the myriad associations around the centrality of subaltern class interests. Both Kerala and South Africa have a dense fabric of organizations in civil society, but as I argue in this study, the Communist Parties relate to civil society in markedly different ways, which shapes the relationship of civil society with the state and economy.

For the greater part of the twentieth century socialism was largely defined through the negation of capitalism. And since capitalism is defined as an economic structure in which the means of production are privately owned and production is oriented to profit maximization through exchange on the market, socialism, then, has usually been defined as state ownership of the means of production (as opposed

to private ownership) and state planning of production and distribution (as opposed to exchange on the market). The problem with posing the opposition in these terms is that both forms of social organization smother the role of civil society. In capitalism the economy wields power over the state and civil society, while in socialism the state wields power over the economy and civil society. However, it is possible to define socialism differently, and in a manner that enables us to see more clearly the development of the CPI(M) and SACP. Socialism can be defined as the dominance of civil society over the state and economy (Wright and Burawoy, 2004: 3–4; Wright, 2006).[24] Under hegemonic generative politics we see the state and economy wielding power over civil society. However, under counter-hegemonic generative politics political parties strive to build institutional mechanisms that help empower civil society in relation to the state and economy, thereby promoting the capacity of civil society to determine state policies and actions and the nature of economic activity.

Recognizing the possibility of the latter disrupts our understanding of how communist parties operate. Historically, communist parties have been largely concerned with capturing state power in order to direct the development of society. As the statism of the Soviet Union revealed its irrationalities, communist parties were forced to reexamine their primary focus on state power and the way in which they related to civil society. While the impetus for transformation must come from civil society, political parties can help coordinate the myriad interests into a coherent alternative social order. In order to play this role, however, communist parties have had to shed their baggage of past ways of relating to their bases of support to become mechanisms for democratic civil society leadership (as opposed to state or party domination) in order to direct the state and shape the broad direction of the economy. In other words, communist parties have to transform themselves into a different type of organization; one that respects the autonomy of civic associations, but at the same time develops synergistic relations with them.

Studying the contrasting political projects of the CPI(M) and SACP not only challenges our understanding of political parties, especially communist parties, it also clarifies the factors affecting the nature of hegemonic generative politics and the possibilities for a counter-hegemonic generative politics. This is particularly relevant at this point in history when dominant visions of alternatives deny a role for both political parties and states, preferring a romanticized role for civil society isolated from the state and political parties.[25] Theorizing internal dynamics of political organizations, the organizing practices of parties, and generative politics helps us understand the conditions for constructing participatory socialist democracy that is emerging in Kerala and to a lesser extent in South Africa.

Outline of Book

In the following chapters I argue that (1) the SACP and CPI(M) developed similar and extraordinary visions of socialist democracy, (2) pursued new and different forms of politics in practice based on their common vision, and (3) offer an explanation for the differences in the efforts to translate their visions into practices that look at organizational capacities in historical perspective and competing political

factions that operate within particular class contexts and political environments. I conclude with a discussion of generative politics at a more abstract level, exploring its application beyond these two cases.

In chapter two I look at the parties' ideological convergence. In the 1990s both parties asked fundamental questions about the nature and content of their understandings of socialism. Out of this reflexive journey the SACP and CPI(M) arrived at remarkably similar understandings of socialist democracy around the following four common themes: participatory democracy, a new developmental state, the coexistence of capitalism and socialism, and an economy oriented toward social needs. Through these four themes the parties elaborated a similar vision of socialist democracy grounded in their local conditions.

In chapters three and four I explore the CPI(M)'s and SACP's efforts to translate their new ideological vision into practice. More specifically, in chapter three I show that the CPI(M) shifted to a counter-hegemonic generative politics in the 1990s by implementing its ideological vision. For the CPI(M), its 1987 election victory marked a turning point. Having been in and out of government and unable to substantially increase its electoral support since the 1960s, by the mid-1980s the CPI(M) was opening itself to new and novel approaches to politics in its efforts to remain apace with the aspirations of the populace. It recognized both the need for economic growth and the limits to redistribution without growth as well as the need to develop programs that involve mass participation and encourage local initiative and self-reliance. The pressure to grow the economy and the failure of old-style politics to address such issues required new initiatives that engendered development. These external conditions played into the party's internal dynamics shifting the balance of power within the party, which ultimately led the party away from state-led development based on mass mobilizing around redistributive reforms toward society-led development enlisting participatory organizing.

In chapter four I turn to the SACP's attempts to operationalize its vision. Unlike the CPI(M), the SACP's shift in the 1990s was toward a hegemonic generative politics of state-led development enlisting mass-mobilizing practices. The party's emphasis was clearly on ideological and strategic developments as the SACP saw its primary role as providing analyses and strategic perspectives as well as strengthening the role of the ANC-led state. The first half of the 1990s was marked by a relatively consistent focus on state-led development, which required an emphasis on policy issues relating to nation building. For example, after the 1994 ANC-led Alliance election victory, the party placed priority on activities that helped solidify the ANC-led state such as the people-driven Reconstruction and Development Program (RDP). After the ANC adopted a neoliberal macroeconomic strategy in 1996, however, discontent within the SACP slowly began to manifest leading the party to question its focus on state-led development. Belying a deep uncertainty in the party the shifting focus from state-led development often led to a return to emotive oppositional politics disconnected from a society-led project despite its ideological commitments pointing it in this direction.

I explain the divergence in their efforts to translate their transformative visions into practices through a comparative historical and ethnographic analysis of the two parties. Comparing the parties over time helps to illuminate subtle differences

and important similarities. I explain the difference in their practices by isolating the most important factors shaping their activities and argue that the particular ways in which the varying factors combine explains the divergent politics of the SACP and CPI(M). More specifically, through an analysis of these two parties over time, I argue that the divergent conditions of economic context and political environments (including relations to other organizations—the SACP's subordinate position in its alliance with the ANC and the CPI(M)'s dominant position in electoral coalitions with Left parties) together with the organizational capacities and competing political factions shaped the possibilities for transformative politics. Using the comparative method strengthens the analysis by focusing attention on the economic context and electoral field. Looking at either party on its own might have pointed to a path-dependent argument drawing exclusively on unique histories. Comparing the parties, however, unambiguously highlights the importance of the broader economic and political fields in which each party is located.

The unique histories and contrasting organizational capacities account for particular aspects of the parties' politics in the 1990s, but neither can alone explain the divergence in their politics. Rather an explanation for the differences in the practices may be attributed to the fact that these dynamics result from particular factions guiding the parties. Factions within the parties act within a field of struggle where the parties address challenges circumscribed by economic and political conditions unique to each place. For one, the class context has importantly shaped political options in both South Africa and Kerala.

The SACP faced a political transformation in which capital was a strong and organized force able to coax leading sectors of the ANC in its favor, while the CPI(M) faced a transformation in which capital was weak and subaltern classes were not only strong and well organized but firmly moored in the state. The particular party-class relations combined with the nature of the electoral fields to affect the politics of the two parties in unique ways. Thus, while organizational characteristics and party histories color the parties' politics in the 1990s, their influence on the particular nature of the two parties' politics is shaped by the political and economic conditions in which each party is embedded. I thus argue that we must look to the confluence of organizational histories and capacities with competing factions and the political and economic contexts in order to understand why the SACP and CPI(M) diverged in their efforts to realize their similar ideological visions. Understanding the concrete and symbolic struggles of the SACP and CPI(M), two political parties deeply involved in the politics of their societies, provides ideal empirical cases to explore the theoretical concepts of generative politics in practice. I conclude by returning to the theoretical questions animating this study: what kind of political parties, organizing strategies, and politics make a counter-hegemonic generative politics feasible in the periphery in an era of global neoliberalism?

In chapter two I explore the SACP's and CPI(M)'s ideological convergence. It is to this ideological journey we now turn.

PART I

Ideology and Practice of Socialist Democracy

There is nothing surprising in the claim that fin-de-siecle socialism was in crisis. Late twentieth-century geopolitics underwent dramatic changes that profoundly transformed the international arena. The collapse of the Soviet bloc marked the end of the Cold War and shifted the international field from a bipolar world to a unipolar world in which neoliberal capitalism dominated the world system.[1] The ascendance of capitalism did not, however, result from the success of the capitalist world economy. Rather the world capitalist economy was in crisis (since at least the 1970s), which could be seen in the dramatic changes within the capitalist system itself. In response to this crisis of capitalism there was an increasing trend toward global integration of financial markets and capital operating on a transnational scale. Through intricate international bodies, legal frameworks, and an ideological bulwark, the powerful triumvirate of the World Trade Organization (WTO), World Bank, and International Monetary Fund (IMF) worked together to alter the way in which countries could engage the world economy. Countries around the world were increasingly constrained as visions of liberalization, globalization, and privatization penetrated the world. These changes had profound and largely negative effects on the countries of the Global South as the notable feature was increased polarization both between and within countries.

In the new international conditions, countries in the South, such as South Africa and India, opened up and liberalized their economies on highly unequal terms, further reducing government protection of local producers and privatizing state assets. Within this context the collapse of the Soviet Union strengthened the grip of the global capitalist economy as the Soviet sphere had been an alternative bloc in terms of international trade, aid, military, and political assistance. For many governments the new world order weakened their sovereignty and restricted the possibilities for development as the ability of the nation-state to regulate capital (especially the flow of finance across borders) and determine the trajectory of a country's development was further eroded with the redistributive role of the state steadily undermined.

These developments did not mean, however, that states no longer play a paramount role in mediating the pernicious effects of capitalist globalization (Evans, 1997). Rather the new world order requires more sophisticated responses and new forms of resistance.

The collapse of the Soviet Union meant that socialist forces no longer had an ally on whom to draw support, ultimately leaving a political and ideological void. For the CPI(M) this signaled a dramatic change in the international balance of forces, which increasingly put pressure on the Indian state to adopt a neoliberal development strategy in which it liberalized the economy, opened domestic markets, and privatized state assets. Despite its efforts to contest the international and national developments, at its 1992 14th Party Congress the CPI(M) concluded that the change in the world situation and the Indian government's economic policies undermined India's role in the world arena (Surjeet, 1998: xix). For the SACP the collapse of the Soviet Union had serious implications for its resources. Gorbachev preferred negotiated political solutions to regional conflicts leading the Soviet Union to reduce (and by 1990 cease) support for armed struggle, which was an important thrust of the liberation movement's struggle against apartheid. On the positive side, the end of the Cold War also meant the diminished strategic significance of South Africa as a bridgehead against communism. Like the liberation movement's loss of support from the Soviet bloc, the apartheid state also lost its crucial support from Western governments, which helped pave the way for a negotiated settlement and multiparty democracy. Thus, the SACP returned to South African soil exactly at a time when the possibilities for transformative politics were being rewritten and dyed-in-the-wool certainties about the struggle against capitalism and the construction of socialism were fundamentally challenged.

At the same time, the demise of the Soviet Union sent a different type of reverberation around the world. During the nineties many socialist and communist parties were forced to engage in a process of ideological and organizational renewal, having to account for the failures of socialist visions and the undemocratic nature of Soviet-style state socialism. While the demise of the Soviet Union initially destabilized socialist and communist parties, it also brought new incentives for parties to envision alternatives that emphasize building socialism democratically from civil society. For the CPI(M) and SACP the change in the international balance of forces opened up new possibilities for rethinking the direction of democratic socialist politics. Thus, the positive effect of the end of the Cold War was that it potentially afforded more space for countries to implement democratic reforms and social and economic development as they were no longer the theater of Cold War politics. Many earlier attempts were crushed by Western government support with the justification of rolling back the "communist threat"; on the other side of the political fence, many socialist and communist parties suffered from an ideological straightjacket imposed by Soviet dominance.

In general, there were two types of responses among communist and socialist parties to the changes in the international context. For many parties, the challenge led to an abandonment of socialist visions shifting instead to visions of social democracy that seek amelioration within capitalism through parliamentary democratic institutions. For some parties, however, the global changes provided an

opportunity for the rejuvenation of radically democratic socialist visions grounded in local conditions and practices. The South African Communist Party and the Communist Party of India (Marxist) are two parties that chose the latter option and met the challenges of the 1990s by creatively engaging their ideological foundations as well as their politics and practices of translating these aspirations into reality. Remarkably, in this process of ideological renewal the CPI(M) and SACP developed strikingly similar ideological visions of "socialist democracy" that placed priority on participatory democratic mechanisms in political and economic structures. Socialist democracy, for the CPI(M) and SACP, came to be similarly defined as the dominance of civil society over the institutions of the state and economy.

In chapter two I turn to the ideological convergence of the SACP and CPI(M) in which both Parties developed indigenous visions of socialist democracy. Given their vastly different locations, it is quite remarkable that their visions of socialist democracy converged around four themes: a deepened and extended notion of democracy, a strong developmental state, coexistence of capitalism and socialism for an indeterminate period of time, and the centrality of civil society in the economy. In chapters three and four I look at the actual practices of the two parties in relation to these four themes. In Kerala, the CPI(M) managed to implement all four themes to some degree, which ultimately shifted party practices toward counter-hegemonic generative politics (chapter three). In South Africa, by contrast, the SACP only focused on implementing two out of the four themes, which ultimately led to hegemonic generative politics (chapter four).

CHAPTER 2

Communist Renewal and Ideological Convergence

The collapse of Soviet communism forced political parties around the world to reexamine their basic beliefs and ask questions about whether an alternative to capitalism was possible. Many parties—such as a number of European parties—shifted to visions of social democracy. Out of this reflexive journey, however, some parties—such as the SACP and CPI(M)—emphasized *socialist* alternatives grounded in democratic principles and practices. There are two important implications of the SACP's and CPI(M)'s ideological journey for this study. First, the political reimagining of the SACP and CPI(M) highlights the existence of another tradition that not only challenges the authoritarian rendition of communism (e.g., Selznick, 1952; Duverger, 1974; Courtois et al., 1999), but also prioritizes the democratic potential inherent in socialism. Second, the reimagining of the SACP and CPI(M) reflects a striking convergence in the thinking of two parties located in vastly different places and faced with challenges unique to each society. Confronted with the failures of twentieth-century socialism, the SACP and CPI(M) arrived at remarkably similar visions of socialist alternatives anchored in participatory democratic practices within representative democratic institutions.[1] In other words, the SACP and CPI(M) envisioned similar responses regarding how to deepen socialist practices through a counter-hegemonic generative politics: rather than the dominance of the state or economy they sought the dominance of civil society over the institutions of the state and economy through radically democratic politics. Drawing on the parties' own language, I refer to this new vision in which ordinary citizens play an increasingly important role through democratic mechanisms as *socialist democracy*.[2]

Socialist democracy, for the CPI(M) and SACP, came to be similarly defined as civil society's subordination of the economy and synergistic relationship with the state in order to increase the decision-making authority of ordinary citizens. Highlighting the importance of democracy, however, was not unique to the SACP and CPI(M). Few parties, however, maintained a more extended and deepened

vision of democracy that included not just the political, but also the economic and social spheres of life. The SACP and CPI(M) were relatively unique, therefore, in integrating a more extensive and deepened understanding of democratic norms and practices into radical visions of socialism grounded in their respective local conditions. With the emphasis on the role of democratic civil society, they were envisioning the constituent elements of a counter-hegemonic generative politics.

In this chapter I explore efforts by the parties to *envision* democratic socialist alternatives. During the 1990s both parties held numerous Congresses, workshops, and conferences[3] as well as produced a plethora of documents in which they worked through their evolving theoretical positions. This chapter is based on a perusal of the materials from this reflexive journey by both parties.

Ideological Renewal: Envisioning Counter-Hegemonic Generative Politics

It is quite extraordinary that the SACP and CPI(M), located in different places and spaces, responded to the challenges of the late twentieth century by theorizing broadly similar visions of socialist democracy. It is not just that they arrived at a similar vision that is noteworthy, but the content of their ideological thinking is also quite remarkable. Their visions of socialist democracy reflect serious engagement with the ideological foundations of the Marxist tradition as well as deep appreciation for the concrete realities of their societies. They have thus pioneered a new notion of socialist democracy from two vastly different societies, each with unique histories.

The parties' ideological renewal grew out of an understanding that socialism could not be conceived of as a predetermined model of social organization, but rather was an undefined process of extending democratic practices of collective decision making and the progressive empowerment of subalterns to participate in the development of society. Visions of socialism that could be reached through either revolution or reforms were abandoned and were replaced with visions of a continuous and undefined process of transformation that progressively eliminates forms of exploitation and oppression through the extension of civil society over the state and economy. Socialism, in other words, requires a long transition consisting of many phases and multiple forms grounded in local conditions; there is no blueprint (CPI(M), 1992: 134; SACP, 1995:13–15). In short, the two parties shifted from a state-centered understanding of socialism based on the Soviet experience to a society-centered vision of socialism that found its moorings in radical democracy. This convergence centered on the following four themes: democracy, the state, the coexistence of capitalism and socialism, the extension of civil society.

All four themes ultimately relate to the expansion of democratic practices of collective decision making and the progressive empowerment of subalterns to participate in the development of society. Moreover, the four themes constitute constituent elements of their socialist vision that build on one another and are integrally interrelated. The four themes represent elements of a counter-hegemonic generative politics and thus provide a compass around which the two parties have oriented their practices to varying degrees. I address each theme by drawing on the parties' documents and written materials.

Deepening and Extending Democracy

Fundamental to the SACP's and CPI(M)'s visions of socialist democracy was a deepened and extended notion of democracy. Neither the SACP nor CPI(M) settled for a narrow vision of democracy limited to political pluralism, but rather developed visions of socialism anchored in participatory democracy in which ordinary citizens are empowered to play a decisive role in all sectors of society. It was a major theme for the CPI(M) in the 1990 Central Committee document "On Certain Political-Ideological Issues Related to Developments in Some Socialist Countries" and the 1992 Congress document "Resolution on Certain Ideological Issues" as well as the 1994 and 2000 Kerala conference papers.[4] For the SACP it is a central theme in its 1995 *Strategy and Tactics* document and its 1998 Program *Build People's Power—Build Socialism Now!* as well as its 1999 and 2000 strategy conference documents. It was also central to the heated debate at the party's 1991 Congress over the slogan of the "dictatorship of the proletariat," which was abandoned in favor of language referring to widening and deepening democracy by the working class and poor. In these documents both parties espoused a vision of radical democracy that extended the control of civil society over the economic and political domains. It is worth noting that a commitment to extending democracy beyond the political domain was not universally shared by communist parties at this time.

Ironically, one of the effects of the simultaneous ascent of neoliberalism and the collapse of socialist economic models was the newfangled emphasis on popular participation in the *political* sphere, diverting attention away from the economic realm. As Gorbachev launched the Soviet Union on a process of *glasnost* and *perestroika*, democracy was hailed as integral to any form of social organization, be it capitalist or socialist. Within the new appreciation of democracy two conceptions of democracy dominated thinking: democracy as a type of political regime (e.g., Schumpeter) and democracy as a mode of social organization that includes the economic and social spheres of life (e.g., G.D.H. Cole). The first view emphasizes the importance of democratic institutions as a framework for managing social and political pluralism. This is a narrow view of democracy, bearing a certain resemblance to the liberal political tradition and largely relying on representative institutions to provide "conflict-regulating mechanisms" that facilitate the peaceful coexistence of competing societal projects (Roberts, 1998: 20). The narrow view conceives of democracy as a form of political regime and confines democratic practices to formal political institutions, allowing social hierarchies and inequalities to remain in all other arenas of life (Roberts, 1998: 28–29). The tendency among many political parties to focus on a narrow vision of participation in the polity, thus, partly stems from withering certainties about a socialist alternative to capitalism. In this political climate many political parties have been inclined to limit efforts at renewal to political, ideological, and organizational issues rather than economic and social issues.

The second view advocates a participatory conception of democracy as the process of popular empowerment of subaltern sectors to make decisions and carry through with implementation in both political and economic domains. This view sees the progressive extension of democratic practices to include participatory forms of self-government, which requires the development of new institutional mechanisms. The

participatory view of democracy sees it as a principle for social organization, and not just a formal regime type. Implicit in the participatory notion is a view of deepening and extending democratic practices to arenas of political, economic, and social life allowing citizens to directly participate in and control decision-making processes in all three domains of social life. Hence, democracy is not simply an end, but rather a continuous process of social organization that directly affects the degree of popular control over collective decision making in political and economic spheres.

As the CPI(M) searched for ways to define a radical program for change anchored in the democratic roots of the socialist tradition, the more extensive understanding of democracy dominated the thinking of certain factions in the party. At this time, the CPI(M) combined its commitment to a multiparty parliamentary system[5] in which political parties contest for state power through free and fair elections with more radical conceptions of democracy in which ordinary people are empowered to make and implement decisions in the political and economic domains of social life (Isaac, 1994: 5). Learning from its own history, the party understood that introducing democratic institutions into local politics without challenging the social and economic power of the landed elite meant that meaningful participation by subalterns was virtually impossible (i.e., political democracy in itself does not ensure the transformation of social relations). Thus, the CPI(M) argued that the institutions of formal democracy had to be underpinned by extending the role of civil society into the political and economic arenas, which requires constant struggle by subaltern classes to secure their right to participate and ensure implementation of democratic decisions (CPI(M), 1990: 302, 308). In order to democratize the political, economic, and social realms, the CPI(M) looked to decentralization as a primary mechanism for advancing this cause (Namboodiripad, 1994: 5).

The vision elaborated in a 1992 Central Committee resolution clearly articulates the culmination of this line of inquiry:

> [The] advance to socialism in any country must be accompanied by increased initiative of the masses both in running the economy and running the state. Lenin's statement "every cook must learn to govern" must be a growing reality. A concrete form of these initiatives in the various stages of development embraces larger and larger number of people. Measures, which free citizens from unnecessary restrictions and provide healthy dialogue within the limits of socialist society, strengthen the society. (CPI(M), 1992: 128)

Statements to this effect, highlighting the importance of popular involvement in both economic and political domains, are found in numerous party documents throughout the 1990s. The participation of ordinary citizens would drive transformation of society. For example, again quoting Lenin, in its 1990 resolution the CPI(M) argued that "only when it enlists the vast mass of working people for this work, when it elaborates forms which will enable all working people to adapt themselves easily to the work of governing the state and establishing law and order. Only on this condition is the socialist revolution bound to be last" (CPI(M), 1990: 309). The party further argued that a range of institutional changes were necessary in order to deepen and extend the possibilities for citizens to exercise democratic

rights: "The widest participation of the people in running the State, administration and economy [...] through self-government and work collectives. Advance of socialism requires reforms of the political structure and the institutions of the State which enrich and strengthen socialist democracy" (CPI(M), 1990: 309). This new ideological orientation was an attempt to continue the struggle within the concrete conditions by extending the power and control of civil society over economic and political activity.

Similarly for the SACP, while it always fought for and highlighted the importance of political and economic democracy, in the 1990s the nature and content of democracy was given more attention.[6] The SACP envisioned a socialism that was firmly anchored in deepening and extending democratic norms and practices as widely as possible. Beginning with SACP leader Joe Slovo's "Has Socialism Failed?" (1990) the party launched itself on a journey in which it fleshed out the importance of democratic politics for the realization of socialism. Democracy had always been treated in generalities and usually referred to either nonracial representative democracy, the "dictatorship of the proletariat," or "organs of people's power." But what these slogans meant in practice and how they related to each other was largely left unaddressed.

The SACP's understanding of the role of democracy stemmed from its conception of the National Democratic Revolution (NDR) and Colonialism of a Special Type (CST). The SACP arrived at its analysis of South African society over a period of many years starting in 1928–1929 when it adopted the Native Republic Thesis, which sought the formation of an African Republic based on majority rule. The Native Republic thesis set the foundation for theoretical developments in the late 1940s and early 1950s linking race and class struggles, which culminated in the CST thesis, which was adopted in the 1962 party program *Road to South African Freedom* (SACP, 1963: 24–70; Slovo, 1976: 161).[7]

Colonialism of a Special Type posited that blacks suffered dual oppression, as the oppression of the black majority was a necessary condition of the exploitation of black workers. CST explained that racial oppression underpinned class exploitation and that blacks from various class locations were united in a similar racial oppression (SACP, 1963). Thus, to fight class exploitation required struggling against national oppression and, hence, the SACP argued that the most appropriate response at this phase was national liberation (Slovo, 1989: 34–35). Clearly, the SACP had an instrumental approach to national democracy and mass power—it was necessary for the realization of socialism—but had not yet defined participatory democracy as a fundamental constituent of socialism.

Similar to the CPI(M)'s commitment to both representative and participatory democracy, in the early 1990s the SACP saw national democracy as not only necessary for the construction of socialism, but a multiparty electoral system, it was argued, was an important mechanism for ensuring accountability and control by the citizenry (SACP, 1995: 7–8).[8] The SACP went further to highlight that the logic and principles of democracy had to be deepened and extended into all other spheres of society—from the political, which included the government and administration, to the economic, social, and cultural spheres (SACP, 1995: 14). Of course, the SACP had been committed to national democracy in so far as it fought for the National

Democratic Revolution the first goal of which was a united, nonracial, democratic South Africa. It had not, however, taken such pains to articulate its socialism to be fundamentally about representative *and* participatory democracy (SACP, 1995: 8, 14).

In the 1990s, however, the party developed a greater appreciation for democracy as a qualitatively important component of socialism. The party was envisioning an extensive role for civil society in governance and over the broad direction of the economy. Participatory democracy became an end in itself and not just a means for achieving a socialist end. Linked to this was the idea that socialism had to be developed and defended by popular movements in civil society and not a bureaucratic state (or party) apparatus. For example, in the Reconstruction and Development Program (RDP)[9] a deepened and extended notion of democracy was posited as a key thrust in the economic and political development of South Africa (ANC, 1994: 120–21; Tripartite Alliance, 1994: 56–57). In short, the SACP was envisioning both an extensive and deepened role of civil society in which it increasingly shapes the political and economic domains of social organization (SACP, 1995: 6–8).

The New Developmental State

Espousing participatory democratic visions of political and economic organization, then, also requires rethinking the state, its role in development, and the party's relation to it. Both the SACP and CPI(M) had been historically influenced by the Soviet Union's statism and thus adhered to notions of an omnipotent state that may have been responsive to demands emanating from below,[10] but did not empower people to deliberate, make decisions, and implement their decisions through state institutions. In the 1990s, both parties abandoned notions of a hierarchical command-structure state with omnipotent powers and in its stead envisioned a state that plays an affirmative role (by which is meant a regulatory and redistributive role) and is responsive to the demands of its citizenry as well as provides institutional space for meaningful participation from below (CPI(M), 1990: 307; SACP, 1998: 49). In their new vision, the state's preeminent role was to create institutions for popular participation and ensure the means through which the citizenry was well prepared to participate. This conception of a developmental state differs from the one commonly found in the development literature. For example, Peter Evans defines the developmental state as bureaucratic, based on highly selective meritocratic rules, and governed by a sense of commitment and organizational coherence.[11] It also presides over industrial transformation and is "embedded" in concrete social ties to society (by which Evans largely means local capital) and "provides institutionalized channels for the continual negotiation of goals and policies" (Evans, 1995: 12). This vision of a developmental state says nothing about the extension of civil society through the active participation in decision making and implementation by ordinary citizens. The CPI(M) and SACP were envisioning a developmental state that was both more inclusive and extensive in its societal project. In order to achieve this vision of a developmental state, the parties looked to participatory democratic mechanisms.

For the CPI(M) its thinking around the developmental state challenged the party's long-held view of the state. During its first term in government in 1957–1959, the

Communist Party believed that holding state power translated into real power that could transform the economic and political power relations in society. It saw the state as the agent of change, working at the behest of the lower classes on whose support it depended. After its bitter experience in government between 1957 and 1959 when the "bourgeois"[12] and landlord forces flouted democratic norms and practices in order to destabilize the government, the CPI(M) came to hold the perspective that state institutions could only be used for agitation and propaganda. It formally articulated this view of the state in its 1967 Central Committee Resolution "The New Situation and the New Tactics" where it argued that the government was an instrument to intensify the people's struggles for land, higher wages, democratic rights, and against the policies of the central government (CPI(M), 1967). Implicitly, and perhaps unintentionally, the CPI(M) was advocating a position that took an instrumental approach to democratic institutions, arguing that they could be used to strengthen the opposition, proselytize the political perspective of the Left, develop popular consciousness, and expand organizational networks (CPI(M), 1967: 649–56). Underpinning this perspective was the view that gaining access to government office did not necessarily translate into real power, and, therefore, revolutionary confrontation was still the primary objective.

By 1987, though still officially supporting the 1967 resolution, the party recognized the need to adjust to new national and international conditions. For example, in Kerala and West Bengal the party regularly held state power, which placed particular demands on the party to deliver concrete changes through the institutions of state. Thus, the party in government in West Bengal and Kerala had to find at least partial solutions to the problems faced by subaltern classes and could not simply use the state for agitation and propaganda. Rather the state had to be used as an agent of change. It began to recognize that participatory democratic institutions could play an important role in creating conditions and institutional spaces for meaningful participation from the citizenry (CPI(M), 1990: 307). Ultimately, the institutions of state would be strongly affected by (even subordinated to) civil society, which would not only give citizens the opportunity to direct developments that affect their lives, but would also ensure greater accountability of state institutions (both representative and bureaucratic) to civil society. These shifts resulted in a new understanding of the state, which was now seen to play a vital role in development, but would be subjected to the control of civil society (CPI(M), 1990: 306–9). One way in which the party conceived the democratization of the state apparatus was through democratic decentralization (Namboodiripad, 1994: 5).

For the CPI(M) in Kerala this translated into practical efforts to transform the bureaucracy and state administration to play a vital role in empowering people to actively participate in the deliberation, decision making, and implementation of development. This required the formation of new participatory bodies that intersected with local government institutions as well as the transformation of local government structures in order for them to be open and accountable. Development agendas were derived from an integrated process of people's participation and local government initiatives. Devolving funds to local government institutions as a first step forced the reorganization of the bureaucracy and state administration to combine its role as an affirmative state with its role as a participatory institution by

opening local government structures to meaningful participation from subaltern classes. The CPI(M) thus moored its developmental state in civil society through extending and deepening democratic institutions. That is, the first two elements of the socialist vision were integrally interwoven.

The SACP's understanding of the eventual transition to socialism rested on a particular assumption about the omnipotence of state power. The party repeatedly explained that once state power was in the hands of the working class the transition to socialism would occur almost inevitably, though it still required struggle[13] (Slovo, 1976: 146–47; SACP, 1989a: 34). The state was the citadel of power and, hence, the working class would have to win for itself the dominant role in the new government to ensure that the direction of the national democratic state was in accordance with the interests of subordinate classes (SACP, 1989a: 40; Slovo, 1976: 148). This formulation of transition drew heavily on the classical Marxist-Leninist path to power in which the party was first to mobilize to attain state power and then to use state power to transform society with both struggles led by a vanguard party (Wallerstein, 1990: 30).

With the state *the* locus of power, other forms of power (e.g., "organ's of people's power") prevalent throughout South Africa were often viewed instrumentally—their utility was measured in terms of whether or not they helped capture state power or as mechanisms to ensure accountability and effective functioning of representative democratic institutions. It had not arrived at a position in which it saw these other forms of power as loci of power in their own right (SACP, 1989a: 34). Grassroots, participatory politics was not yet seen as a qualitatively important component of democracy. Thus, in the late 1980s the SACP still adhered to a mechanistic view of state-led development strongly influenced by the Soviet experience in which priority was given to an omnipotent state in controlling, leading, and guiding the economy and development. This top-heavy view of the state provided little institutional channels for grassroots participation.

In 1993 the party acknowledged its overemphasis on a state-led orientation in an Alliance discussion paper where it argued that "despite the Freedom Charter's broad social and economic perspectives, we tended to have a statist (that is, state-centered) approach to the NDR. The NDR would come about when an ANC-led National Liberation Movement (NLM) smashed the apartheid regime, assumed state power (which we tended to equate with the 'transfer of power to the people') and then implemented its programme" (Alliance, 1993a: 4). By the mid-1990s the party shifted its perspective and viewed other sites of power as significant and not just as an auxiliary to state power (SACP, 1995: 13–14). Power was no longer seen to reside only in the institutions of the state, but was seen to be enormously diffuse, and, therefore, contesting it would occur in multiple spheres by multiple forms of movements (SACP, 1999: 4). In other words, though the state continues to be a major locus of power, power does not lie solely with the state and holding the reins of state institutions might not translate into real power (SACP, 1999: 3–4; Alliance, 1997c; Moleketi, 1993: 16).

The party (along with its Alliance partners) was redefining the NDR to be much more than the transfer of state power to include the ongoing process of "popular self-empowerment." Forums for such involvement had to be developed at the

various levels of government and the transformation of the state itself was seen to be dependent on mass participation and had to be people driven (Alliance, 1993a: 6). The party further argued that popular forces had to actively engage the new institutions through local development forums, people's housing programs, workplace forums, school governance structures, and other similar forums (SACP, 1998: 49). This understanding of the state reflected the party's shift from a monolithic view of the state to an understanding of the state as a complex set of semi-independent (autonomous) institutions with multiple sites of power as well as a more inclusive understanding of social power rooted in myriad institutions in civil society and not simply the organized working class. The SACP saw local government as a crucial site for deepening democracy. The transformation of local government shifted significant powers to it as a constitutionally mandated tier of government with original powers (i.e., not just a function of provincial or national levels) and hence provided tremendous potential for citizen participation through institutional channels (SACP, 1999: 24–25).

These shifts in its vision of the state are seen in the elaboration of the 1995 *Strategy and Tactics* document, the 1998 party Program, and the 1999 strategy conference documents as well as the Reconstruction and Development Program, which became a major thrust in SACP thinking in the mid-1990s. For example, in the RDP a new vision of a developmental state with a great deal of emphasis on participatory institutional mechanisms was articulated. In all its documents the SACP placed significant emphasis on the role of community-based organizations in development and formulated an economic and social program to develop, expand, and stabilize the economy through meeting the basic needs of the people (Nqakula, 1994: 8). The state's role envisioned in the RDP and other documents was to facilitate and create institutional spaces for democratic action, while the main thrust of transformation was society centered (SACP, 1995: 8). The institutional spaces created for such participation include standing, hearing, and theme committees in parliament, the National Economic Development and Labour Council (NEDLAC),[14] Local Development Forums, Shopfloor-based Workplace forums, Housing and Electricity Forums, and University Transformation Forums. In addition, the transformation of local government created institutional space for participatory governance (Carrim, 2001: 33–35). The role of political and community organizations was to capacitate, train, and educate people to take advantage of these spaces created by the state and policy makers. Thus, the state was not to subordinate civil society, but rather would create institutional spaces and nurture conditions that would encourage popular participation and ultimately civil society's inclusion in governing and economic activity. For example, in its 1998 Program the party argued that the strength of the state was dependent upon the strength of civil society and its ability to build social cohesion around a development program (SACP, 1998: 27).

The SACP succeeded in consolidating a vision of the character of the state as developmental, by which was meant an activist state with institutional avenues for mass participation. The party thus simultaneously espoused the extension of civil society into economic and political domains, but also pushed for more active state involvement in the economy (SACP, 1999: 7). The SACP summarized its understanding of the active role of a developmental state to include the provision of

essential services (e.g., health, education, and welfare), the creation of conditions for a developmental growth path (including human resource development and democratization and participation), the promotion of redistribution (of income and wealth), and countering the effects of market failure (e.g., unemployment and jobless growth) (SACP, 1998: 45). This included strong state intervention when necessary and in some cases the state might have to go beyond facilitation and support and act by "pressuring and cajoling capital, as well as taking active steps to transform ownership patterns" (SACP, 1998: 41). In short, the state was to act as a catalyzer and strategic coordinator and, when necessary, actively intervene in the economy in order to realize the nation-building, democratic, social, and economic objectives of the NDR. Transformation, however, was to be society centered with civil society increasingly participating in the political and economic realms.

Coexistence of Socialism and Capitalism

Moving from issues of governing and the state, the CPI(M) and SACP also developed their thinking on issues relating to the economy. With their commitments to participatory democracy and a developmental state moored in civil society, it is clear that both parties were, at least for the foreseeable future, jettisoning visions of revolutionary rupture with the capitalist system (CPI(M), 1992: 120–21 and 1990: 293–94; SACP, 1999: 3). Indeed, both parties envisioned a transition in which capitalism and socialism would coexist for an indeterminate period of time. The parties were finding a route between the orthodox view of a revolutionary break with capitalism and accommodationist reforms within capitalism.[15] The parties similarly argued that the conditions for and transition to socialist democracy would have to be created on and through the terrain of capitalism by developing socialist logics alongside the predominant capitalist logic through democratic politics (CPI(M), 1990: 293–94; SACP, 1995: 13–16). Both parties translated this element of their vision into practice through creative efforts at securing the necessary capitalist development to nurture economic growth while simultaneously creating the conditions to develop alternative logics of accumulation. In both Kerala and South Africa the parties actively sought the creation and extension of micro-production units based on cooperative principles.

In Kerala, the CPI(M) married these efforts to the decentralization campaign and provided backward and forward linkages for local-level production. While the CPI(M) placed special emphasis on nurturing the conditions for developing alternative logics of accumulation, given Kerala's rudimentary capitalist development, the CPI(M) also sought capitalist investment in areas in which Kerala enjoyed comparative advantage and areas that tapped its high human development capacity such as the information and technology sector (Isaac and Franke, 2001: 32–33). Thus, socialism and capitalism, the CPI(M) envisioned, would exist simultaneously.

Protracted class struggle remained at the heart of its vision of transformation in which the transition to socialism would include the prolonged existence of both a capitalist logic and socialist logic (CPI(M), 1990: 293). While the two forms of social organization would simultaneously coexist, the period would be fraught with continuous confrontation "between the counter-revolutionary forces which wish to preserve the exploitative capitalist order and the revolutionary forces that seek to liberate humanity" (CPI(M), 1992: 120). This marked a significant shift from its

earlier position positing an immanent revolutionary break from capitalism. While the party still ascribed to the long-term objective of a revolutionary break, in the medium term (which could last a long time) socialism and capitalism would exist together. Indeed it went even further to argue that elements of socialism must be constructed in the current conditions and through the process of transformation. Clearly, the CPI(M) was advocating a processural view of socialist construction based on the concrete conditions in India.

In South Africa, the Communist Party argued that under South African conditions a transitional phase of national democracy was necessary, which was a long transition in which the foundations and capacity for and elements of socialism must be built from within society through a process of revolutionary reforms (replacing the "political economy of capital" with the "political economy of the working class") (Zita, 1993; Cronin, 1994: 39–41). This view of the coexistence of capitalism and socialism was further articulated in the early 1990s (SACP, 1995: 13–14). Thus, a noticeable feature of the SACP's formulation, and similar to the CPI(M)'s vision of simultaneous existence of capitalist and socialist logics, was the processural construction, through revolutionary reforms, of the conditions for socialism.

The SACP was explicit about the absolute interrelation between the NDR and socialism. At the 9th Congress in 1995 the SACP clarified that the attainment of state power provided the conditions for developing socialism in the current context. While the 1994 democratic breakthrough indicated a strategic defeat of CST and a political defeat of the apartheid regime, class exploitation continued to characterize South African conditions. The National Democratic Revolution was, therefore, conceived as a protracted struggle that included the continuous and simultaneous struggle for both democratic and socialist transitions in which capitalist and socialist logics would coexist for an indefinite period (SACP, 1995: 13). Thus, the SACP highlighted the importance of delinking,[16] to a degree, from world capitalism, but acknowledged that socialism was a long-term, historical struggle to shift the balance of class forces in favor of the subaltern sectors (especially the working people) and would have to be built on a terrain dominated by capitalism (SACP, 1995: 5–6 and 1998: 60). While the SACP developed a vision about South Africa's place in the international system, it was slow to develop its ideas about economic transition within the national context. It was only in the new millennium that the SACP addressed such questions. Moreover, during the 1990s the party paid too little attention to the contours shaping the economy in favor of capital's interests. For example, in the 2001 Gauteng Provincial Congress document "Building a People's Economy in Gauteng" and the 2005 Central Committee Special Congress document "Class Struggle in the National Democratic Revolution: The Political Economy of the Transition in South Africa, 1994–2004" questions about capital's hegemony over the transition and building alternative logics of accumulation were addressed. Thus, similar to the CPI(M), the SACP envisioned transformation in which socialist logics would be built in and through the current capitalist conditions.

The Role of Civil Society

For many people socialism is first and foremost about the central role of the state, and state ownership, in production and distribution in the economy.[17] The failures

of this "statism" (and state ownership) forced a reinterpretation of the role of the state. Faced with many new challenges in the economic arena, both the CPI(M) and SACP turned their attention to clarifying their understandings about the transformation of the economy from one dominated by economic (or political) elites to one dominated by civil society. There are two dimensions to their thinking on the way economic resources are allocated, controlled, and used that are relevant to our discussion. One concerns the extension of civil society over economic activity and the other concerns the state's control (often in response to pressure from civil society) over economic activity.

On the first dimension and linked to their vision of deepening and extending democratic decision making into the economic domain, the parties supported the increased role of civil society in determining economic activity and thus sought the creation of cooperative forms of economic organization, work collectives, democratic management, and decision making in production (CPI(M), 1990: 308–9 and 1992: 136; SACP, 1998: 42–43, 50). For the economy to be organized in such a way so as to serve the needs of ordinary people, rather than political and economic elites, it must be controlled to a certain extent by ordinary people. The CPI(M) and SACP thus elaborated the importance of various forms of ownership that challenged the binary contrast between socialism and capitalism where state ownership is the alternative to private ownership of the means of production. The parties continued to support the idea of social ownership of the means of production and socialized production as among the primary ownership forms, but, the parties insisted, they were not the only forms of ownership. The CPI(M) and SACP argued that under socialism at least the following three forms of property would exist: state, cooperative and collective, and individual ownership (CPI(M), 1990: 315–16; SACP, 1995: 15 and 1998: 70).

On the second dimension, the state was also to play a crucial role in determining economic activity. The state was to ensure redistribution, facilitate alternative logics of accumulation, and regulate the management, control, distribution, and use of economic resources. Hence, the state was to be actively involved in the economic arena as well as nurture the increasing control of civil society over economic activity. Both parties were clear that any vision of anticapitalist economic activity had to take into consideration the role of markets, but argued that markets had to serve the needs of the populace, which could be secured through the decommodification of certain services (e.g., health and education), the promotion of cooperatives, and hence a degree of state intervention in the economy (CPI(M), 1990: 314–16 and 1992: 138–40; SACP, 1995: 15–16). Both parties saw the failures of the Soviet Union's planned economy (CPI(M), 1990: 298) as well as the deleterious effects of the free-market system in the West and thus argued for a system that combined the strengths of each (SACP, 1995: 15). Markets were necessary, but had to be regulated to ensure they served societal needs and not just profit maximization (CPI(M), 1992: 138–40; SACP, 1998: 39–46, 49–50).

For the CPI(M), the failure of the Soviet economy together with the fact that the Indian capitalist economy had grown over the previous 40 years forced the party to rethink and nuance its approach to economic development. In its 1992 ideological resolution, the party acknowledged that it had overstated the likelihood of

capitalism's imminent collapse and had underestimated the tenacity of the system as well as the potential of technological revolutions (CPI(M), 1992: 120). The party had to acknowledge that in India capitalist development had achieved significant economic growth since independence. The party now argued that it had the responsibility to try to achieve economic growth within the capitalist system in the most democratic and egalitarian way possible while simultaneously struggling to transcend capitalism through establishing alternative logics of accumulation (Isaac and Franke, 2001: 33). The CPI(M) envisioned a socialist economy in which civil society plays a central role through ordinary people organizing various aspects of economic activity, and not just shaping the deployment of economic power (CPI(M), 1989: 142–43; Isaac, 1994: 59). For example, in Kerala the CPI(M) has promoted small-scale cooperative production units, pushed for the decommodification of social services such as health and education, and established an extensive public distribution system of ration shops that provide subsidized staple foods to all households.

The party supported the idea that markets were pivotal, but insisted that planning is necessary to coordinate the management of the national economy into a single whole to meet social needs and to properly direct markets for social ends. Left on their own, markets produce immense pernicious effects such as economic irrationalities and negative externalities ranging from the failure to provide adequate public goods, the inability to reproduce the labor force, environmental degradation, regular economic crises, and increased suffering of large numbers of the world's population (Wright and Burawoy, 2004: 1). In order for markets to play a positive role, however, they have to be properly regulated, which requires state intervention (CPI(M), 1990: 315). In other words, the CPI(M) envisioned an integration of planning and markets:

> Socialistic planning pursues the aim of increasing the socialized productive forces so as to ensure increasing goods and welfare services of the citizens. Within this framework, the central plan and market relations should not be seen as opposing principles of regulation. The plan should utilize the market relations and regulate it for the immediate economic goals corresponding to the stage of development. (CPI(M), 1990: 314)

The party was, thus, directly challenging free-market dogma that advocates a minimal role for state intervention in the economy. At the same time, the party was also challenging the idea of centralized planning in all aspects of the economy. Thus, the CPI(M) maintained that state intervention and markets have positive roles to play in the economy, but at the same time civil society had to play a greater role in shaping economic activity.

In South Africa, the SACP was also aware of the urgent need to formulate alternative economic proposals to the hegemonic neoliberal development models permeating thinking in the early 1990s.[18] However, when the SACP returned in 1990 the liberation movement had not worked out an official economic policy. While the SACP was committed to a mixed economy (outlined in the late 1980s), by 1990 it had not developed a coherent economic program. The 1994 democratic breakthrough meant that the Alliance had to confront the complexities of translating

popular aspirations for economic transformation into concrete policies. Over the course of the 1990s there were a number of articles in the SACP's theoretical journal, *The African Communist*, indicating serious reflection about the nature of economic development.[19] Like the CPI(M), the SACP pushed for both the increased role of civil society (especially the working class) in determining economic activity as well as the importance of the state (which ideally is accountable to ordinary citizens) in controlling the direction of the economy (SACP, 1995: 15–16; Satgar, 1997: 68–73; Carrim, 2001: 39–41).[20]

The party rejected arguments against state involvement in the economy and argued that "there is no example of a developing country achieving high growth, let alone improving human development, on the basis of a minimalist state" (SACP, 1998: 44). While the SACP was clear about the pivotal role the state had to play in the economy (especially in redressing the extreme inequality and poverty generated by the apartheid economic and social system) in order to put the economy on a new trajectory of sustainable development, it was careful to qualify the state's role.[21] The party argued that state intervention in the transformation of the economy had to be policy driven (e.g., industrial, sectoral, and labor market policies) (SACP, 1999: 14).

In addition to the importance of state involvement, the SACP also articulated the need to maintain anticapitalist class struggle by transforming economic power relations. Deracialization of capitalism was only justifiable within a broader transformation program that extended democratic control to the working class. It, therefore, indicated the importance of structural reforms that help shift the balance of class forces by undermining the core of capitalist power. Among the top priorities were redistribution and restructuring production, which included production for social needs, democratization of management, broadening the empowerment of workers, and a labor-intensive emphasis (rather than capital intensive) (SACP, 1995: 17).

For the SACP, building socialism in the current conditions included the socialization of a predominant part of the economy, decommodification of essential services, freedom and equality, and participatory planning (SACP, 1995: 16–17 and 1998: 69). Thus, the party envisioned a fundamental role for ordinary people in economic activity in order to ensure that socialization of the economy was not just formal ownership, but was the real empowerment of working people (SACP, 1995: 14–15). The SACP envisioned cooperatives as potentially shifting the vector of power from economic elites to ordinary people through democratic principles of production, ownership, and management (Satgar, 2001: 64). To be clear, the SACP envisioned a cooperative movement that challenges the dominant structures of accumulation; if they fail to challenge capitalist accumulation patterns, cooperatives simply become shock absorbers for the poor and unemployed (SACP, 1999: 46–47).

The SACP also saw the importance of markets, but argued for their regulation in order to ensure they served societal needs and not simply the profit motive (SACP, 1995: 15). The party argued that markets have an important regulating and distributive function in the economy, but significant areas of society such as healthcare, education, and public housing cannot be left to market forces (i.e., they have to be decommodified) (SACP, 1995: 16). In short, the party defined its economic vision consisting of a society in which "the socialized sector of the economy

is predominant, democratic, rational planning is increasingly possible, a democratic culture and practices reach deeply into every sphere of social life, and there is a substantial equality of income, wealth, power, and opportunities for all its citizens, and thus a growing freedom for all" (SACP, 1998: 71). Thus, both the CPI(M) and SACP envisioned an activist state strategically intervening in the economy in the interest of social needs and an increased role for civil society in controlling economic activity.

Implications for Political Practice

The CPI(M)'s and SACP's four themes of socialist democracy represent the constituent elements of an alternative politics. The combination of the four themes—participatory democracy, a developmental state, coexistence of capitalism and socialism, and the increased role of civil society in the economy—are, thus, the concrete articulation of a counter-hegemonic generative politics. It follows, then, that the ideological renewal has significant implications for political practice. While the SACP and CPI(M) converged in their ideological visions around these four elements of socialist democracy, the attempts to implement their visions varied. The CPI(M) managed to translate, to some degree, all four elements of its socialist vision into practice, while the SACP only managed to implement, to varying degrees, two out of the four themes.

What this suggests is that by mapping the SACP's and the CPI(M)'s practices as different configurations of the four themes we can begin to think about the concrete articulation of generative politics. In the case of the SACP, the party stopped short of thoroughly implementing its vision through practice and has emphasized state-led development rather than society-led development, allowing the democratization process to remain segmented and narrowly confined to representative institutions. The CPI(M), by contrast, has attempted to translate its radically democratic visions into practice through participatory organizing practices that mobilize civil society, unleashing a wave of new initiatives in the political, economic, and social realms. The divergence in the implementation of their theoretical views resulted in different forms of generative politics. The SACP's practices led to a hegemonic generative politics, while the CPI(M)'s practices represent a counter-hegemonic generative politics. It is to these developments that I now turn in chapters three and four.

CHAPTER 3

The Counter-Hegemonic Politics of the CPI(M)

The 1990s saw the CPI(M) elaborate a new ideological vision that emphasizes democratic norms and practices and grassroots-oriented development. In this vision it placed tremendous value on educating and training subalterns in order to meaningfully extend and deepen democracy to all spheres of society. The CPI(M) rejected the idea that "nothing could be done" until a national revolution occurred, arguing instead that it was in and through the current conditions that a socialist democracy would be forged. In practice, this meant the party had to find concrete ways in which it attempted to contest the predominant capitalist logic and construct alternative socialist logics through participatory democratic norms and practices and democratic state institutions. In this chapter I look at the ways in which the CPI(M) in Kerala utilized the space afforded by the new ideological developments to initiate a new type of transformative politics.

I begin with an overview of the party's shift from hegemonic to counter-hegemonic generative politics. Using the four themes of socialist democracy as reference points, I explore the CPI(M)'s attempt in the 1990s to pursue a new politics anchored in civil society and mass-based organizations. The CPI(M) used the state to help reconstruct civil society in order for civil society to play a more active role in governing and thereby making the allocation of state resources more democratic. At the same time, the CPI(M) organized subordinate groups in civil society into small-scale production units and hoped such cooperative forms of production would eventually amount to an alternative logic accumulation. The CPI(M) was reconstructing state institutions in order to stimulate the mobilization and organization of subordinate groups in civil society, which, then, increases civil society's impact on politics and the economy.

Redistributive Struggles Yield to Democratic Decentralization

In the late 1980s conditions in Kerala came to a head. The combination of international and national developments ultimately led the Kerala party to shift

from hegemonic to counter-hegemonic generative politics. To understand Kerala's shift to counter-hegemonic politics one must first appreciate the extent to which the CPI(M) had used protest politics along class lines for the better part of the twentieth century to reinforce a hegemonic politics. Kerala is perhaps best known to scholars for its impressive achievements in human and social development measured by "human needs" and "physical quality of life" (e.g., in 1991, Kerala had 90.6 percent literacy compared to the national average of 61 percent, infant mortality of 13 per 1,000 live births compared to the national figure of 62, and life expectancy of 73 compared to the national level of 63 and 77 of the United States of America) (United Nations Development Program, 2004; World Bank, 2004 and 2007; GOK, 2000; Isaac et al., 1998). These accomplishments have been achieved despite aggregate low income and slow economic growth, defying common assumptions about development espoused by the World Bank and Western development agencies. Indeed, under the organizational impetus of the Communist Party, subaltern mobilization and hegemonic state institutions have combined to yield high levels of human and social development.

The mobilizational history of the CPI(M) roughly divides into three periods. From 1930 to the mid-1950s communists organized subaltern sectors around caste, class (primarily agrarian), and independence movements into one coherent movement that successfully dismantled some of the most abhorrent social indignities on the subcontinent. In this first period the party emphasized participatory organizing and spent a great deal of energy educating and conscientizing the populace (e.g., its library movement helped set up reading rooms in villages throughout the state where it taught political education through literacy classes).[1] In the 1960s and 1970s the party organized more explicitly around class issues (i.e., agrarian and industrial) and forged a strong "working class" movement out of disparate class elements (Heller, 1999). These struggles precipitated an agrarian transition that dissolved precapitalist social and property relations on the land and introduced social and economic reforms with impressive gains in industrial unions in the public sector and public employees associations (Herring, 1983). The organized militancy of lower-class sectors thus dismantled traditional power structures and helped set the stage for effective state intervention. These struggles and the concomitant interactions between the state and lower-class groups within a competitive electoral democracy also helped institutionalize lower-class power within the state (Heller, 2000: 69–70) and thus can be characterized as building the basis for hegemonic politics in which the state plays the pivotal role in economic and political development.

During this second phase of its history protest politics came to dominate party practices as strikes and demonstrations were widely employed in labor and redistributional struggles.[2] This lower-class movement dynamic was intensified between 1960 and 1980 due to the fact the CPI(M) was only in government three years in this whole period.[3] This placed the CPI(M) in a continuous position of political opposition and encouraged it to shore up support in civil society (Herring, 1983: 209, 237). Heller captures the implications of this succinctly: "As a democratic oppositional force with broad-based if not majority support, the Communists busied themselves with the task of occupying the trenches of civil society, building mass-based organizations, ratcheting up demands, and cultivating a noisy but

effective politics of contention" (Heller, 1999: 15). While this "politics of contention" certainly secured working-class victories in land reforms and labor market interventions as well as redistributive and social reforms, it also helped precipitate a crisis of accumulation (Heller, 1999).

The successful lower-class mobilization thus also had its shortcomings. As Heller explains, "High wages, state-enforced controls on mechanization, rigidities in labor deployment and high levels of social consumption have all contributed to either driving capital away or creating significant barriers to internal capital accumulation" (Heller, 2000: 72). By the mid-1980s (the third period of mobilization) Kerala was at a crossroads unable to reinvigorate its lagging economy. The "Kerala Model of Development" was coming under fierce criticism from academics, activists, and politicians who argued that Kerala's development trajectory was unsustainable. The state's dismal record in terms of economic growth was the evidence most often cited to corroborate such criticisms. Even the CPI(M) had to admit that the redistributive demands were increasingly difficult to sustain in the face of the state's low economic growth and the neoliberal assault on the national economy. Moreover, the redistributive demands had expanded the role and size of the state as well as the power of the bureaucracy, both of which ultimately circumscribed the possibilities for popular civil society initiatives (Isaac and Heller, 2003: 85). Hegemonic politics in which the state dominates were thus stifling Kerala's celebrated politics of community activism.

In response, CPI(M) intellectuals argued that the Kerala model of low industrial development was sustainable, but acknowledged the need to attract and create new forms of economic development. Within this debate there was the recognition that the party's focus on old-style protest and hegemonic politics proved impotent in either facilitating or generating economic growth. Some within the party started looking to ways in which a generative politics enlisting new practices and strategies could be engendered. In an effort to stimulate productive investments and expand the economy, the party began rethinking the way in which it pursued sustainable economic development. In keeping with its commitment to promote growth without jeopardizing the hard-won redistributive and social gains, the CPI(M) began developing ways in which the social and institutional advancements (e.g., the vibrant civic associations, robust political climate,[4] legitimate state institutions, capable bureaucracies, and human capital) could be harnessed for economic and political development.[5]

Thus, after two and a half decades of hegemonic politics around redistributive reforms, by the late 1980s a new emphasis on counter-hegemonic generative politics began to emerge, reflecting the party's attempt to spark sustainable local economic development in which civil society is the driving force. The 1987 election victory of the CPI(M)-led Left Democratic Front (LDF) government marked a turning point. The CPI(M) recognized the need for economic growth and the limits to redistribution without growth as well as the need to develop programs that involved mass participation and encouraged local initiative and self reliance. Party activists realized that popular campaigns and volunteerism around nontypically class issues (e.g., literacy) could be harnessed for developmental projects and participatory democracy at the village level.[6]

In response, the CPI(M) launched a series of initiatives meant to mobilize and activate energies of the mass base and began investigating the possibilities for democratic decentralization in which people's involvement would drive social, economic, and political development.[7] As initial footsteps in this direction in 1987–1991 the CPI(M) launched a series of novel initiatives (e.g., a literacy campaign, a people's resource mapping campaign, group farming initiatives, and a limited democratic decentralization process[8]). These and other initiatives laid the foundation for the 1996 People's Campaign for Democratic Decentralization (discussed in detail later). These initiatives yielded to a new phase of development, one marked by counter-hegemonic generative politics. Some scholars have interpreted these events as class conflict evolving into class compromise much like a Western social-democratic model in which the working class compromises with capital to ensure capitalist development (Heller, 1999).

While there is truth in this characterization of the transition within capitalism from "despotic" to "hegemonic" forms of labor-capital relations (Heller, 1999: 10), this rendition misses a significant element of the picture. It is not simply a shift to class compromise that the CPI(M) and the subaltern sectors desire, but rather the CPI(M) is attempting to navigate a new and uncharted path to social, political, and economic development that seeks to establish noncapitalist relations within the current conditions. In other words, it seeks to establish a counter-hegemonic politics that fundamentally refashion relations in the economic and political arenas based on the experiences and aspirations of subaltern classes. In practice these relations have to both interact with and transcend the capitalist logic, which requires developing new institutional and political mechanisms for ensuring mass-based participation. Hence, I would argue that the shift in the 1980s is better captured by locating it within a shift from hegemonic politics in which the state is the driving force to counter-hegemonic politics, which focuses on constructing new institutions and channels for substantive participation in political and economic structures.

I refer to this shift as counter-hegemonic because the party is attempting to set up alternative forms of political engagement as well as alternative logics of accumulation through extending the role of civil society. For Gramsci hegemony is the combination of force and consent, which is ensured through specific institutions in civil society (e.g., education, trade unions). But Gramsci's notion of civil society also allows space for opposition to hegemony to be mounted within civil society, which I call counter-hegemony. I specifically define counter-hegemony as an attempt to set up alternative forms of social organization that break with the capitalist hegemonic forms prevalent in society and ultimately seek to subordinate the state and economy to civil society. While Heller only saw a hegemonic politics in the 1990s that sought to secure further concessions within the dominant capitalist system, I see the initiatives of the 1990s significantly attempting to establish new forms of political and economic engagement. Through the expansion of alternative political and civil society institutions the party was attempting to create spaces that would then become levers for societal transformation from below, which it did by devolving significant financial and administrative powers and decision-making authority to lower tiers of government. Because the efforts in the 1990s sought a new type of transformative politics, and not simply an accommodation within capitalism,

I would, therefore, argue the party was attempting to establish counter-hegemonic generative politics. Thus, the CPI(M) inaugurated a new phase of politics based on participatory democracy, which continued to ensure subaltern sectors were, to make a play on Heller's phrase that referred to the working class's role in *capitalist* development, "the engine of democratic development" (Heller, 1999: 3).

Reinventing the Developmental State

One of the key features of the innovations in the late 1980s and early 1990s was the focus on participatory organizing as the grassroots faction was able to gain enough influence within the party to redirect energies away from the mass-mobilizing practices of the previous two decades. As I mentioned earlier, the 1987–1991 CPI(M)-led government marked a turning point as the emphasis was now on programs that involved mass participation and encouraged local initiative and self-reliance, shifting focus from a hegemonic politics (i.e., struggling against existing exploitation through state-led initiatives) to a counter-hegemonic politics (i.e., struggling to construct new institutions for civil society initiatives).[9] In both phases, protest politics played a key role. Thus, the party was trying to implement its vision of a deepened and extended role for mass participation in the polity and economy.

Reflecting its new ideological orientation the 1987–1991 CPI(M)-led government initiated the following three campaigns that were meant to galvanize and incorporate subalterns in the development process: the Total Literacy Campaign, group farming, and the People's Resource Mapping Program. The campaigns also reflected the party's willingness to try nonconventional forms of activities that went beyond narrow class struggle to include broader issues in social, economic, and political development. It was trying to construct alternative logics of social organization on the current terrain of capitalist hegemony.

All the campaigns shared a common commitment to activate and educate the mass base as well as galvanize a middle strata of society into volunteering their time and labor. For example, the Total Literacy Campaign, which began as a KSSP-led (or People's Science Movement as it is called in English)[10] pilot project in Ernakulam district in December 1988, was launched as a mass movement with popular committees formed in every ward. The original pilot project began with 50,000 activists visiting 600,000 households to determine who was illiterate. The investigative efforts were then followed by 18,000 volunteer instructors offering literacy classes to the illiterate members of the district (Tornquist, 2000: 122). After just a year, the Prime Minister V.P. Singh declared Ernakulam the first completely literate district in India. The impressive (and high-profile) success of this pilot project further enhanced the grassroots faction's stature within the party and helped lay the foundation for the campaign to be replicated throughout the state. In rolling out the state-wide campaign the party worked closely with KSSP, which helped mobilize 350,000 volunteer instructors to teach thousands of hours of literacy classes. The statewide initiative was equally successful[11] and by the early 1990s Kerala was just shy of 100 percent literacy.[12]

In addition to the literacy campaign, the grassroots faction pursued an equally innovative campaign that attempted to activate and educate subalterns through a

long-term process of acquiring development knowledge.[13] This second initiative, known as the People's Resource Mapping Program, had two intentions. First, it was meant to establish a database on the human and natural resources of every area. Activists and volunteers from the community collected data on land, water, vegetation, and environmental problems (e.g., flooding, mosquitoes, etc.) from every plot of land in villages as well as socioeconomic surveys of every household. Village resource maps were devised out of the mass of information accumulated, which would later assist in determining and prioritizing appropriate development initiatives.[14] Second, it was a tool to raise people's awareness about their natural environment and spark thinking about the possibilities for socioeconomic development in their communities. Thus, the village resource maps were developed from the data collected with local participation in every stage of the campaign.[15] The act of collecting data and drawing up resource maps was a vehicle for consciousness raising about local resources and environmental issues[16] (Isaac and Franke, 2001: 41). In addition to these campaigns focusing on human and community development (i.e., literacy and people's resource mapping), the party also directly tried to galvanize farmers and increase production in agriculture.

Despite Kerala's successful land reform, agricultural production and productivity stagnated for almost two decades. In the late 1980s the agricultural growth rate increased, but the productivity of individual crops remained far below the national average and Kerala's potential. In addition, while Kerala is primarily rural, the scope for agricultural production was minimal given the especially high density of people on the land.[17] Thus, despite comprehensive land reform, agricultural production deteriorated and people have increasingly turned to nonagricultural production for their livelihoods. In response to the low productivity on the land, the party launched a "group farming program," where its erstwhile commitment to cooperative farming was replaced with the idea of group farming. The idea behind the program was that individual farmers maintained private ownership of farms, but aggregated agricultural operations especially for procurement and marketing activities. This was an attempt to enhance production by encouraging farmers to come together in agricultural operations in order to take advantage of economies of scale.[18] In addition, the party initiated certain market regulations for agricultural laborers, who were guaranteed a certain amount of work and higher wages in return for agreeing to a degree of mechanization. The initiative further included water regulatory measures, organic recycling, collective use of farm machinery, quality seed production, and integrated pest management. Again, KSSP activists played a critical role in these efforts.

In addition to these initiatives, in 1990 the CPI(M)-led government initiated a democratic decentralization process in which it gave more responsibilities and powers to district councils and thus embedded the developmental state in civil society through participatory democratic mechanisms. Local government institutions include municipalities and three tiers of rural government (district, block and grama panchayats[19]). In Kerala there are 14 district panchayats with 300 elected representatives, 152 block panchayats with 1,543 elected representatives, and 990 grama panchayats with 10,720 elected representatives (Isaac and Franke, 2000: 87). In addition to these rural local government bodies there are 58

urban municipalities. Municipalities and grama panchayats are the lowest level of democratic representation and have populations ranging from 10,000 to 30,000, which are divided into 10 to 15 wards each with its own councilor. The government recognized that a participatory approach to development was essential and Kerala's extensive network of mass organizations and vibrant civil society could easily be tapped for this end (Namboodiripad, 1994). Similarly, it was redefining the developmental state's role to both engender economic development and create institutional mechanisms for local government institutions to become participatory institutions. In other words, the party was contesting capitalist hegemony by extending the scope of civil society to play a critical role in local government institutions.

In 1986 Rajiv Gandhi's national government provided an additional opportunity as it tried to introduce a constitutional amendment decentralizing power to the local level. Rajiv Gandhi's proposed amendment, however, was problematic as it decentralized power at the expense of the state government. It strengthened the link between the central government and local governments making state governments powerless and ineffective, and thus the CPI(M) opposed this form of decentralization. The CPI(M)'s vision strengthened and increased efficiency of state government by empowering local government institutions and the mass base. The amendment did not pass and was significantly changed before it came into being in 1993. But this early attempt helped create an atmosphere for decentralization both at the national level and within Kerala.[20] In Kerala, KSSP and grassroots party activists studied the proposed amendment in order to understand the radical potential existing within it and launched a campaign explaining decentralization to ordinary citizens through a range of media such as seminars, discussions, pamphlets, and street theater.[21] Thus, the national government's local government legislation opened the space for the grassroots faction to push for a new politics.

The party had a long history of supporting decentralization which began with its first term in office in 1957 when it drafted a bill for decentralization[22] (the government was dissolved before the bill could pass). The bill for decentralization was taken up again in 1967 when the CPI(M) was in government, but little was achieved until the 1980s. In 1987–1991 the Left Democratic Front government decided to form district councils—which had been legislated for in the 1970s by Congress government—and held the first elections in early 1991. The elections were a stunning victory for the CPI(M) with 13 out of 14 district councils voting for the CPI(M)-led LDF. However, the CPI(M)'s luck quickly turned. Largely due to a sympathy vote for Congress after Rajiv Gandhi's assassination, in the June 1991 state elections the Congress-led United Democratic Front (UDF) coalition won the majority of seats and formed the government. The Congress-led UDF government was threatened by the overwhelming control of the LDF in district councils and thus immediately abolished the district councils.[23]

In 1993 the central government adopted a constitutional amendment, sections 73 and 74 of the Constitution, empowering municipalities and panchayats (rural municipalities) by devolving certain powers to local bodies and making provisions for involving people in the decision-making process.[24] Though the central government passed the amendment, it was clearly ambivalent as it erected a significant

obstacle to implementation. It required each state pass its own separate legislation before a predetermined cut-off date. Kerala passed its own legislation under the lead-' ership of the UDF government at midnight of the last day.[25] In September 1995 local elections were held and the CPI(M)-led LDF won 60 percent of the seats. These local bodies were given some power, but no (financial or human) resources. Thus, when the CPI(M)-led government came to power in 1996 it immediately busied itself with devolving resources and decision-making authority to lower tiers of government.

By this point the CPI(M) was serious about embedding the state in civil society and strengthening the decision-making role of ordinary citizens in local economic and political developments of their communities. Thus, in 1996 the CPI(M)-led government constituted the Sen committee (named after its chair Dr. S.B. Sen) to overhaul local self-government legislation. The Sen Committee laid down a comprehensive vision of decentralization that strengthened both the powers of local government and people's participation. It delineated the importance of autonomy, subsidiarity (i.e., "what can be done best at a particular level should be done by that level"), role clarity, complementarity, uniformity, people's participation, accountability, and transparency (Parmeswaran, 2000: 246). In 1999 the government comprehensively amended the Kerala Panchayat Raj and the Kerala Municipality Acts of 1994 based on the recommendations of the Sen Committee. The amendments clarified and refined the powers and functions of the different tiers of government, gave the local self-government institutions a greater role in planning, and secured the autonomy and accountability of the local self-government institutions[26] (Isaac and Franke, 2001: 199; Isaac and Heller, 2003: 87). In other words, the CPI(M) was redefining the developmental state.

While the 1987–1991 CPI(M)-led government was a turning point in terms of deepening participatory democratic institutions and reconfiguring the power relations between the state and civil society, even in opposition the debates around this new type of politics continued. Whether the CPI(M) or Congress was leading the state government, the fact remained that Kerala was facing a developmental crisis with economic stagnation threatening to undermine the democratic polity and redistributive gains of the past.

Antecedents of Counter-Hegemony: Pilot Experiments, Debates, and a Plan

While it was out of government between 1991 and 1996, the CPI(M) continued to develop its thinking around democratic decentralization. In an effort to inspire debate and critical thinking, the party initiated a debate in the daily newspaper on the measures needed to make decentralization effective (Namboodiripad, 1991). In these debates it was argued that development policies had a class bias and, therefore, even while operating within a framework of a capitalist path to development, it was necessary to prioritize the rights of people and to provide their due share in the fruits of development. A lively public discussion followed among leaders of political parties (including the opposition), administrators, and academics.[27]

In addition to encouraging debate and critical thinking, the party supported a number of pilot experiments, which provided the basis on which the 1996 statewide

democratic decentralization was based. The most important experiment was in the northern panchayat of Kalliasseri in the district of Kannur, which has a long history of party and KSSP activism. In addition to the history of activism in the region, the party is the dominant political formation and consistently receives 80 percent electoral support in Kannur. Its strength stems from struggles for land reform (which were especially fierce in this region) and the fact that many popular leaders such as A.K. Gopalan hail from the area.[28] Kalliasseri panchayat mirrors the vibrancy of the district and offered a few additional incentives for locating the lodestar pilot project in the area: the party's uncontested dominance in civil society and the local government with close to 95 percent electoral support,[29] its strong organizational capacity in the region, as well as the strong links between the party and KSSP.[30] On my field visits to the area, I witnessed the party's prevalence in a variety of ways. For example, people across the political spectrum spoke positively about the party and its people-centered approach. In one discussion with a Muslim League supporter, he explained that the CPI(M) is the only party that has consistently fought for the interests of the average person. When I questioned why he did not join or vote for the party, he answered that he is happy it exists, but his party is the Muslim League. The CPI(M)'s presence was also felt in the ubiquitous posters plastered throughout the region. I also saw the party's support for local activities such as children's plays and village festivals that it helped organize.

The Kalliasseri experiment was led by grassroots-oriented party activists and was underpinned by the idea that development involves a dramatic increase in the production of material goods and services in a sustainable and equitable manner and hence subtly began constructing a counter-hegemonic logic of social organization. In other words, there was a recognition that development requires a finely tuned confluence of economic growth, sustainability, and equity, which had to be driven and led by ordinary citizens (Kalliasseri Report, 1995: 1). Again, the combination of party and KSSP structures drove the experiment. But what is especially interesting about the party's involvement is that it went to great lengths to de-emphasize the party's role in the development projects. The party took special precautions to ensure that all political and mass formations participated in every phase of the development projects and that the pilot experiment did not seem to be a party-political project.[31] Rather it emphasized decentralizing power and decision-making authority to ordinary citizens regardless of their political affiliation.

The participatory organizing approach was incorporated into every sphere of local government activity, deepening the local government's linkages with civil society. The project began by asking community members to list pressing issues facing the community and how the aspirations of the people could be realized. The KSSP/CPI(M) activists conducted a number of studies in which they developed surveys (about consumption habits, human and natural resources, etc.), held group discussions, looked into secondary sources, and trained local volunteers in a range of activities (including people's resource mapping).[32] The importance of developing strategies that directly address local conditions was highlighted. For example, the income-generation strategy adopted was eclectic and addressed the particular conditions of the area. For example, one of the studies on the consumption habits of residents revealed that 20,000 eggs are consumed monthly, but not

a single egg is produced in the area. In response small-scale egg production was encouraged.[33]

With 30,000 people living in an area of 60.7 km², the population density on the land in Kalliasseri is 493.2 km².[34] The region is characterized by a dense web of housesites with most people owning 15–20 cents land,[35] making agricultural production extremely difficult on such small plots of land and no vacant land to expand agricultural production. In addition, the land in the area is largely (60 percent) coastal plain and thus possesses sandy soil. Despite these conditions, most of the land is under small-scale agricultural production (mainly paddy and coconut crops), but few people depend on agriculture for their livelihoods. The panchayat, therefore, explored other avenues of income-generating activities, many of which targeted women since they tended to be unemployed and were willing to accept lower wages in the initial stages of the projects.[36] The income-generating activities focused on traditional industries such as handloom production and garment-making ventures and targeted local markets. These income-generating units were organized on cooperative principles and were facilitated in various ways by local government. For example, I visited a production unit making notebooks that was given space in the municipal office building.[37]

On the political front, neighborhood groups were another novel innovation developed in the project to consolidate linkages between civil society and local government institutions. The neighborhood groups consisted of 40–50 households organized into wards[38] and served as the bottom tier of local planning. The neighborhood group representatives had a general assembly from which a 25-member executive committee was elected, which also includes the panchayat-elected representatives. One of the ways the neighborhood groups were directly involved in the development process was through the Development Society, another institutional innovation. The Development Society provided another forum for citizen involvement and attempted to make the development process as inclusive of all political and civic formations as possible.[39] In the Development Society's by-laws it requires representation from all parties, the KSSP, and two members (one woman and one man) from every neighborhood group. While not officially a local government institution, the Development Society is integrated into local government by the overlap of members (all elected representatives of the panchayat are also included in the Development Society). The office bearing positions of the president and vice president of the panchayat are carried over into the Development Society (e.g., president of the Development Society is the panchayat president), while the secretary is a KSSP activist.

The role of the Development Society is largely to facilitate implementation of decisions taken through the decentralization process.[40] Part of the impetus to establish such an inclusive institution was the grassroots faction's recognition of the latent dangers in any one organization wielding unrivaled authority in civil society and the structures of government.[41] To make any development project owned and led by ordinary citizens and supported by all civic and political formations the process had to ensure avenues for inclusive participation. Thus, the Development Society was one such attempt to ensure mass participation and inclusiveness. The grassroots faction in the party was trying to ensure that the new political project would be

seen as representing universal interests, and hence was trying to construct a counter-hegemonic political project.

A canal works project illustrates the inclusive role of the Development Society in implementation. It also illustrates the synergistic relation between the party and KSSP in their combined efforts to enlist participatory organizing. The canal works project, conceived at the grassroots and elaborated in the Development Society, required thousands of volunteers to clean up and build new canals. Meetings were convened to introduce and discuss the canal project with all political parties and mass formations. After the project had gone through a deliberative process with all the local structures, the question of implementation posed a serious challenge as no resources were available. While all the political and civil society organizations offered volunteers, they were still short by a large number. Grassroots-oriented activists approached official party structures and it responded by providing the majority of the volunteers for the project.[42] In addition to providing nearly 1,000 foot soldiers to construct the canal, the party used the high-profile nature of canals to educate and popularize the importance of mass collective volunteer projects and to gain support for community development. Thus, grassroots party and KSSP activists introduced the idea to formal party structures. The party then chose what it could support and the role it could best play.[43] It then followed up the process by using the canal project as a tool for education and conscientization. The success of projects such as these helped gain popular support for mass participation in development and strengthened the stature of the grassroots faction.[44]

It took three years for the Kalliasseri experiment to produce a tentative village development plan, and by September 1995 a comprehensive report on participatory planning in Kalliasseri was issued.[45] Again, reflecting the grassroots faction's commitment to learn collectively and develop a cohesive vision of the way forward, a two-day seminar was convened at the Center for Development Studies to review the Kalliasseri report. Seminar participants highlighted a number of lessons from the Kalliasseri experiment with the most important being the latent potential in voluntary action, the necessity for creating new institutions for participatory development (e.g., neighborhood groups), the difficulties of integrating institutions in civil society with institutions of government (hence the formation of the Development Society), and issues on the relation between politics and local development (Isaac and Franke, 2001: 55). Based on lessons learned in this experiment, grassroots party and KSSP activists drafted a vision of decentralization for the state. At this point the draft plan was an exercise in learning as the actual possibilities of implementing it were very limited since panchayats had no financial support and limited administrative powers. And since the CPI(M) did not control the state government, activists could not expect the situation to change favorably until at least the next election in 1996.

In the meantime, the party continued to develop and nuance its political vision through public debates in the various print media as well as through seminars and conferences. The party brought together political activists, scholars, and experts to look into the possibilities for participatory development through decentralization. In 1994 the CPI(M) held an international congress on Kerala Studies at the AKG Center for Research and Studies. In his Presidential Address at the Conference E.M.S. Namboodiripad highlighted the need to reach consensus on the way

forward through a fresh approach to the situation and the need to draw up a new agenda. Old ways of doing development and politics were thus no longer sufficient (Namboodiripad, 1994: 5). The congress was attended by 1,600 people, 700 of whom were scholars from abroad and other parts of India. Through deliberations and papers a broad perspective emerged. It was generally agreed that Kerala was in a serious crisis that encompassed not only the economy but also the political, social, and cultural spheres. It was also agreed that a reorientation of planning toward enhancing material production and improving quality of services, which would require a radical overhaul of the sectoral policies, was necessary. Industrialization and infrastructural development required state-level intervention, yet basic services and petty production sectors might best be served through a decentralized development strategy (CPI(M), 1995b; Isaac and Franke, 2001: 32). The seminar helped bring the new streams of political thinking of the grassroots faction into the main-stream Left.

By the mid-1990s all the discussions, debates, and experiments laid the basis for developing a coherent strategy. The party accepted the coexistence of capitalism and socialism for the foreseeable future and thus argued that private capital would be encouraged to invest in electronics, light engineering, rubber processing, agro-industries, and any other industries where there was comparative advantage. The other pillar of the strategy was mass involvement to increase productivity in small-scale sectors and enhance quality in public services; that is, it increased the role of civil society in the economy, which included ensuring that markets serve societal needs. The way the party was conceiving democratic decentralization was to extend democracy beyond making demands to making decisions about development and production as well as addressing questions of improving people's lives.[46] The way in which it developed its strategy reflected the party's synergistic relation to the mass base as well as its willingness to play a guiding role while leaving space to learn from below and through mistakes.

In addition to the paramount role of grassroots-oriented activists, the importance of political will from the CPI(M) must be highlighted. Transformative political projects must be championed by an ideologically coherent and programmatically strong political party. The state-level political vision was based on the fact that Kerala has a vibrant and active civil society that is of a democratic-promoting type[47] and is organized around class-based politics. The CPI(M) in Kerala moreover refused to adopt a defeatist attitude despite its awareness that real socialist democracy could not be created as an island in Kerala.[48] It also refused to adopt the attitude that efforts toward a socialist democracy could only be built once the Indian revolution occurred (Isaac, 1994: 59). Rather it was committed to building elements of social-ism within the current conditions by utilizing the strength of organized civil society and political consciousness of the people—it was constructing a counter-hegemonic politics. For such a vision to be implemented the party had to provide the incen-tives to and build the capacities of ordinary citizens as well as create the institu-tional structures for such involvement. The party was waging a war of position that focused on transcending the political and economic configuration under capitalism, in which civil society increasingly comes to exercise influence over the economic and political spheres. In this regard party leader and intellectual Thomas Isaac argued

for a new program that revised "the development policies pursued within the state, creating new democratic institutions within the sphere of production, integrating modern science and technology in a manner to promote sustainable development and reorienting the mass organizations themselves" (Isaac, 1994: 59). This vision culminated in the "People's Campaign for Democratic Decentralization."

Within the party the grassroots faction had captured enough power to nudge it enough to adopt a clear position on decentralization. Based on the lessons learned in Kalliasseri it was clear that without resource devolution decentralization would remain an exercise in learning (Kalliasseri Report, 1995). Anticipating the 1996 election victory, the grassroots faction raised the idea with E.M.S. Namboodiripad,[49] who had a history of supporting decentralization, and suggested it could be the CPI(M)-led Left Democratic Front government's contribution to the next five-year plan.[50] Getting E.M.S. to support the idea was crucial as his stature in the party would at least temporarily silence the trade union faction's opposition to it. E.M.S. brought the idea to the party leadership and strongly encouraged its adoption. It was subsequently approved by the state secretariat and later presented to the CPI(M)-led coalition, the Left Democratic Front as a *fait accompli*.[51]

It should also be noted that while there was a discernable shift in the party's practices toward counter-hegemonic politics enlisting participatory organizing, it also continued to mount protest politics and mass-mobilizing campaigns during this period. Between 1991 and 1996 the CPI(M) enlisted a number of oppositional activities, anti-Congress campaigns, and fought policies in the legislature. The agitational activities largely targeted the programs and policies of the Congress government in the state and the central government's neoliberal policies.[52] For example, mass demonstrations, darnhas (sit-ins), anticommunal campaigns, strikes, and marches were regularly staged throughout the state.

Nonetheless, while the party participated in protest politics, the grassroots faction continued to pursue counter-hegemonic generative politics through pilot projects and local activism that heavily relied on participatory organizing. These efforts ultimately yielded into the 1996 Democratic Decentralization Campaign that devolved significant state funds to lower tiers of government.

Building Counter-Hegemonic Generative Politics: The People's Campaign

The twin emphasis on hegemonic and protest politics placed the CPI(M) in the 1990s in an especially propitious position to deepen the participatory democratic reforms that require not only government support, but also, and very importantly, a highly politicized and educated base. By the mid-1990s the grassroots faction had developed a coherent strategy for decentralization wedded to local economic development through its experiments, seminars, and public debates. Once again in government, in 1996 the CPI(M) initiated a radical democratic decentralization campaign that attempted to transform political institutions, deepen democratic practices, and promote alternative forms of accumulation. The "People's Campaign for Democratic Decentralization" (referred to as the Campaign) was a bold attempt to widen participatory democratic institutions to include a broader spectrum of

society, extend participation beyond the political to include the economic realm, and thus marked a shift to counter-hegemonic politics.[53]

The Campaign included devolving discretion of 35 percent to 40 percent of the state's annual plan budget (untied funds) from state level to local village committees. As a result of the democratic decentralization, local communities became actively involved in deliberating and implementing initiatives to meet local needs and foster sustainable development. Indeed, it was part of a larger struggle for self-reliance and was meant to deal with the most keenly felt needs of people through their participation in every level of the process. I regularly asked villagers whether people had become more active as a result of the Campaign. I was consistently told that many people had become more involved, but that not everyone participated. For example, in one village I visited approximately 30 kilometers outside the capital city of Thiruvananthapuram, members of the community held regular neighborhood meetings to discuss issues germane to their community's needs and had started micro-production projects (e.g., making clothes, soap, and notebooks) with the assistance of local government. Approximately 2,500 women were involved in 96 women's self-help groups and 174 neighborhood groups in the area.[54] The Campaign represents the operationalization of the CPI(M)'s four ideological themes and is thus part of a larger effort to develop participatory institutions, promote a democratic political culture, as well as encourage local economic development.

To appreciate the novel aspects of the CPI(M)'s attempt, we must understand how it differs from decentralization pursued in many places around the world. First, democratic decentralization is also about local economic development, which refers to a process of building the structure of and managing the local economy by tapping local skills, knowledge, and resources and subordinating the economy to the needs of society. For the CPI(M) the goal of local economic development is ultimately to build an alternative logic of accumulation. Such an accumulation strategy requires active participation of citizens, addresses basic needs, and utilizes alternative technologies where appropriate, while at the same time attempts to harness people's energies for economic development. Creating economic activity, however, is not enough to engender development.[55] Structural changes such as the dual economy, agricultural reform, restructuring of local government institutions, and development of participatory local-level planning must also be addressed. In the CPI(M)'s vision, local economic development is thus a complimentary part of a counter-hegemonic generative politics.[56] In this effort the party argues that new social and economic relations that empower disadvantaged communities are the most hopeful avenues in the pursuit of more just and equitable development (Namboodiripad, 1991, 1994). The party was using the state to initiate the development of alternative forms of production. For example, 45 percent of devolved funds were designated for production, which in practice meant the creation of small-scale producer cooperatives. The party was attempting to integrate sustainable local economic development with democratic decentralization and in the process create alternative, counter-hegemonic logics to the predominant capitalist logic.

The party's vision of democratic decentralization is unlike the decentralization espoused by the World Bank and IMF, which have placed tremendous pressure on developing countries to decentralize. Because there are many attractive arguments

in favor of decentralization (e.g., making government more responsive to local needs, ensuring accountability, providing better public services, generating economic growth and employment, promoting popular participation and democracy, and increasing equality), the trend around the world has been to adopt some form of decentralization (Isaac and Franke, 2000: 231). But what kind of decentralization? Decentralization has often served a neoliberal agenda in which structural adjustment programs (e.g., reduce government spending, liberalize imports, remove restrictions on foreign investment, privatize state enterprises, devalue currency, and freeze or cut wages) have been pushed simultaneously with decentralization. In this vain, decentralization simply serves to weaken states and strengthen international organizations' influence over national development.

The party's vision, by contrast, highlights the vital role of an effective, society-led developmental state capable of pursuing society-led projects and in the process challenge the limits of representative structures and bureaucratic apparatuses. Decentralization, then, is a form of empowerment that facilitates genuinely participatory development and makes states more accountable to the populace. For it to be democratic, the party argues, both the representative and participatory forms of democracy must be strengthened through powerful and active civil society organizations, state-level commitment (including government officials), elected representative accountability, and the meaningful involvement of ordinary people (which requires conscientization and collective action).[57] For these changes to take place, the CPI(M) recognized that far-reaching institutional innovations had to accompany the legislative reforms and popular mobilization. A great deal of effort went into establishing participatory institutions that provided citizens multiple avenues through which they could deliberate, formulate, and implement development projects.[58] Thus, the Campaign was underpinned by the following two basic principles: (1) local government institutions had to become governing institutions with financial, functional, and administrative autonomy (rather than conduits of service delivery for schemes dictated from above), and (2) representative and direct structures of democracy should coincide and complement each other (Isaac and Heller, 2003: 80). The party's attempt at decentralization in Kerala was clearly in line with its theoretical vision of a strong developmental state that acts as a catalyst for participatory development and provides institutional space for citizens to make and implement collective decisions.

There are three principal forms of administrative decentralization (Isaac and Franke, 2001). The weakest yet most common form of administrative decentralization in the developing world is "deconcentration," in which central offices of line ministries transfer certain decision-making authority to regional or subregional offices. The second form of decentralization is "delegation," in which the government authority for particular tasks is transferred to semiautonomous or independent organizations (e.g., state-owned enterprises, public utilities, or private enterprises). The third and most comprehensive form of decentralization is "devolution." In devolution the authority and power to plan, make decisions, raise revenues, employ staff, and monitor activities is devolved to autonomous or semi-autonomous local government institutions. In addition, for decentralization to be truly participatory it must ensure collective self-government through an active and

informed citizenry and the construction of institutional channels through which citizens can engage in significant forms of participation. Meaningful democratic decentralization thus includes devolution of powers and finances, and simultaneously strengthening of participatory and representative democratic institutions through empowering citizens to participate in decision-making processes. In addition, the decision-making process must be made transparent and elected representatives held accountable to the electorate. In this way, decentralization holds a radical potential as it provides multiple avenues for people to confront and challenge systems of power within society.

To achieve meaningful decentralization, according to James Manor, change along the following three axes must occur: the administrative structure, the allocation of functions and powers, and the control of resources (Manor, 1999). Reform in all three areas is necessary and, ideally, should be introduced simultaneously. Conventional wisdom, however, conceives of a sequential model in which decentralization must begin with the creation of administrative support structures, and only after their establishment can the devolution of financial resources begin (these administrative preconditions, however, are seldom met) (Isaac and Heller, 2003: 81). This approach was challenged by the CPI(M)'s radically democratic vision of decentralization in which it reversed the sequential model. Rather than waiting for the incremental building of administrative capacity, the CPI(M)-led government took the risk and devolved funds as a first step.[59] This compelled the government and administration to carry out necessary reforms and create conditions for financial devolution.[60] It also helped generate pressure from below to bring about the necessary institutional changes. In addition to reversing the sequence, the Campaign gave local self-government institutions[61] the autonomy to formulate and implement projects within their clearly defined capacities. These measures firmly committed the party to a process in which citizens play a vital role in the functioning and development of both the local government as well as local development. Citizens were, in other words, being called on to play a driving role in both economic and political development.

The party had a long history with decentralization and thus it did not represent some radical sea change. The initiatives in the 1990s, however, vary in scope, depth, and commitment to an alternative model of development that not only marries decentralization with local economic development, but, very importantly, empowers people to participate in and shape the direction of economic and political institutions. The party was attempting to realize the radical potential in its theoretical vision that argued for developing elements of socialism in the current conditions by putting into practice all four elements of its vision simultaneously. In these efforts the party delineated a vision of political and economic development that was both people centered and people driven and simultaneously engendered economic growth. One aspect of the shift was, obviously, legislative fiat in which appropriate institutions and channels were constructed for mass participation and in which the devolution of financial and decision-making authority was given to local government institutions. Just as important, however, was creating capabilities in order for ordinary citizens to participate in every aspect of economic and political development at the local level (e.g., deliberation and decision making,

implementation, monitoring and sharing of the benefits and responsibilities of governmental activities). As party leader Thomas Isaac explained: "Fundamental reforms cannot be merely legislated. Legislation remains empty phrases unless powerful movements oversee their implementation. Legislation is necessary but not sufficient for decentralization" (Isaac, 2000). Thus, an important component of the Campaign was to build local-level capacity to conduct project assessments and formulate development plans.

In its efforts to capacitate the citizenry the party relied heavily on participatory organizing practices to educate and galvanize people.[62] Thus, a great deal of party activity focused on developing ordinary citizen's capacity to participate in the planning and implementation of development in their communities. This required, for example, an infinite number of workshops, political education seminars, and study groups. In 1997–1998, over 300,000 participants received training in "development seminars" where a range of skills were taught (e.g., self-governance skills) and nearly 4,000 pages of capacity-building material (e.g., handbooks and guides) were prepared and distributed in various training programs.[63] In addition to the formal training, informal learning also increased. In my field visits to villages, ordinary citizens and elected representatives often mentioned the increased opportunities for learning since the Campaign. For example, in one community I visited in central Kerala activists held an informal meeting at the village library every morning that began with a public reading of local newspapers. The meetings then turned to discussions about particular problems facing the community. These informal meetings were purely informational, but the people I spoke with explained how they helped them better understand issues and helped prepare them to participate in Grama Sabhas (village assemblies at the ward or panchayat level).[64]

Invoking its understanding of a developmental state anchored in participatory institutions, the CPI(M) redirected the way in which development is pursued. A unique feature of the decentralized planning is its focus on formulating projects rather than schematic sectoral allocations. From the very beginning of the Campaign there were efforts to steer development investment away from road construction and expansion of social services into production (Isaac and Franke, 2001: 114). To ensure the appropriate allocation of funds in the different areas of development, specific guidelines were drafted for allocation between the productive sector (45–50 percent of the budget was for productive projects in agriculture, animal husbandry, fisheries, and small-scale production), social spending or service sector (30–40 percent was for education, health, sanitation, drinking water, and housing), infrastructural sector (10–25 percent), and programs targeting women (10 percent) (Veron, 2000: 222). These demarcations, however, were somewhat porous as there was often overlap across sectors. In the service sector area, for example, a great deal of the funds went into infrastructural development.

Informed by its theoretical understanding of increasing the role of civil society in the economy, the CPI(M) spent a great deal of energy on creating the conditions for alternative logics of accumulation. With the largest percentage of funds earmarked for economic activities a great deal of effort was put into steering these initiatives into bridging decentralization with economic development through the

establishment of micro-enterprises (e.g., small-scale vegetable production, soap and candle production). The microeconomic initiatives have an anticapitalist logic that places workers in control of the means of production. The production units are based on cooperative principles[65] and are the first step in developing an alternative logic of social organization that contests the predominant capitalist logic. While private initiative and ownership was recognized as important, the CPI(M) encouraged development based on cooperative forms of ownership, especially small-scale cooperatives,[66] which produce for local markets and attempt to break the vulnerability to external forces.[67] The CPI(M)'s efforts to economically empower subordinate groups through democratic ownership of the means of production represents an attempt to build economic institutions that are based on different principles than capitalist enterprises. These efforts, thus, represent an attempt to *build* an alternative logic of accumulation.

While there was a great deal of success in the area of small-scale production, there were also some serious problems. Questions relating to marketing were generally overlooked, undermining the survival of many of the fledgling production units.[68] For example, the rapid expansion of vegetable production without adequate storage and marketing facilities led to a sharp decline in the prices of perishable commodities. Initially local government institutions did not develop complementary projects to assist in marketing products (Isaac and Franke, 2001: 157), but this failure was addressed by many local government institutions within the first couple years of the Campaign.[69] For example, I visited a village in Kannur where the panchayat assisted local production units by procuring their products and assisting market linkages with other institutions such as local schools to buy uniforms and notebooks. The CPI(M) learned the importance of integrating markets with planning, a point the party had acknowledged in its theoretical documents. Markets, it was acknowledged, played a vital role in questions of distribution and, therefore, needed active state intervention to help steer them to serve societal needs. Given the emphasis on production it was clear to party activists that questions of marketing and distribution were the linchpin to the success of small-scale production units. The issue of markets was highlighted as a primary concern by 15 out of 17 party activists and local government officials I spoke with in Kannur.[70]

The CPI(M)'s practices were fundamentally informed by its vision of participatory democracy in which ordinary citizens participate in decision-making processes. Thus, fundamental to the CPI(M)'s process of decentralization was the insistence on mass participation and transparency,[71] which required both the creation of new institutions as well as immense organizational support. For example, Grama Sabhas are utilized in each stage of the development process and serve as a key forum for ordinary citizens, elected representatives, and technical experts to come together to deliberate, formulate, and implement the development programs. Other institutional innovations such as development seminars, citizen-led task forces, and local governments all serve to increase the avenues for citizen participation (Isaac and Heller, 2003: 79). Making beneficiaries responsible for implementation is crucial to ensuring that funds are spent appropriately (i.e., not by corrupt contractors). For example, one of the means through which beneficiaries ensure transparency is a daily bulletin board listing the accounting of each project. In one panchayat I visited

in central Kerala a road construction project had a bulletin board next to the road being constructed detailing the specifics of the project including who was constructing it, the total cost, the amount paid to date, and the expected completion date.[72]

The Campaign was consciously trying to reconfigure the bureaucratic, hierarchical structure that dominated the state government and in its stead was attempting to create a new participatory model of local-level governance that simultaneously made the state government more efficient and effective as well as more fair, participatory, and accountable (Fung and Wright, 2003a: 6). The participatory institution of the Grama Sabhas, however, had many limitations as they were too large, their boundaries were purely administrative, and they only met a few times a year.[73] Based on the success of the neighborhood group model in Kalliasseri, neighborhood groups of 20–50 families were formed below the Grama Sabha with each family having a male and female member in the group. Many neighborhood groups assumed many of the powers of the Grama Sabhas, met regularly to discuss and deliberate issues, and eventually became an unofficial substructure of the Grama Sabha (Isaac, 1999). While activists encouraged the model to be adopted in all areas, it spread to around 200 (out of approximately 990) panchayats with varying degrees of effectiveness.[74] The sustainability of participation in these local participatory bodies was a serious problem and eventually led to the formation of women's neighborhood groups (discussed later).

To address the tremendous needs for organizational support thousands of volunteers were trained.[75] Despite Kerala's thriving civic culture, volunteers were necessary in order to educate and mobilize people to participate in the people's assemblies and the overall development process. In 1997, 300,000 participants received training in development seminars, 100,000 volunteers were trained to assist in formulating village projects, which were condensed into village plans with the assistance of 25,000 volunteers (Fung and Wright, 2003a: 14). Thus, in the first year of the Campaign seven rounds of training were held at various levels of government providing training to 15,000 elected representatives, 25,000 officials, and 75,000 volunteers (Isaac and Heller, 2003: 83).

The party understood that inaugurating participatory democratic institutions required a great deal of oversight to ensure that the democratic potential was not hijacked by political and economic elites. Thus, to ensure transparency and mass participation in plan formation and implementation a series of phases were drawn up by the State Planning Board with each phase having distinctive objectives, activities, and training programs (GOK, 1996). Every phase required numerous preparatory activities such as preparing handbooks, organizing training programs, developing methodologies for participation and empowerment, and guiding the process through an array of local and statewide political interests (Isaac and Franke, 2001: 36). Each phase thus required intense political mobilization and organization and a high degree of capacity from below. While the party guided the process through training and clearly delineated phases, it did not have a blueprint of the outcome. Indeed it envisioned an undefined process that reflected the particularities of each area.[76] It thus continually stressed that each area should develop its own priorities and project plans (since 1997 local governments have formulated and implemented their own development plans each year) (Isaac and Heller, 2003: 79). Similarly, it

encouraged activists to continually learn and adapt to developments from below.[77] In this way, the party was trying to develop meaningful party-society synergies that shape the direction of development. This included convening regular Grama Sabhas and establishing sectoral task forces of experts, elected representatives, officials, and citizens to prepare reports, develop projects, and draft plans.[78]

The first phase mobilized the maximum number of people possible to attend Grama Sabhas in order to identify local problems and priorities as well as to discuss the resource potential for addressing them.[79] The Grama Sabhas brought together approximately 1,500–2,000 residents in a community forum in which technical experts, elected representatives, and activists participated with local residents in the deliberation and planning of development projects.[80] The effective functioning of the Grama Sabhas was crucial to ensuring transparency and accountability in plan preparation and implementation. The central role of Grama Sabhas reflected the CPI(M)'s commitment to providing institutional spaces for public participation and citizen engagement with state institutions. To this end an array of popular media (such as festivals, jathas (marches), newspaper advertisements and articles, leaflets, radio talk shows, and television slots) were used to publicize the new forums and inform citizens.[81] To ensure the quality of local projects and plans small groups based on sectoral development (e.g., agriculture and irrigation, animal husbandry and fishing, education, drinking water, sanitation and health, industry, transport and energy, housing and welfare, culture, women's development, Schedule Caste/Tribe welfare, cooperatives and resource mobilization) were formed out of the Grama Sabhas. Every sectoral group had one or two trained resource people from the community. The groups discussed issues guided by semistructured questionnaires, which were meant to spark thinking and discussion. A crucial dimension of the Grama Sabhas was to facilitate critical thinking within the community about local problems, resources, and possibilities for development.[82]

To deal with the organizational demands of training resource people a three-tier training program was formulated: state-level training for Key Resource Persons (KRP), district-level training for District Resource Persons (DRP), and panchayat/municipal training for the Local Resource Persons (LRP). Approximately 600 state-level resource persons received 20 days of training, 12,000 district-level resource persons received 10 days of training, and more than 100,000 local resource persons received at least 5 days of training (Isaac and Heller, 2003: 83). A second round of training was given with the objective of equipping resource persons to guide the various tasks of the planning process such as undertaking local studies, preparing participatory development reports, and organizing development seminars. In addition to training resource personnel there was an overall commitment to educating and training ordinary citizens through action research, seminars, and active participation in the process.[83] There were also great efforts to inform all political parties and administrators of the Campaign through a series of conferences. A detailed overview of the Campaign was sent to almost every mass organization (students, youth, women, workers, farmers, agricultural workers, teachers, government employees, heads of research institutes, vice chancellors of universities, engineers, doctors, and managers and officers of selected voluntary organizations).

The second phase moved from the subjective aspirations of the people to developing a perspective of "what is to be done?" for each locality. This phase consisted of development seminars and participatory studies of the local human and natural resources. Out of the participatory studies assessments of local problems and needs were drawn up in "Development Reports," which were discussed at development seminars by delegates from the Grama Sabhas who collectively drew up proposals for development action.[84] Fifteen-chapter development reports were written for each area. From these proposals formal project proposals were formulated by task forces set up from every local body in the third phase. There was a task force for every development sector, which included elected representatives, officials, experts, ordinary citizens, and activists. This phase proved the most difficult and many municipalities failed to come up with new projects, copying model projects from the handbook or adapting the ongoing schemes of the line departments (Isaac and Franke, 2001: 100).

In the fourth phase the proposals were submitted to elected representatives who made the final choice from the range of proposals, with the rationale for the final choice written in a formal plan document and presented to and discussed at the Grama Sabha. This phase had to deal with the problem of incorporating the broad framework of development adopted by the state government into the local plans without infringing on the autonomy of the local planning process. There was another round of training during this phase, which included the key resource persons, municipal presidents, and secretaries. Training proved to be an important part of the Campaign at every level and lends credence to the argument that meaningful development requires a continuous process of education and learning. The fifth phase consisted of the higher tiers of government preparing their plans out of the proposed plans of the lower tiers. And finally, the sixth phase was a technical and financial evaluation of the plans and projects.[85]

The sixth phase presented serious technical challenges in that final plan evaluation required a systematic process of appraisal, which was impossible for the line departments to provide for so many projects. The State Planning Board came up with a novel idea to form "voluntary technical corps" made up of retired technical experts—and with the state's 55 retirement age the pool of candidates was vast.[86] Again, this is a vivid example of ordinary citizens in civil society extending their role in and complementing the efforts of local government institutions. The State Planning Board put a full-page advertisement in the newspapers calling for applications and held conferences to attract working professionals and technical experts to volunteer their time. Thousands of qualified applicants applied providing the State Planning Board a highly motivated and qualified pool of technical experts from which to draw (see table 3.1).

The issue of transforming the state to a developmental state anchored in civil society was pivotal to the Campaign's success. Threatened by the changes in the authority and decision-making structures, many officials in the state bureaucracy resisted the integration of the different levels. A truly participatory government requires the bureaucracy to work with nonofficials, ordinary citizens, and elected representatives, but this intersection of the bureaucracy with democratic institutions is one of the most resilient to transformation. Cooperation from the administration

Table 3.1 Campaign phases and activities

Phase	Activities and objectives
1. Grama Sabha	Convene Grama Sabha to identify and prioritize needs
2. Development seminar	Participatory studies, development reports and seminars; formulate development strategies
3. Task force	Meetings of task forces to prepare projects
4. Plans	Plan formulation of elected panchayat representatives
5. Plans of higher tiers	Plan formulation by elected block and district representatives
6. Volunteer technical corps	Expert committee meetings by 5,000 volunteers to appraise and approve plans

is thus crucial and administrative officials were, therefore, encouraged to participate in every phase. Not surprisingly, areas in which administrative officials were supportive were some of the most successful in the state. This point was made patently clear to me during my visits to communities. For example, in Kunnathukal Grama Panchayat an innovative labor bank was developed as a response to the decrease in agricultural production on the land. Many farmers had ceased to engage in agricultural activity due to the diminishing profits in the face of increasing competition. The local agricultural officer, Ginish Kumar, proposed the idea of the labor bank: farmers resume production if workers agree to a marginal reduction in wages (but a guaranteed number of workdays a year). In the months in which the laborers had no work they would join the labor bank from which the local government and communities would draw for public works projects, community development projects, and so on. The workers were paid slightly less in these jobs as well in return for a guaranteed number of workdays a year. The labor bank was highly successful and was expanding every year. Other panchayats were experimenting with similar ideas.

A further issue that hindered local plan integration was the narrow consciousness of ward councilors. Every elected member wanted a share from every possible project for his/her ward without regard to the larger development agenda. I witnessed this in a number of ward councilors with whom I spoke. Many councilors were only concerned for his/her ward's needs, often competing with neighboring wards for resources. To counter these trends, the party tried to imbue a broader consciousness in the elected representatives through workshops and training classes[87] as well as participation in panchayat plan formation.

Coordination among the different tiers of local self-government also proved a challenge.[88] While the grama panchayat provided the space for the most integrated, direct participation of ordinary citizens, the block and district levels also included important mechanisms for citizen involvement. By the third year of the Campaign the districts' role was clearly defined: to provide macro-perspectives for sustainable development in the district, consolidate lower-tier plans and identify gaps and duplications, and provide a long-term strategic vision (Isaac and Heller, 2003: 102). The serious attention the CPI(M) gave to ensuring widespread support is a concrete example of its attempt to build society-wide inclusivity. The Campaign was

an attempt at subaltern-led economic and political development that represented wide-ranging and diverse interests.

With the opposition controlling a significant number of local government institutions (e.g., in 1995 the UDF won 40 percent of local government seats), its participation was fundamental to the Campaign's success. To bring the opposition into the Campaign a "High Level Guidance Council" (HLGC) was formed, which included the 140 Legislative Assembly members, Kerala's 20 national parliament members, senior state government officials, leaders of mass organizations, artists, literary figures, cultural leaders and all former Chief Ministers (Isaac and Franke, 2001: 57). The party was trying to shore up support and avoid as much opposition as possible to the Campaign. It, therefore, actively encouraged the participation of all political formations and simultaneously ensured mass participation from below. I found it difficult to believe that party preference did not matter in such a highly politicized society. I thus regularly asked ordinary residents whether or not one's political party affiliation affected participation in, access to, or fund allocation in the Campaign. To my surprise, most people insisted that party affiliation did not matter. A couple of neighborhood groups I visited even said they did not know which party other members supported. This, of course, is not the case in areas where one party is dominant.

In essence the party was radically realigning the way in which development was done. It combined decentralization with state-led development and envisioned government institutions becoming integral part of community, social, and political development.[89] Historically, state-led social welfare reforms followed centralized and hierarchical departmental chains of commands and hence represented hegemonic generative politics. The democratic decentralization process fundamentally broke from this structure and placed the government machinery under the control of elected representatives at lower levels and made them accountable to their constituents.[90] The party, however, emphasized that democratic decentralization was not a substitute for national- and state-level planning (especially in areas such as foreign trade, infrastructural and industrial development) and warned against romanticizing local-level planning as the panacea for development problems. Rather, while the party maintained a commitment to an integrated, complementary approach among the national, state, and local levels, the party envisioned decentralization to help engender a more just and equitable world through a combination of planning and participation from below.[91] Social and economic planning was meant to make government spending more efficient and to incorporate market forces and private entrepreneurs. The effort to educate and empower citizens to play an informed role through institutional mechanisms coupled with the mass political mobilization helped to ensure egalitarian-oriented development. But the objective of the Campaign was not simply to develop plans from below. The entire process was also meant to transform the character and role of the state, the nature of participation, and the way in which political and economic development was pursued. It was, thus, a counter-hegemonic generative project as it shifted the terrain of struggle to civil society and extended the power of citizens over local government institutions and local-level production.

One of the implications of the Campaign for the party was in the way in which it related to the mass base. While continuing to officially hold a traditional vanguard

understanding of the party guiding from above, in practice the party was not only placing emphasis on learning from below, but was providing the conditions that necessitated a synergistic relation between the party and its base. The grassroots faction consistently maintained that if the party wanted to lead society then it must remain apace with developments in society, which requires constant study and incorporating new ideas addressing changing societal conditions.[92] The Campaign was trying to do exactly this as it took the decision-making and implementation role of the party (and state) out of the party's (and state's) hands and vested it in the people. One of the leaders of the grassroots faction succinctly explained: "Mistakes should not be the privilege of political parties. Let the people make mistakes and let us all learn from them."[93] The party was not pushing discrete innovations designed to address particular policy problems nor was it pushing for bargaining with or making claims against the state. Rather it sought a radical, unbounded participatory approach to economic and political development that placed society at the helm.

In the following section I look specifically at women's neighborhood groups in order to provide a further example of the ways in which the counter-hegemonic project extended the role of civil society into both the political and economic domains.

Counter-Hegemonic Generative Politics: Women's Neighborhood Groups

Grama Sabhas were an important participatory institutional innovation and provided a crucial avenue for ordinary citizen participation in the decision making and implementation of development priorities in their areas. While Grama Sabhas were a pivotal institutional innovation, they were still too large to ensure effective participation of ordinary citizens. Women's neighborhood groups[94] were thus encouraged to form as subsets of the Grama Sabhas and eventually came to play an important role in linking local government institutions with grassroots participation and economic activity (Seema and Mukherjee, 2000). CPI(M) activists saw the potential for women's neighborhood groups becoming a powerful mechanism for ensuring participation in formulating and implementing development plans and thus actively encouraged their formation. In addition, because the decentralization campaign allocated 10 percent of the devolved funds to projects that directly affected (and were managed by) women, women's neighborhood groups mushroomed throughout the state.

The women's neighborhood groups were an attempt to develop links between women's groups and local government institutions and deepen the democratic potential in the micro-credit programs. Thus, in addition to the role they play as micro-credit and micro-enterprise organizations, women's neighborhood groups were also an effective instrument for women's empowerment more generally as they directly linked women to political and economic structures in the community and helped provide a basis from which women could participate in the public realm.[95] To ensure that the women's neighborhood groups were organically linked to local self-governments and local plans as well as to ensure that they were both a means for small-scale production and an effective tier of participatory governance a tremendous amount of training and education was necessary. Party activists played the

primary role through education in seminars, informal meetings, training manuals, and training classes for groups and individuals.[96]

In Mararikulam (in the central part of the state) CPI(M) activists assisted a number of initiatives by women's neighborhood groups by providing numerous forms of training. Mararikulam is one of the poorest areas of the state with nearly 60 percent of the population living below the poverty line. Ironically this high level of poverty has also seen (and perhaps encouraged) a great deal of innovation and enthusiasm around decentralization. For example, the panchayats in Mararikulam have been at the forefront of the Campaign in terms of physical outcome, quality of participation, transparency, and innovation.[97] After the initiation of the Campaign women's neighborhood groups began to form throughout the area.[98] In late 2002 there were approximately 1,500 Kudumbashree women's neighborhood groups with 31,000 families as members[99] with approximately 75 percent of households represented in the women's neighborhood groups (Isaac et al., 2002). The socioeconomic characteristics of the members broadly reflected the region's socioeconomic pattern with the notable absence of middle- and upper-class women. In the women's neighborhood groups 70 percent of the members came from below-the-poverty-line category.

The Mararikulam panchayats developed extensive networks of women's neighborhood groups and with the assistance of local grassroots party activists women's neighborhood groups became an important part of the decentralization and economic development in the area. Party activists put enormous energy into training the groups to both participate in political structures and engage in viable economic activity. Regular classes were held in bookkeeping, financial management, production techniques, and organizational procedures (e.g., minute taking and record keeping, collective decision making, etc.). Party activists also encouraged local government officials to facilitate linkages with and support for the groups. For example, in Kanjikuzhy panchayat the local agricultural official regularly visited the neighborhood groups engaged in vegetable production, offering assistance in solving agricultural-related problems.[100]

In a number of groups I visited[101] meetings were held in gardens, empty paddy fields, and vacant land. While the groups looked informal at first glance, all the groups had rigorous bookkeeping methods, kept minutes of their meetings, and ran the meetings professionally. Some groups were more effective at making and implementing decisions than other groups, but all the groups I visited maintained high organizational standards and were actively involved in local developments and engaged in some form of economic activity. At minimum, all the groups reported discussing political issues and development priorities. Some groups were quite effective at making their views known in the Grama Sabhas and played important roles in development initiatives. Party activists and local government officials were often asked to come to the groups to assist in particular matters. Most of the groups highlighted the importance of training and education received by local party activists in the effective functioning of their groups. For example, a rural development center run by party activists held regular training and aftercare programs and facilitated ongoing linkages between the women's neighborhood groups and local government as well as other relevant actors

and specialized institutions (e.g., various government bodies, training providers, Kerala Agricultural University, Integrated Rural Technology Center, etc.).[102] I attended a meeting in which a local party activist was giving follow-up training to the women's group in agricultural production. The group had successfully harvested a range of vegetables, but wanted to diversify its planting and thus asked for assistance in this process. At the meeting I attended, the party activist was discussing the various options with the group such as the benefits and drawbacks of different crops (e.g., water needs, harvest times, etc.).[103]

The Mararikulam groups consisted of one woman per family in the neighborhood and tended to be younger members of households (e.g., 27 percent are below the age of 30, and 43 percent are between the age of 31 and 40, and less than 6 percent are above age 50). The educational level of the members was also fairly high: 55 percent had school-leaving certificates, 13 percent had pre-degrees, 7 percent graduate degrees, and about 1 percent had postgraduate degrees. There were hardly any members (less than 1 percent) who were illiterate, and those who were illiterate came from the older generation.

Most groups were systematic in their functioning (e.g., held weekly meetings and maintained registers). The bookkeeping and registers were an important aspect of their functioning: 99.9 percent of the groups had minute books and 81 percent claimed to have maintained detailed minutes; 91 percent had proper financial registers and 94 percent had membership registers; and 90 percent maintained separate loan registers. Within a short period of existence the women's neighborhood groups had taken to systematic functioning, regular savings, and circulation of savings through micro-loans to members. All the neighborhood groups collected weekly savings (10 rupees per member) and deposited the collection into the group's collective bank account. Seventy-five percent of the groups maintained their accounts with branches of the Cooperative Banks. None of the groups were receiving loans from the banks, which meant all the groups were circulating most of their savings and most charged 24 percent per annum interest on the loans.[104]

The women's neighborhood groups' activities quickly expanded beyond savings and loan to include political discussions of international events, national issues, and local concerns including the development priorities of their communities as well as micro-production ventures.[105] A recurring theme brought to my attention was the importance of self-confidence imbued through their participation in the women's neighborhood groups. Members often alluded to the fact that before they joined the groups they had no knowledge of politics and felt insecure in asserting themselves. Through their participation in the groups (including the weekly discussions about politics, the economy, and personal issues) they were empowering themselves to participate in formal political institutions and become active and efficacious citizens. In the words of a young woman I spoke with:

> I used to feel that I did not have anything to contribute to community meetings. In the past if a foreigner like you came, we [the women in the village] would have hid in our homes. We did not think we had anything to share. But now you are meeting our group and we have lots to tell you about. We contribute to our village meetings. We got the library built.[106]

Party activists encouraged the women to debate local issues and collectively decide what should be raised at the neighborhood groups and Grama Sabhas. In 16 out of 20 groups I visited in the area, the women said that participating in the group had helped inform them of national and international issues. In addition, many of the groups I visited were engaged in micro-enterprise initiatives in agriculture, coir products, soap making, candle making, and food processing (e.g., pickled vegetables) and while some groups were economically viable making a regular surplus other groups were able to produce enough to make a small difference in the women's lives by supplementing family income. For example, in vegetable production the harvest time was short and while many of the groups produced enough vegetables to feed their families, they were also able to bring produce to market. During harvest time I visited the farmer's market—set up by local government to sell small-scale producers' products during harvest time—where a range of locally grown vegetables and pickled products were sold.

The women's neighborhood groups held tremendous potential for linking local economic development and decentralization to help make participatory institutions more viable and are a concrete attempt by the CPI(M) to capacitate and empower people to participate in local economic and political development. Moreover, the women's neighborhood groups are a constituent part of the party's counter-hegemonic generative politics and thus were part of a larger political project aimed at fundamentally changing the balance of power among the state, economy, and civil society.

Conclusion

Facing formidable challenges that threatened to undermine Kerala's impressive development achievements, by the mid-1980s the CPI(M) was opening itself to new and novel approaches to politics. The Campaign represented a fundamental shift for the CPI(M) in which it implemented all four areas of its theoretical vision—participatory democracy, a new developmental state, socialist logics alongside capitalist logics, and increased role of civil society in the economy. It thus increased the role of civil society in both the political and economic domains, which ultimately resulted in a counter-hegemonic politics.

What explains the shift that led the CPI(M) in Kerala (or at least elements of it) to embrace dramatic changes in its political practice? The party had achieved a great deal of success in its earlier hegemonic and class-based forms of protest politics such as land reform and the vast gains made in the industrial unions in the public sector and public employees' associations. Indeed, Kerala boasts a unique history of social and political activism that helped usher in progressive initiatives throughout the twentieth century, which helped ensure the high levels of social and human development and extensive public infrastructure that have gained Kerala international recognition. What, then, led the CPI(M) to shift its emphasis in the 1990s?

It is clear that the KSSP played a crucial role in developments in the 1990s. But it is not the existence of KSSP that explains the changes in the party. Rather the balance of power within the party shifted toward the grassroots faction, which had firm links with KSSP. It is the shifts within the party that explain the change in

orientation. The CPI(M) both recognized the need for economic growth and the limits to redistribution without growth as well as the need to develop programs that involved mass participation and encouraged local initiative. The impotence of old-style politics to address the challenges facing the state required new initiatives that engendered development. These external conditions played into the party's internal dynamics facilitating the shift in the balance of power within the party toward the grassroots faction. Indeed, the grassroots faction prevailed in the 1990s, which, after two and a half decades of mass mobilizing around redistributive reforms, shifted the party to emphasize counter-hegemonic politics enlisting participatory organizing. The People's Campaign combined pluralistic, participatory politics with new and novel attempts at fostering economic and social development, and in the process helped nurture a civic culture that promotes grassroots democratic institutions. Moreover, it is the CPI(M)'s attempt to operationalize the four elements of socialist democracy. As a result the terrain of struggle shifted to civil society and extended the power of society over the state and economy ultimately initiating a counter-hegemonic politics.

What led to the shift in the balance of power in favor of the grassroots faction in the 1990s? The answer to this question is addressed in chapters five, six, and seven. Before we get to the explanation, however, in chapter four I discuss the SACP's practices in the 1990s.

CHAPTER 4

The Hegemonic Politics
of the SACP

The South African Communist Party faced daunting challenges in the 1990s. The international balance of power was unraveling in favor of the U.S.-dominated West with its claims of economic superiority and ideological hegemony. South Africa's fledgling negotiations were precariously under threat with the possibility of civil war becoming increasingly palpable and the simultaneous need for the liberation movement to forego armed struggle in favor of negotiations. After 40 years of clandestinity the SACP also faced the imperatives of reestablishing direct links with a popular base and open membership in completely new terrain. To make matters more difficult, unemployment and poverty had become constant features of life for many South Africans. In response to these challenges, the SACP, like the CPI(M), articulated a vision of socialist democracy that placed priority on participation of ordinary people in the realization of democratic egalitarian politics.

In practice, however, the SACP fell short in implementing its vision. Unlike the CPI(M), the SACP's efforts at participatory democracy and a new developmental state focused on the legislative arena and neglected to galvanize civil society to participate in the new institutional spaces created. It fared slightly better in its efforts to translate the other dimensions of its theoretical vision into action. First, like the CPI(M), the SACP accepted the fact that socialism and capitalism would have to coexist for a period, which it articulated in its programs of action as a medium-term vision and a minimum socialist program. Second, as part of its efforts to expand civil society's control over economic activity and softening the deleterious effects of the market, the SACP pushed for the decommodification of social services, the reform of financial institutions, and the development of cooperatives.

In this chapter I discuss the SACP's shift from protest politics to generative politics. This shift is especially important as it launched the party on a dramatically new path away from its struggle past to the construction of a new nation. I then look at the SACP's engagements in the 1990s. I argue that, unlike the CPI(M)'s counter-hegemonic

generative politics, the SACP pursued a hegemonic generative politics enlisting mass-mobilizing practices.

Protest Politics Yields to Generative Politics

To appreciate what the shift to generative politics entailed it is useful to review the politics of protest that characterized the greater part of the SACP's history. South Africa is perhaps best known to students of African studies for the impressive character of its national liberation struggle and the relatively peaceful transition to a democratic South Africa. Despite the brutal practices of the apartheid regime, the liberation movement succeeded in forcing the regime to give up power through a negotiated transition. With the oldest liberation movement on the continent, South Africa has been in a near-century-long state of struggle, much of which has been guided by the Communist Party.

The mobilizational history of the SACP can be divided into three periods. From the 1920s to the 1950s[1] the Communist Party was at the forefront of labor and community struggles in which it consistently enlisted nonviolent methods of opposition both in terms of participatory organizing and mass mobilizing.[2] For example, communists played crucial roles in the most important oppositional campaigns of the period such as the 1946 mineworkers strike, the 1952 Defiance Campaign against racial laws, the 1955 "Congress of the People" (which ratified the Freedom Charter[3]), the pass burning campaign, and a general political strike. These campaigns injected a spirit of defiance and raised awareness for the need to directly challenge the apartheid state. Communists were also very active in community politics, held regular political education and literacy classes, and went to great lengths to pursue issues that spoke to the daily lives of ordinary citizens.

With the increasingly hostile and repressive methods of the apartheid regime, in the early 1960s the mood among black South Africans turned more defiant and dissatisfied with the politics of nonviolence. Reflecting the shifting sentiments, the SACP and ANC concerned themselves with directing the frustrations bubbling up from the populace and thus channeled the mood "in terms of armed rather than spontaneous violent activities" (Slovo, 1976: 169). The ANC's and SACP's joint decision in 1961 to launch Umkhonto we Sizwe (MK, the armed wing of the ANC and SACP) reflected a strategic turning point for the movement and attempted to direct popular sentiment into a coherent form of opposition. While they shifted to violent opposition, the SACP and ANC did not give up their commitment to minimize the loss of life. MK's *modus operandi* was to direct violence in the form of sabotage campaigns against hard targets (e.g., infrastructure such as electricity pylons and rail lines), explicitly avoiding the loss of life. Thus, the shift from the 1950s to the 1960s in terms of oppositional activities can best be characterized as a radicalization of practice that encouraged a confrontational approach. But this also provoked a response from the apartheid regime, which intensified its efforts at destroying all opposition structures and resistance efforts. By the middle of the 1960s the apartheid regime had decimated internal structures of opposition, forcing both the ANC and SACP into exile.

During this second phase of the SACP's mobilizational history, the emphasis increasingly shifted to oppositional activities enlisting mass mobilizing. Over the

course of the 1960s and 1970s the party (together with the ANC) focused on military action, despite repeated appeals about the importance of mass political formations. The role of armed struggle had shifted from a defensive mechanism wielded against the hostile apartheid regime to the primary strategy for seizing state power. For example, in the party's 1962 Program, *The Road to South African Freedom*, the question of armed struggle was officially raised for the first time, but the discussion of it was brief. While it supported armed struggle as a defense against the state's attacks, the party was at pains to clarify that it was not rejecting other forms of nonviolent, political methods of struggle. By the 1970s, however, armed struggle had eclipsed political activity as a primary emphasis in the party and ANC.

The situation came to a head in 1978 when top leaders of the movement went on a study tour of Vietnam.[4] The study tour eventually led to an official statement recommitting the liberation movement to political activity out of which military activity would grow. The ANC's Politico-Military Strategy Commission's 1979 document entitled *Green Book: Thesis on Our Strategic Line*[5] emphasized the importance of developing political mobilization and organization within civil society and marrying political struggle to military action. However, despite this official commitment to the primacy of political activity, which was flourishing in communities within South Africa, in practice the SACP continued to focus on armed struggle.

Despite the apartheid regime's attempts at despotic control, spaces of opposition continued to exist as the 1970s exploded in cycles of resistance from trade unions, students, and communities across the country. By the 1980s trade union politics had evolved into a formidable force challenging the apartheid regime. By the time COSATU formed in 1985 labor was organizing at the political level in which it represented universal interests that combined community and labor struggles into the broader national liberation project. In addition to overt forms of resistance, everyday forms of resistance also existed in families, churches, schools, and workplaces. In conjunction with structures forming within the country, by the mid-1970s the ANC and SACP had reestablished underground units sprinkled throughout the country. The internal structures of the party were small cell structures or semiformal groupings. Most of the work of internal party activists at this time was propaganda work and information dissemination (e.g., letter bombs).[6] While the SACP and ANC were slowly reestablishing internal structures and networks, community resistance was intensifying throughout the 1970s and early 1980s.

In 1983 the United Democratic Front (UDF) formed as the organizational umbrella of the multitude of formations bubbling up throughout the country. In addition to building an organizational structure that spanned from the local to the national and coordinating the panoply of protests and campaigns, it also promoted the profile of the underground and exiled structures of the ANC and SACP (Seekings, 2000: 3). From its genesis, the UDF was overtly oppositional in orientation. While the UDF's original goal was simply to organize opposition to the Tricameral parliament elections and the Black Local Authorities,[7] it quickly broadened its scope to include school and rent boycotts that yielded into urban uprisings and insurrectionary tactics and eventually led to "ungovernability" in the townships (von Holdt, 2003: 22–23). The activities of the 1980s were protest in nature and focused on confronting and challenging the apartheid state and its abhorrent policies.

After returning from exile in 1990 the SACP had to shift its political imperative from protesting against the apartheid state to participating in the construction of a democratic South Africa, marking the third period of its mobilizational history. This required an extensive reorientation for the party as it had just adopted a new program *The Path to Power* (1989) in which it highlighted the primacy of capturing state power through insurrectionary action (SACP, 1989a: 57). While insurrectionary seizure of state power was certainly the main thrust found in *The Path to Power*, the last section of the program also pointed to the likelihood of negotiations. In this section the SACP underpinned the importance of armed struggle and mass actions to achieve meaningful negotiations, arguing that the apartheid state would not give up power without real pressure through mass political and military action (SACP, 1989a: 58). But as history would show, this combination of military action and negotiations was unsustainable and by the early 1990s the party had to reorient itself away from protest politics toward a generative politics of societal reconstruction. Indeed, the party warned against becoming an oppositional force that undermined the democratic transformation and long-run socialist project (Cronin, 1992: 88–89; Eidelberg, 2000: 139). Drawing on its recent history of mass mobilizing, however, the SACP continued to stage big events and mass actions in the form of large rallies, public speeches, and marches to support the negotiations process.[8] While old-style protest politics and armed struggle increasingly lost legitimacy as the movement was no longer trying to destroy the apartheid government through insurrection, shifting to a constructive politics around negotiations and nation building was not an easy transition after so many years of protest politics. The SACP struggled to develop generative politics enlisting participatory organizing practices.

The negotiated settlement and the 1994 ANC-led Alliance election victory meant that the party had no choice but to shift to generative politics and engage in new practices and activities. In a 1992 Consultative Conference Document the SACP argued for expanding popular control:

This raises the whole question of the role of the masses in making their own history. [...] The type of democracy that we want to build will require permanent mass struggle. Now the word mass action has come to be associated with action against the regime, a battering ram type of power and it is a weapon.

But what we are struggling for is a new nation, where the people make their own history, where they are truly empowered under a constitution which enables them to build what they really want and have what they really need. (SACP, 1992b: 8)

It was now forced to confront viable alternatives grounded in concrete realities of South African conditions. The party had two roles in this process of building a democratic South Africa. On the one hand, with a disproportionate number of the movement's intelligentsia in its ranks, the party was deeply involved in the negotiation process and played a crucial role in developing the foundations of the new nation (e.g., the Constitution, the Labor Relations Act, and the *Reconstruction and Development Program* (RDP)). On the other hand, as a mass-vanguard political party with access to state power through its alliance with the ANC, the SACP had

to engender people's participation in the development and reconstruction of South Africa. Its primary activities could no longer focus on oppositional politics against the old systems of oppression and exploitation, but rather had to construct new institutions and practices in the development of a democratic and socialist South Africa. Thus, the party had to shift from protest politics to a generative politics in which it emphasized developing new institutions and channels for mass participation.

Building Institutions for Participatory Democracy and a Developmental State

Creating the conditions for a new developmental state and participatory democracy were fundamental to the SACP's vision of socialist democracy. The SACP, therefore, placed a great deal of energy in shaping legislation and ensuring the creation of institutional spaces for mass participation. With the statist faction securing sufficient control within the party, one of the notable features of the party's activities in the 1990s was its focus on issues of strategy and governing (SACP, 1994b: 4). In the period between its 1991 Congress and the 1994 democratic elections the party's attention was largely focused on negotiations, issues of nation building, and the civil war in KwaZulu Natal and thus it played a central role in elaborating the contours of the negotiated settlement and the Government of National Unity.[9]

In 1993 and 1994 the party's focus turned to securing an ANC election victory and the twin demands of building organizational structures and constructing fledgling democratic institutions (SACP, 1992b: 7). The party focused on gaining as much access to state power as possible for the ANC-led Alliance despite the fact that the ANC ultimately shaped the character of the developmental state. Unlike the SACP's vision of a developmental state moored in civil society, the ANC-led state drifted in the direction of a state that drives development on behalf of the people rather than in conjunction with the people. Why, then, did the SACP think it could influence the character of the ANC-led state? The SACP was still working under the illusion of its past. The SACP's close relation to the ANC dates back to the 1940s and 1950s when the party sought to radicalize and build the ANC into a mass-based opposition movement. The relation between the two organizations solidified over the years in exile when the party held a preeminent place in the movement. In three separate interviews with movement stalwarts, each spoke about the high-caliber party cadres and the influence of the party in the movement during exile.[10] One respondent claimed that "to move up in the ANC you had to be a party member. It was like a badge of honor."[11] Similar sentiments were expressed repeatedly by members who had been involved since the 1970s and 1980s. After returning to South Africa in the 1990s the ANC and SACP formalized their relationship in the Tripartite Alliance (the Alliance as it is popularly called) with COSATU. While officially working together in the Alliance, the ANC has increasingly shown itself willing to disregard Alliance agreements when it suits its interests (discussed in chapter seven). One of the areas that the ANC and SACP were at variance related to the role of the state.

The election process raised a number of issues that had not been adequately addressed by the party for much of its existence. For example, the party's blind focus

on capturing state power reflected an inadequate understanding of power (and the state) in which it collapsed nonracial parliamentary democracy with a qualitative transfer of power to the people and belied a monolithic understanding of the state. After the ANC-led Alliance's election victory the party began to recognize that the picture was more complicated and power more diffuse. For one, the negotiated settlement translated into a slow and evolutionary process of transferring power to the new government (which the party did not control). For example, in securing a relatively peaceful transition the Alliance agreed to "Sunset Clauses,"[12] which left a large portion of the civil service unchanged for a transitional period. The state bureaucracy would, thus, only be seriously transformed at the beginning of the new millennium.

The realities of the concrete conditions led the SACP to question what it meant to hold state power and whether controlling the state actually translated into real power.[13] The party was increasingly coming to the view that while wielding state power was crucial, it was insufficient and did not reflect the completion of the democratization process (SACP, 1992b: 9). Moreover, its focus on state power was at variance with its vision of a developmental state that is accountable to subaltern classes and subordinated to civil society. A dynamic civil society, the party acknowledged, was crucial in any effort to transcend advanced capitalism. And conversely, too much state control, as history has shown in the Soviet Union, tends to smother civil society. It thus began questioning its overemphasis on state power as well as its assumption that the ANC-in-government would necessarily represent subordinate classes.[14] Reflecting the evolution in its thinking a document from its 1992 Consultative Conference argued that the goals should be "(a) not just the transfer of power but fully taking over and wielding state power in the interests of the masses of our people; and (b) empowering ordinary people and organs of people's power, including trade unions, to take this struggle further" (SACP, 1992b: 10). The party attempted to embed subaltern classes in the state by ensuring that the entire election process was democratic and open to mass participation. For example, the SACP insisted on a transparent, bottom-up nominations process for the ANC election lists. It also urged the elaboration of an election manifesto "based on a clear program for national democratic transformation" (SACP, 1994a: 2).

The SACP was trying to ensure that the developmental state was moored in civil society through the plethora of newly created institutions and forums for extending the scope and depth of civil society's participation.[15] For example, parliament standing committees, hearings, and theme committees were formed as well as a number of institutions were created such as the National Economic Development and Labor Council[16] (NEDLAC), which institutionalized consultation and bargaining procedures between business, labor, community-based groups, and government. For example, it was in NEDLAC that the 1995 Labor Relations Act was discussed clause by clause. Forums for direct participation of ordinary people were also created such as Local Development Forums, Housing Forums, Electricity Forums, and University Transformation Forums (Tripartite Alliance, 1995: 10). The SACP supported the creation of the myriad institutional and organizational spaces giving ordinary citizens avenues for direct participation, which were legislated by the ANC-led state. The SACP's role in implementation

was, however, unclear. While there were many new institutions created, the thrust of many of the new institutions ultimately extended the role of the state over the institutions of civil society. For example, at a community meeting I attended in Soweto people expressed frustration about the local government's unresponsiveness to residents' demands and complained that they were called to meetings to be told what is going on by the councilor and other government officials. Residents were informed of decisions, but not part of the decision-making process.[17] Similar sentiments were expressed in three interviews with participants of development forums in Johannesburg.[18]

Another arena that provided tremendous potential for mass participation was local government.[19] To appreciate the potential for participatory processes at the lower tiers of government, a brief discussion of provincial and local government is in order. The administration of the nine provinces in South Africa have a fair amount of authority and power to administer a range of services, are allocated approximately two-thirds of the national budget (after repayment of national debt), and employ the vast majority of public servants. For example, out of the 1.1 million public servants 750,000 are employed in regional administration. In the 2001–2002 financial year, R117 billion out of a total revenue of R273 billion was assigned to the provinces in the form of block grants,[20] which the provinces can spend as they choose (Lodge, 2002: 32–35).

With a significant portion of the state's funds allocated to provincial governments, it is not surprising that provincial government is responsible for the range of aspects of government that affect the everyday life of citizens such as health, pension payments, education, and housing.[21] Not surprisingly, most provincial expenditure is on health, education, and social security with the other major expense going to salaries (a situation aggravated by the increases in public sector wages over the 1990s)[22] (Baskin, 2000: 146–47). With priorities given to basic services and salaries, capital expenditure decreased between 1994 and 2002. Most departments lack adequate technical skills and professional integrity and suffer from the legacy of inefficiencies from the past (Lodge, 2002: 33–35). At the same time, more people have made claims on government, increasing the strain on provincial administration (Lodge, 2002: 36–37). Ultimately these constraints have meant that provincial governments have not been able to support the massive service delivery required.

Below provincial government is municipal or local government (the lowest tier of government in South Africa), which is responsible for a number of public goods such as clinics, street lighting, water-borne sewage, public spaces, electricity supply, public transport, and roads. While provincial government has had its challenges, the balance sheet for municipal government activity is even less flattering as most local governments struggle to meet their responsibilities and are in financial straits. Unlike provincial government, local government has a number of sources of independent finance such as raising revenues by increasing local taxes, cross subsidizing, improving remittances for services, service cut-offs, and rate increases. In tight fiscal times many local governments have tried to ameliorate their financial situation by shifting the burden to consumers through rate increases and service cut-offs. Many of these attempts, however, have provoked a response from civil society. For example, SANCO organized widespread resistance in Johannesburg against rate

increases and service cut-offs (Lodge, 2002: 89), and social movements such as the Soweto Electricity Crisis Committee emerged and began challenging the local state. Another response by local government to financial crisis was to reduce spending on infrastructure, privatize, and borrow from banks (Lodge, 2002: 91). For example, Johannesburg's development strategy, Egoli 2002, was based on such a privatization formula. Together these factors have earned local government a poor reputation for being ineffective at governing and unaccountable and unresponsive to their constituencies. Despite these problems, a participatory local government is enshrined in the South African Constitution.

The Constitution specifically outlines the objectives of local government "to provide democratic and accountable government for local communities" and "to encourage the involvement of communities and community organizations in the matters of local government."[23] In 1998 and 2000 local government legislation was passed (the Municipal Structures Act of 1998 and the Municipal Systems Act of 2000), outlining a comprehensive program of institutional reform. Local authorities were to govern developmentally, provide vision and leadership to coordinate operations of public agencies and the private sector, encourage participation of the citizenry, and prioritize needs through holistic, integrative development planning, which should guide budgeting decisions (Lodge, 2002: 93). The legislation included a provision for local government to establish participatory democratic institutions in the form of ward committees (Houston et al., 2001: 206).

Ward committees are community structures linking municipalities with the needs, aspirations, and problems of communities. They are the bridge between local government and communities and are the main tool available to municipalities to increase participation of ordinary citizens. Ward committees are chaired by the ward councilor and are composed of not more than 10 community members. In addition to ward committee meetings, local councilors are supposed to hold regular report-back meetings (at least four a year) open to the public. While ward committees provide a potential avenue to construct new networks of representative bodies and increased participation of ordinary citizens, they also have their problems. The national legislation requires that local municipalities enact municipal by-laws or resolutions establishing ward committees and leave the responsibility for implementation to ward councilors. In practice, this has led to serious stumbling blocks in the implementation of ward committees as many municipalities do not have adequate capacity to enact the necessary by-laws and a great number of ward councilors have not understood their roles (IDASA, 2006).

While the SACP fought for the institutional creation of ward committees, it has not played a role in ensuring their effective implementation nor has it participated in popularizing community involvement in ward committees. For example, in all the branch meetings, district and provincials councils, political schools, seminars, and workshops I attended in 2001, the issue of ward committees rarely came up.[24] In only three interviews (out of 81 interviews with party members) did respondents discuss the importance of ward committees and the need for the party to educate the public about them.[25] Further indicating the party's neglect of ward-level institutions, in 2003 I attended four ward meetings in Johannesburg and Durban in which very few SACP members were present despite the wards being in areas where

there are strong SACP branches. The SACP members that did participate were there as residents (i.e., not in their capacities as party members). After one meeting I attended in KwaMashu, I asked an SACP district leader why the party was not actively engaging residents around ward-level institutions. His reply is telling: "We plan to get more involved in them and to let people know they should participate. We just get caught up in other things. It is hard to get comrades involved in these things."[26] The sentiments of this party leader aptly capture the party's relative disinterest in ward-level institutions.

Clearly there is space for participation of ordinary citizens in local government structures and with the amount of powers and funds allocated to provincial and local governments it is clear that these lower tiers of government offer ample opportunity to pursue alternative political projects. Indeed, it is exactly at this level of governing that the CPI(M) in Kerala intervened and pursued its counter-hegemonic generative politics. The SACP has failed to take up this opportunity.

Antecedents of Hegemonic Generative Politics: Mass Mobilizing from Above

While it focused on constructing the contours of a new democratic developmental state, the SACP launched its first public campaign after returning to South Africa. The Housing, Health, and Hunger Campaign (The Triple H Campaign as it is popularly called) was an outcome of a resolution adopted at the party's 8th Congress in 1991 and tried to ground the party in the most keenly felt needs of the populace as well as draw direct links to the party's practices of the 1940s that emphasized participation of ordinary citizens (SACP, 1992a). In the 1940s the party led militant mass activities for socioeconomic issues and it was this history that the SACP was now trying to reclaim.[27] The party was trying to establish its moorings in legal activities around bread and butter issues and local concerns and thus redirect the party away from armed struggle to concrete issues that require new practices. As one Central Committee discussion document on the Campaign explained: "The party needs a programmatic approach to campaign work, rather than merely a responsive attitude to struggle" (SACP, 1992a: 1). It further argued that new methods were necessary as "many cadres are skilled in methods of struggle no longer suitable to the climate of legality; others have learnt their politics under State of Emergency conditions. The skills needed for organizing in the present context must be shared among all our members" (SACP, 1992a: 4). The Campaign was meant to galvanize people around issues of housing, health, and hunger, and to anchor the party in local communities. The theme of the campaign certainly offered the potential to enlist participatory organizing that strengthens civil society as it called on people to participate with the state to ensure a new dispensation. For example, the party argued that "we must consult, educate, mobilize, and organize so that we can build a people's solution to the problems of the homeless, the sick, and the hungry" (SACP Western Cape Region, 1993: 1–2).

Documents of the Campaign repeatedly make reference to the importance of the Campaign as a means through which the party can embed itself in civil society. The party argued that "the masses must build organization, identify day to day issues

and struggle around concrete demands to achieve this dual goal" (SACP, 1992a: 1). Indeed, it argued that the best way to politicize people is through successful campaigns that address local needs linked to national political demands. One of the suggested activities was action research and data collection. Party activists were to collect data on the most keenly felt needs (squatting, lack of access to clean water, etc.) in order to expose the conditions under which people suffer as well as develop appropriate responses. I could not find any evidence to suggest that any data was ever collected.

While the party had a number of public events supporting the Campaign such as high-profile visits by top leaders (such as Chris Hani the general secretary) to hospitals, clinics, and communities, it failed to develop a clear plan of action for implementation of the Campaign. It offered rhetorical generalizations about the need to "combine mass work, campaign work, propaganda, political education around the socialist perspective on solutions to housing, hunger, and medical care and skills training around organizing methods, public speaking, and house visits, etc." (SACP, 1992a: 2). Yet despite the party's plan to develop speaker's notes and other training material to assist activists in taking the Campaign forward, it never developed the material. Similarly, while the party acknowledged the need for a strategy workshop to figure out how to carry out the Campaign as well as the need to develop a clear perspective on the long-term and short-term goals of the Campaign, it never organized such a workshop.[28] Without a clear vision and strategy, the Triple H Campaign merely amounted to a populist slogan that did not receive meaningful popular support. It thus never took off and fizzled out within a short period of time.[29]

A number of rank-and-file members I interviewed had heard of the Triple H Campaign, but very few could even name what the three "H's" stood for. Even fewer could claim to have participated in any activities surrounding the Campaign and those that had participated mentioned mass actions such as rallies or public speeches by leaders.[30] According to party documents there were three methods of action used in the campaign: (1) symbolic actions such as bread eating in business clubs, (2) "welfare actions" such as the distribution of bread to pensioners; and (3) mass actions such as marches, demonstrations, pickets, and rallies. All three methods of practice do little to educate and empower people to develop solutions to their problems. Rather the party continued to view practices in terms of winning demands from an identifiable benefactor (such as the state or employers). While the issues of housing, health, and hunger could certainly have been built into a transformative politics aimed at building a democratic state anchored in active participation of ordinary citizens, the general thrust of the activities were protest actions enlisting mass mobilizing (SACP, 1992a: 4). After the Triple H Campaign the party did not launch another campaign until the new millennium. In the intervening years the party primarily focused on issues of governing and developing its own programmatic and strategic perspective.

While the party acknowledged the importance of ordinary people's participation, the issue of capacitation and education of the citizenry (including government officials) to play this new role continued to be a secondary concern. Almost as an afterthought a 1992 draft document raised the issue of people's participation: "We

need to urgently address how the people will be actively involved in taking forward the process of democracy after there is a democratic constitution" (SACP, 1992b: 8). An active and empowered citizenry involved in the deliberation and implementation of development requires a range of skills that were not adequately developed through the protest politics of the previous half century. Yet despite its awareness of the need to build capacity, the party put very little attention into this area. Reflecting this ambiguity and confusion, the party's practices lacked a coherent strategy enlisting participatory organizing, but rather primarily relied on mass-mobilizing practices. For example, only 8 interviewees (out of 81 interviews with party members) spoke of engaging in participatory organizing practices in the 1990s. All 81 respondents, by contrast, recalled participating in internal debates, government functions, and mass actions such as rallies and demonstrations. As these numbers attest, the challenge of preparing the citizenry to actively and meaningfully participate in the new institutional arrangements was sorely neglected, ultimately thwarting participatory development initiatives.

The practices of mass mobilizing (e.g., high-profile, large events) can be used for either state-led or civil society-led protest politics. In civil society-led protest politics mass mobilizing is often geared toward challenging or destroying political or economic power. In state-led protest politics mass mobilizing is usually used to create solidarity among the population and as a propaganda tool to popularize and galvanize energy around particular issues. In both the type of campaigns and activities are chosen for their symbolic and propaganda value as much as for what they achieve. Seeking a limited view of participation, mass mobilizing does not attempt to empower people to participate and make decisions that affect their lives, but rather seeks to channel popular support for decisions already made. Participatory organizing, on the other hand, seeks to prepare people for participation (i.e., to deepen and extend ordinary citizens' capacity to participate in decision making and implementing policies that directly impact on their lives). In this way, the goal of participatory organizing is integrated into the practices themselves. Thus, participatory organizing is fundamental to counter-hegemonic generative projects that seek to extend civil society's control over political and economic institutions. In other words, participatory organizing seeks to develop popular initiative to transform society, while mass mobilizing seeks popular support for particular campaigns.

The party gave relatively little attention to developing practices that complement and advance the party's socialist aspirations. Party theorist and strategist Jeremy Cronin's discussion document on the different strategies of struggle exemplifies the party's failure to envision a participatory organizing approach around a counter-hegemonic generative politics. Cronin outlines three strategic approaches: (1) "don't rock the boat," (2) "turning on the tap," and (3) "the Leipzig way" (Cronin, 1992). Cronin argues that symbolic protests (the first two approaches) demonstrate either legitimacy or illegitimacy for a particular government or movement and might also help create a space for elites to bargain over transitional processes. He juxtaposes this to mass acts of popular self-empowerment (the Leipzig way). While Cronin saw the mass acts of popular self-empowerment as an alternative, all three strategies are mass mobilizing in character. The three types of practice converges in form and content, but diverges in their timing and duration. Reflecting an even deeper

failure, Cronin displays ambivalence as to whether the SACP was still in a phase of protest politics or had shifted to generative politics. His preferred choice, the Leipzig way, is oppositional in nature and essentially consists of a mass uprising that ultimately develops organs of people's power in opposition to the state. While Cronin was penning this document the party was simultaneously envisioning a transformative project enlisting people's participation in constructing and guiding the nation's development trajectory (SACP, 1992b).

Reinforcing the party's focus on developing institutional spaces rather than creating capacity of citizens to participate was the fact that the majority of leaders were employed in government and hence focused on state-led initiatives. In Gauteng, for example, provincial leaders were disproportionately represented in Gauteng government structures and all three provincial secretaries during the 1990s were Members of the Executive Council (MEC), the provincial equivalent of the cabinet.[31] A similar trend is seen at the Central Committee level. The 1998 Central Committee had 28 out of 30 members employed in government positions ranging from ministers and members of parliament to national and provincial bureaucrats and local government officials. Thus, with so many leaders occupying key positions in government it is hardly surprising that the party did not focus on civil society-led initiatives, but preferred state-led initiatives.[32]

Thus, while the party influenced the creation of institutional mechanisms for mass participation, it fell short in educating, training, and empowering ordinary citizens to take advantage of the new institutional spaces. Like many on the Left, the SACP seemed to idealize the capacity and latent skills within South Africa's celebrated civil society. While it is certainly true that many people were educated and politically trained through struggle, civic organizations, and trade unions, the question of whether this knowledge base could be translated from struggle mode to developmental initiatives was rarely asked. Yet it was widely acknowledged that there was a dearth of capacity among the majority of people who were not equipped for the demands of a democratic polity. For example, in three separate interviews with top-level leaders I asked about the capacity of the base and all three respondents cited this as a serious problem and felt the party was not doing enough in this regard. However, none of the three interviewees were too concerned about it nor were they doing anything to change it.[33] Such failures notwithstanding, the party did slowly develop an appreciation for participatory organizing practices: "We need, urgently, to begin to give more concrete content to what we mean by terms like 'a mass-driven RDP'. We cannot simply leave it at the level of generalities. We need in many practical ways to help people become active participants in the process of transformation" (SACP, 1994b: 13).

Despite such acknowledgments the party did not capacitate and educate people to participate in the various institutional arrangements (e.g., local government, local economic development, participatory forums). In 2001 I attended 21 branch meetings in Gauteng and KwaZulu Natal (KZN). The issues of education and capacity building were raised regularly, but usually referred to internal party structures. On one occasion the Johannesburg Central Branch—an especially vibrant and high caliber branch—organized a public information event in Yeoville, Johannesburg. On the chilly winter morning only one party member (out of nine that agreed to come at

the branch meeting) showed up. After waiting for about an hour, the party member, frustrated with the situation, told me that it is really hard to get people (both leaders and rank-and-file members) to do participatory organizing work. Members are more likely to turn up for a rally or demonstration than for the thankless work such as precinct walks, door-to-door canvassing, and information dissemination. In general, the party has focused on ideological and strategic developments and mass mobilizing rather than participation in local-level issues. One party leader explained that the party's approach was more like a war of position within the Alliance than a war of position in civil society.[34]

Indeed, a noticeable feature of the party's practices was its lack of community activism, relying instead on instrumental mass-mobilizing practices that call on the base to support high profile events. For example, out of 81 interviews and numerous informal discussions I had with party activists only nine interviewees mentioned participatory organizing activities, but all respondents recalled participating in mass-mobilizing events in the 1990s. During my fieldwork in 2001, I attended 15 mass actions and not a single participatory organizing event organized by the Head Office. Except for the 2001 anti-privatization strike, which was a protest action against the neoliberal policies of the state, most of the mass actions supported state-led initiatives. For example, a Financial Sector Campaign rally I attended in KwaZulu Natal was organized together with the local councilor to popularize the campaign, which had state support in NEDLAC. The emphasis on mass mobilizing (and the concomitant failure to develop participatory organizing) ultimately underpinned the party's emphasis on the legislative arena. The other primary activity that occupied party structures during the 1990s was internal discussion and debate. In 81 interviews with party members, all respondents mentioned the vibrant culture of debate in the party. Members placed a great deal of emphasis on the importance of healthy discussion as conditions were changing and the party had to study and analyze the situation in order to offer the movement guidance. I witnessed the culture of debate at branch meetings, district and provincial councils, political schools, seminars, and workshops. While debate was considered crucial, a few interviewees complained that the culture of tolerance was diminishing. Indeed, by 2006 the list of individuals disciplined and criticized for voicing unpopular opinions (i.e., opinions the head office did not like) had grown to the point that it is difficult to claim the party has maintained a culture of open debate and plurality of opinions.

While the party focused on state-led initiatives, the party continued to articulate the need for a counter-hegemonic generative politics that attempted to subordinate the state and economy to civil society. Gauteng provincial party leader Jabu Moleketi[35] argued: "It is this process that must fundamentally change the lives of ordinary people in terms of access to political institutions, freedom from socioeconomic hardships, that empowers people to have control over their own lives and over the structures of society. Active, dynamic and autonomous organs of civil society and the democratic state are co-drivers of this process" (Moleketi, 1993: 17). What Moleketi was essentially arguing was the importance of extending civil society's role in the social, political, and economic realms.

In addition, in 1994 the SACP clearly outlined the importance of extending civil society's role in the economy through participatory democratic mechanisms while

confronting capital's neoliberal agenda. In this struggle, the party believed it had the capacity to influence the ANC to represent working-class and poor interests over capital's interests. Thus, in 1994 the party argued:

> In mobilizing and organizing for socio-economic transformation the Left in South Africa has two primary tasks: the task of carrying through consistently and continuously a class critique of the neo-liberal agenda; and moving beyond critique, to posing concrete, viable and sustainable programs to address the needs of the majority. As a Left in South Africa we need to place ourselves at the very center of the struggle for democracy, reconstruction and development. [...] Democracy is the continuous and deepening self-empowerment of the great majority of our country. (SACP, 1994c: 37)

Despite these declarations in support of civil society-led politics, the party did not translate these aspirations into practice. Rather, SACP activity focused on leaders addressing rallies around a range of issues such as governing, the right to education for school children, and squatter camps. Indeed, the national-level structure largely limited its engagement to mass rallies and attempts to influence the ANC's strategic perspectives without constructing mechanisms within the party to help implement its vision. One stalwart I interviewed bemoaned the party's focus on the financial sector campaign as it was not in touch with the needs of the people. The interviewee was certain that the party chose it because "the ANC government gave it the go-ahead. The ANC knows it is not a campaign that will strengthen the base of the SACP."[36]

The movement's thin relation to the mass base is reflected in the poor performance in the first years after the election of many of the participatory institutions (e.g., parliamentary standing and theme committees and hearings, NEDLAC, Local Development Forums, Housing Forums, Electricity Forums, University Transformation Forums). In the 21 branch meetings, 11 political education schools, and 8 provincial and district councils I attended in Gauteng and KwaZulu Natal the poor status of the participatory institutions was raised a couple times, but never became a serious point of discussion. The Alliance acknowledged its failures and argued that "we have generally failed to elaborate a clear mobilizational program for our mass constituency. Over the past three and a half years, formerly active and mobilized constituencies have often been marginalized spectators and anxious would-be recipients of delivery. This is a recipe for confusion, disgruntlement and a lack of shared understanding of where we should be going" (Tripartite Alliance, 1997a: 12). It called for a more concrete elaboration of the strategic tasks faced both in government and outside of it. The Alliance document further argued for elaborating a practical program of action

> that is capable of organizing and mobilizing our constituency in ways that converge with what we are seeking to achieve in government. We need, also, to appreciate that mass mobilization should not be narrowly equated with "marching in the streets." The variety of participatory forms that we have begun to evolve in the context of, for instance, the legislative process, must themselves be seen as mobilizational work. (Tripartite Alliance, 1997a: 12)

In this formulation Alliance partners were being called on to *implement* change, which requires participatory organizing practices.

Civil Society-Led Development to State-Led Development: GEAR Eclipses the RDP

The SACP's emphasis on mass mobilizing and state-led development converged with the ANC's shift to a neoliberal macroeconomic strategy. The 1990s saw the state shift from people-driven development articulated in the RDP to delivery of development targets in which the state is the driver of change and people's participation is limited to "consultative" forums in which citizens are informed of development projects. While many scholars and activists argue that the ANC dramatically shifted directions in 1996 with the adoption of the *Growth Employment and Redistribution Strategy* (GEAR), the contours of this development can be traced to the beginning of the decade.[37] For example, a discernable move by the ANC can be traced from its 1990 joint ANC-COSATU Harare workshop proposal supporting "an extension of public ownership, state regulation of credit, a prescribed high-wage economy, and a central role for organized labor in policy formulation. Redistribution would serve as the principal agency of economic growth" (Lodge, 2002: 21).[38] In 1990, thus, the ANC envisioned the restructuring of the economy guided by the principle of "growth through redistribution." In 1991, by contrast, ANC economists began singing from a different hymnal and by its 1992 Draft Policy Guidelines the ANC suggested the possible reduction of the public sector, acknowledged legal protection of property rights, and displayed a concern and sensitivity to the demands of international competition for manufacturing[39] (Lodge, 2002: 22). This was the beginning of a shift from priority given to the popular national liberation project based on redistribution to a neoliberal project advocating a free-market economy underpinned by the principles of a narrowly defined democracy.[40]

While ambiguity can be seen with regard to policy issues, the *Reconstruction and Development Program* was unambiguous about mass participation.[41] The RDP specifically outlined the importance for the involvement and empowerment of ordinary citizens in development projects, which themselves should be a result of popular initiatives and grassroots consultations (ANC, 1994: 4–5). Development, it was argued, should be led and driven by ordinary people (ANC, 1994: 8). It promised structural consultation processes at all levels, which led to the formation of NEDLAC and regional and local development forums that include all stakeholders (ANC, 1994: 60–61, 80–81; Baskin, 1996; Webster and Macun, 2000). Thus, the RDP had a strong participatory democratic thrust and the institutional mechanisms were being developed to support it. In line with the SACP's theoretical vision of a developmental state, the RDP envisioned the state as the major catalyzer and enabler in integrating growth with reconstruction and social development, while empowering people to play an equally important role. The RDP argued that "development is not about the delivery of goods to a passive citizenry. It is about active involvement and growing empowerment. In taking this approach we are building on the many forums, peace structures and negotiations that our people are involved in throughout the

land" (ANC, 1994: 5). This resonated with the party's own understanding as it saw the extension of popular control as paramount to transformation.

The Left saw the RDP as a decisive break with past (apartheid) policies and tended to emphasize the sections in the document that highlighted the importance and value of state intervention in the economy and the expansion of civil society's role.[42] The conservative interpretation pointed to the aspects of the document that provided for restricting the growth of the public sector and endorsing privatization. The ambivalent language in the document gave license to both interpretations as the state was to be a "partner, catalyst, and facilitator" rather than a direct provider of growth or in the provisioning of welfare and utilities (Lodge, 2002: 56).

Despite the duality found in the RDP, many on the Left, including the SACP, were not prepared for the ANC's shift to a more orthodox macroeconomic orientation found in the 1996 *Growth, Employment, and Redistribution Strategy*. GEAR committed South Africa to macroeconomic measures emphasizing deficit reduction, government "rightsizing," tariff reductions, privatization, and productivity linked to wage rates. GEAR marked the official shift from growth led by infrastructural development to export-led growth and private sector investment, especially foreign direct investments (Hart, 2002: 18–19). Thus, by 1996 the ANC's official economic policy had acquired an overt class character as GEAR was an investor-friendly macroeconomic strategy.[43] The controversy surrounding GEAR was more than just its content, however. It was drafted secretly and presented to the ANC's National Executive Committee (NEC) in mid-1996 as a *fait accompli*. Before the NEC saw it, then-Deputy President Thabo Mbeki was shown a draft in March 1996, while the ANC National Working Committee (NWC) and the NEC's economic transformation subcommittee only saw the final draft in mid-1996. A selective group of COSATU and SACP officials were presented the final version shortly before it was released publicly on June 14, 1996. The Alliance thus only engaged the final product and never was included in its drafting, which further fed the sentiment that GEAR represented an abrupt turnabout in the ANC.[44] Its original goal, however, was to reconcile the progressive goals of the RDP with macroeconomic needs of investment and financial markets. But history was to work against the Left and the final version was affected by the currency crisis resulting from Trevor Manuel's appointment to minister of finance (Eidelberg, 2000: 147).

While GEAR was being formulated, the RDP was simultaneously emasculated. Mandela's government firmly committed itself to the RDP with the establishment of a special RDP ministry located within the presidency. COSATU leader Jay Naidoo was appointed minister of RDP tasked with policy formulation, coordination of different development projects, and to further develop institutions to advance the goals of the RDP (ANC, 1994: 138–39). Approximately two years after its inauguration, the government closed the RDP ministry on March 28, 1996, dividing its responsibilities between the Department of Finance and different government departments. The closure of the RDP ministry signified a shift from the more holistic program integrating different department projects through a senior politician to a more piecemeal approach through line departments. The temporal proximity of the RDP ministry's closure and the adoption of GEAR were widely interpreted as a dramatic shift within the ANC from its previous commitment to social equity and participatory

integrated development involving ordinary people. The adoption of GEAR was not only a shift to market-related development, it also signaled a shift in the ANC's class orientation (Hart, 2002: 19). The SACP, for its part, failed to effectively challenge this shift, often settling for adding class content to the ANC policies without championing a coherent alternative project.[45] Thus, with the drift away from the RDP the commitment to society-led development withered and the state increasingly shifted to state-led delivery targets. In the process civil society was increasingly demobilized and called on to support state-led programs. In other words, citizens became beneficiaries of programs rather than active partners in development.

In the period between the 1995 and 1998 party Congresses, the SACP developed its critique of neoliberalism, participated in developing the National Framework Agreement and Labor Relations Act, and engaged debates around the 1997 COSATU Congress and 1997 ANC Mafikeng Conference.[46] The party achieved many gains in areas of labor relations, local government, integrated development plans, and the idea of a local developmental state. However, after the ANC's adoption of GEAR the SACP found it increasingly difficult to justify the pro-capitalist policy direction of the ANC. The SACP began slowly, and ambivalently, fluctuating from hegemonic generative politics to moments of protest politics. For example, in 2001 the SACP and COSATU took a confrontational stand against the ANC's privatization policies, which culminated in a two-day national strike. The strike attracted thousands of people, especially workers, across the country, and was an important marker of the degree to which Alliance relations had disintegrated. The SACP supported COSATU in the strike, but was at pains to try to ease tensions between its alliance partners. The SACP was fluctuating from seeing itself as a political party in power with the ANC and an oppositional force trying to push the recalcitrant ANC to adhere to Alliance programs and commitments. This ambivalence about its own position and role ran deeply in the structures of the party and increasingly manifested in internal battles within the party.

Hegemonic Politics in Transforming the Economy

The 1998 SACP Congress marked a turning point. The party developed its own Program rather than relying vicariously on the RDP to form its central programmatic thrust. In this new Program the party showed subtle signs of reverting to a more classical Marxist-Leninist state-centered development vision in which the working class is the primary agent, a reflection of the shift in the balance of power in favor of the trade union faction. It also included some of the new thinking of the 1990s such as socialization of the economy, decommodification, and the promotion of cooperatives. This Program also marked a subtle but noticeable uncoupling of race and class in which a class-on-class analysis was articulated. These ideological developments were further elaborated in two Strategy Conferences held in 1999 and 2000. Together the 1998 Congress and the two Strategy Conferences elaborated an ideological line that also facilitated a rapprochement between the SACP and COSATU. Moreover, it marked the end of the project of renewal as the party's modus operandi was no longer a dynamic process of questioning and rethinking its ideological and programmatic orientation.

With the trade union faction leading the party by 2000–2001 the party was focusing attention more directly on the central terrain of economic transformation. In its 2002 Program of Action the party argued that

> the SACP has sought to relate to this reality through programmatically and ideologically focusing, directing and harnessing working class and popular mobilization towards the building of what we refer to as a people's economy. This has primarily focused on the defense and extension of the public sector, the transformation and diversification of the financial sector, the building of co-operatives and social capital and the elaboration of an industrial strategy perspective. (SACP, 2002)

Thus, the party shifted its gaze from the political domain to directly addressing the economic questions in its ideological renewal. In line with this perspective, the party launched its second major campaign since returning to South Africa.

The Financial Sector Reform Campaign was implemented under the leadership of General Secretary Blade Nzimande. In direct response to the macroeconomic program and coming out of the party's two Strategy Conferences in 1999 and 2000, the SACP with the support of COSATU tabled the issue at NEDLAC[47] in 2000. The SACP then launched a campaign to reform financial institutions, which highlighted the inaccessibility of banks and lack of services to the working class and poor as well as the need to transform the financial sector to play a developmental role in communities. The party called on the government to develop community reinvestment and support cooperative banks. Part of the rationale behind this campaign was the party's attempt to take advantage of its strategic position within the Alliance as well as its recognition of banks as a major pillar of power in society. The party continued to place emphasis on the state arguing that "the state must play a leading role in coordination and driving such a growth and development strategy premised on a strong, democratic and accountable public sector" (SACP, 2003a).

The campaign was largely implemented through mass-mobilizing practices such as mass rallies, public speeches, and propaganda work with very little participatory organizing around the campaign. In addition to high-profile visits to communities by party leaders the campaign held a series of marches in 2001 calling for financial sector reform. For example, one event I attended in Alexandra Township in northern Johannesburg began with a march to the local community center. Provincial and national leadership began the rally with speeches about the importance of reforming the financial sector.[48] Residents were then given a chance to voice their grievances. At three marches I attended the grievances expressed were not mainly about the financial sector, but rather were about issues more germane to their daily lives such as jobs, housing, and transport. Similar marches were organized around the country and culminated in a ceremonial presentation of a memorandum of demands to the Banking Council of South Africa and the minister of finance. The central demand was for government to convene a financial sector summit bringing banks, government, labor, and community groups to the table to map out a strategy to diversify and transform financial institutions as well as set a new legislative framework for financial institutions. The SACP outlined the following three pillars to its

program: (1) to transform the financial sector, (2) to build a strong, democratic, and accountable public sector in the context of elaborating a state-led industrial strategy, and (3) to meet basic needs through local economic development. All three pillars focused on the state and private sector initiatives with little emphasis on the role of people's participation. The party's emphasis on negotiations and mass mobilizing through NEDLAC indicates a slide into trade union tactics and bargaining. The SACP was, in effect, working within the contours set by the ANC-led state.[49]

The SACP joined (and heads) NEDLAC's community sector through a Financial Sector Campaign Coalition, which is a multi-class coalition of forces consisting of 40 member organizations. One of the main aims of the Coalition is to "build a mass social movement and front of people's power for the fundamental transformation and diversification of the financial sector in South Africa" (Financial Sector Campaign Coalition, 2003: 16). Ironically, the Coalition's approach has been top-down and has not integrated ordinary people into the process despite the aim of building a popular movement. It is a state-centered approach that targets elite-level pacting to push transformation. Yet the outcome is meant to bring a degree of societal control over markets. The party's 2002 Program of Action outlines the role of the populace as "mass mobilization in support of, and in order to influence, shape and direct the negotiations process. In this regard, key tasks are the popularization and consolidation of our demands before and after the NEDLAC Summit by the SACP branches, districts, and provinces" (SACP, 2002). The mass base is called on to support the process, which is to be popularized through SACP structures. Unlike the CPI(M), which simultaneously secured policies and legislative reforms while ensuring subaltern classes are actively involved in shaping the process, the SACP seeks support from subalterns for strategic decisions and policy interventions made on behalf of its base. Moreover, the campaign itself is far from resonating with the lives of subordinate classes, many of whom are unemployed and poor. One event I attended in Inanda, KwaZulu Natal, exemplifies the disjuncture between the campaign and ordinary citizens. The rally was held in the middle of a squatter settlement in which the majority of the people were unemployed. About 100 people showed up. After the rally I informally spoke with residents and asked what they thought of the rally and the campaign to reform the financial sector. Without exception none of the people I spoke with had any understanding of the campaign and had come to the rally simply to watch. Many of the people in this squatter settlement did not have regular sources of income and, therefore, a bank account was a distant concern. One man aptly captured the mood: "Once I have a job and can feed my family, then I will worry about a bank account."[50]

The Summit was a principal goal of the campaign and was meant to pressure government to ensure the diversification and transformation of the financial sector to align with the developmental goals of society. With its focus on government-led transformation and the lack of citizen participation, the Financial Sector Reform Campaign is an example of the SACP's hegemonic generative politics. The NEDLAC-convened Financial Sector Summit was held on August 20, 2002. Ultimately the achievements of the Summit were limited. It was generally agreed that banks need to contribute more to development as well as the importance of the long-run viability of the financial sector. It was also agreed that many of the

problems were due to external constraints, thus conceding limited responsibility of banks in creating the current conditions. One tangible result of the Summit was the commitment to hold another summit on Growth and Development, which was held on June 7, 2003. The Growth and Development Summit was meant to take forward the agreements from the Financial Sector Summit and develop cooperatives. Government thus initiated the process to draft and finalize legislation on cooperatives and a strategy and policy for cooperatives. The campaign achieved a very significant goal in the establishment of the Mzansi account, which provides free banking to the poor. In short, the campaign succeeded in getting the state to ensure the (limited) transformation of the financial sector.

The Financial Sector Reform Campaign was the party's main campaign by the second year of the new millennium. While the campaign sought to transform the existing system along the lines outlined in its programmatic and strategic perspectives, all its efforts were aimed at state intervention through the institution of NEDLAC. It did not align the campaign with participatory organizing on the ground to help subaltern sectors to participate in the new institutions, which would extend democracy beyond formal political institutions to economic and social spheres. Very few rank-and-file party members I spoke with had knowledge about the campaign that could be communicated to their communities. Almost without exception it was party leaders and officials that could speak knowledgeably about the campaign (and not all leaders could do it either). Reflecting the convergence of the statist and trade union factions' practices, by 2003 the party had not engaged in local-level initiatives and participatory forums to empower people. The trade union faction has focused on summits and high-level negotiations, which belies its emphasis on the state's role in leading transformation with little attention to organize participation in civil society. For example, in 2003 it put great hope into "the Ekurhuleni Alliance Summit" (SACP, 2003a).

The SACP's ability to successfully launch the Financial Sector Reform Campaign demonstrates the conducive political environment for state-led development. Rather than focusing on greater control of the economy by civil society, the party limited its efforts to getting the state to act on behalf of subaltern classes. Thus, even with the rise of the trade union faction within the party, the SACP's focus on corporatist bargaining relations with the Financial Sector Campaign as a primary form of action continued the hegemonic generative politics of the statist faction. The campaign attempted to win concessions from the state and capital within the capitalist terrain, but it did not marry this to organizational efforts to galvanize and educate the citizenry to take the transformation further by developing alternative forms of banking in communities such as cooperative banking. The leadership was more focused on state-led institutional forums and mass mobilizing than grassroots participation in counter-hegemonic alternatives.

While the party pursued hegemonic generative politics, it also slid into overtly oppositional protests such as the anti-privatization national strike in 2001. The strike provoked a vicious response from the ANC (a reminder that consent is *always* backed by force). While the vitriolic exchange between Alliance partners represented a low point in the ANC's and SACP's relationship, what is striking about the SACP's involvement is not, as many commentators have noted, its willingness to directly

challenge the ANC.[51] Rather what is more striking about the SACP's position is the lack of a coherent strategy. The strike was anticapitalist in that it was against privatization, but it was not clear what alternative was envisioned beyond the rejection of privatization due to the resulting job losses (i.e., trade union interests). The twin thrusts of the Financial Sector Reform Campaign and the anti-privatization strike reflects the SACP's contradictory location: it collaborates with the ANC and state through corporatist arrangements and simultaneously contests the ANC and state through mass actions to promote class struggle. It has ultimately overseen a hegemonic generative politics in which civil society has been increasingly subordinated to the state and economy and has largely pursued top-down practices around a leader-led agenda.

Despite these shortcomings, the party also made initial footsteps in the direction of alternative projects in the economic domain that empower civil society. For example, the party launched an effort to build cooperatives.[52] Initial efforts to promote cooperatives included a three-day education workshop for party activists to educate and train cadres on the fundamentals of cooperatives.[53] Approximately 100 people attended the workshop and it was an important event to educate COSATU and party members. What effect it had is difficult to assess. I met one man from the workshop a month later at a meeting in KwaZulu Natal where he reported on the workshop and told of his plans to set up two cooperatives in his area. He explained that the cooperative members would be SACP members and that 10 percent of the surplus of the cooperative would go to the party. As I listened to him excitedly tell about his plans for cooperative development, I could not help but wonder where the democratic ownership and collective decision making would come in. His decrees were completely antithetical to what a cooperative is and were not the message of the workshop. When I checked a year later, he had not set up a single cooperative. In 2003 the party set up a cooperative resource center, the Dora Tamana Cooperative Center, which promotes cooperative development and in May 2004 it launched the Dora Tamana Cooperative Savings and Credit Union.[54] And indeed, there have been some concrete successes in establishing cooperatives and empowering subalterns to participate in cooperatives in their communities. The actual initiatives of cooperative development, however, have been scattered and depend on particular individuals at the local level rather than reflecting a coherent and effective national-level party approach.[55] Indeed, the neighborhood meetings and participatory organizing events I attended were the initiatives of individuals from the grassroots faction working in the local structures of the party.

Counter-Hegemonic Generative Politics at the Local Level

Looking at the grassroots faction's politics in Gauteng and KwaZulu Natal it is clear that while the grassroots faction may not have significant presence at the top of the organization, it is busying itself at the local level. In 2001 the grassroots faction made its debut in Gauteng when a new provincial leadership was elected at a hotly contested Congress.[56] The grassroots faction secured enough presence in the top provincial leadership (Provincial Working Committee) to shift the direction of the party. The new leadership wasted no time and immediately began implementing

alternative political projects that linked local participation to economic and political development. It began with literacy forums and sustainable development forums that educated party cadres about the need to organize and empower subaltern classes.[57] The new provincial leadership broke with the old emphasis on mass mobilizing, placed a great deal of energy on developing participatory organizing practices, and aligned the provincial Program of Action with policies and programs of government in order to implement progressive policies already on the books. For example, the province's vision for local economic development outlined in its 2001 Congress document, "Building a People's Economy," was integrated into its Program of Action and implemented through provincial and branch structures. In addition, the provincial party structures prioritized grassroots activities around the cooperative movement and linked these activities with the local economy. In this effort, a few branches were involved in setting up producer cooperatives in townships and aligning these initiatives with government programs.[58] For example, I visited 6 cooperatives in the Vaal area and 12 cooperatives in Ivory Park that grassroots activist had been involved in forming.

The new leadership also placed priority on implementation. A key issue at the political school held in October 2001 was the need to put emphasis on practice and the PEC circulated a discussion document about the relation between theory and practice. The discussion document opened debate around the party's tendency to emphasize theory and its failure to go to the ground and implement its strategic visions.[59] These initiatives coincided with concrete programs guiding branch activities. This was one of the few political schools (out of the 11 I attended) that addressed the need to concretely implement the party's visions. In this effort, the province identified beacon branches (one in each district) to act as an anchor for party programs and advanced training.

In addition, the provincial leadership studied spaces and opportunities available at various levels of government. With the fledgling local government legislation, opportunities for development had been created, but not yet realized. For example, by mid-2003 the Gauteng party had spent a great deal of energy studying the possibilities for intervention in areas of local economic development, Integrated Development Plans (IDP), ward councils, and various alternative forms of development such as food security. The provincial structure held a conference, *Socialism and Sustainable Local Economic Development*, which brought together government officials, political leaders, academics, environmentalists, community organizations, and branch members to debate, educate, and develop connections across structures. The conference clarified the socialist content in developing self-reliant and sustainable communities and linked township communities to initiatives in housing, food security, IDPs, sustainable local manufacturing, and the local cooperative movement.[60] It was among the only events I attended in which ward-level institutions were discussed at length and an attempt was made to educate party members about the importance of them. In response, many branches set up IDP committees and engaged local government. Food security resource packs were distributed to branches that guided members on how to establish food production projects and community food security forums, which were linked to the Department of Agriculture and Environment's Homestead Gardens Program. By 2003 food security forums

had been established in two branches in two districts in the province. I attended both launches of the food security forums where approximately 50 people from the communities attended. At the launch in a township on the West Rand the local councilor attended and committed to give full support through the council.

The Gauteng party also held ongoing workshops for its members on local development issues such as Integrative Development Plans, ward committees, and local economic development. For example, after the July 2003 conference the party continued to discuss in workshops the implementation of integrated development plans through local-level structures. At the same time, pilot projects were started, one of which was in Emfuleni district in the Vaal Triangle. The municipal council of Emfuleni was trying to be civic oriented and had a number of councilors who were committed to their constituents (rather than just party-political), and thus it provided fertile ground for the grassroots faction to pursue alternative projects that align local government support with community-based development.[61] One aspect of the party's approach has been to galvanize and educate both community residents and ward councilors on the potential of local government. With the Emfuleni council's financial and political support party activists established the first industrial hive complex in the country where local manufacturing organized on the principles of cooperatives was set up. The industrial hive consists of five production units and houses a branch of the community cooperative bank. Party activists pursued an integrative approach that ensured that hive production units gave back to the local community in terms of cheaper products (e.g., the bakery unit sells bread cheaper than local stores, and the toilet paper making unit produces for the local council). Because local government was the main initiator, party activists ensured they remained involved. For example, over a period of four months I attended weekly meetings of the Emfuleni Local Economic Development department, the cooperative leadership, and the grassroots party activists involved in the project, where they discussed very concrete issues of day-to-day running of the cooperative as well as longer-term progress and problems. Like CPI(M) activists, grassroots activists in the SACP did not advertise they were SACP members, but rather worked through a grassroots nonprofit organization involved in cooperative development. In late 2004 the industrial hive approach (based on cooperatives) was adopted by Ekurhuleni Metropolitan Municipality, which launched a major initiative that set up 10 industrial hives on the East Rand.[62] Again, through their work with the nonprofit organization, party activists were integral to these initiatives. For example, I attended three five-day workshops party activists held with the beneficiaries of the projects. The workshops facilitated cooperative education and training, the registration process, and did business plans and marketing strategies.

While the provincial leadership in KwaZulu Natal did not pursue counter-hegemonic generative projects that extend civil society's role, it did shift the party to emphasize participatory organizing and began focusing on developing contacts with a base of support. For example, in 2001–2002 the province launched a campaign on social grants, with the main thrust of its activity focused on popularizing the issue and pushing the implementation of government policy. The party sent out "red brigades" (named because of the red SACP t-shirts they wore) signing people up for social grants, which became a means through which the party forged

independent links with citizens. For example, out of the social grants campaign an issue that came to the fore was education. People told party activists that social grants were important, but the real issue facing the poor was the *de facto* lack of access to education due to unaffordable school fees. The KZN party took up the issue and launched a Right to Learn Campaign holding meetings with teachers, parents, and school administrators to inform them of the violation of the constitution and children's right to school whether or not they can afford to pay school fees. This initiative was followed by an anticorruption campaign that helped raise the profile of the party and won it positive media publicity.[63]

Unlike the SACP in Gauteng where the grassroots faction captured the leadership positions, in KZN the grassroots faction is only active at the local level. However, the KZN party has allowed flexibility at its district and branch levels, providing the grassroots faction ample space to pursue its politics. Each district is responsible for setting up and running its own campaigns (which are meant to align with the provincial program and strategies).[64] This has often translated into local efforts around issues germane to a particular locality. For example, in Newcastle the party focused on land and rural issues (e.g., the right for farm workers to bury the bones of deceased on farms), whereas the North Coast district dealt with community issues such as a campaign to stop the implementation of a tollgate in the community.[65] The Pietermaritzburg district was engaged in innovative campaigns that were not typically communist-type issues, but were relevant to the local community. For example, the party championed a campaign to help the growing number of mentally ill people on the streets (a few years earlier many mental institutions closed). The party played a behind-the-scenes role in getting various actors to deal with the issue (e.g., they met with the MEC for health, hospital administrations and doctors, the health department, and church organizations). Activists were careful not to publicize the party's involvement, but rather emphasized the plight of the mentally ill and the community's responsibility in finding solutions.[66]

KZN districts have also pursued cooperative development in a number of areas. Work on cooperatives has excelled due to the efforts of certain members, especially in Durban and Pietermaritzburg, and are linked to municipal programs. For example, since the late 1990s communists have worked in Cato Manor township in Durban with the Cato Manor Development Association (society), a European Union (EU)-funded "presidential project." Through EU funding a number of building projects have been undertaken—building schools, community centers, and libraries.[67] The project also included the construction of industrial complexes for local production enterprises, which are meant to help stimulate the township economy and local production through small-scale initiatives. Using a livelihoods development approach, the party has been involved in a broad range of financial management training (including life skills training). For example, party activists trained people about homeownership (e.g., loan procurement, financial responsibility and accounting, and the different options for procuring materials and building homes such as private contractors, local initiatives through sweat equity, etc.). The activists emphasize the bottom-up nature of their work and the painstaking work involved in attracting community involvement.

Through these efforts party activists helped start a number of cooperatives. For example, a skills cooperative and a cooperative crèche were developed with the assistance of party activists. A cultural cooperative was set up that encourages local cultural groups such as art, dance, and music groups and has received funding from the local council and foreign donors. In addition, there are a number of food gardens—all based on cooperative principles—that produce on fallow land around the community (e.g., next to the highway, on uninhabitable slopes of hills, etc.).[68] The party activists explicitly avoid party identification in their development work[69] and do not set up the cooperatives linked to the party (though many cooperative members are party members). Nevertheless, the party has grown through this work due to the fact that the team members are key leaders in their branches. The party is seen by residents to be active in their local issues and concerns, which has translated into the growth of party branches. The party activists provide the links with local government, councilors, and development groups for local initiatives and thus play an important facilitating role, but not a strong visionary role.

All of these initiatives seek to empower community residents and subaltern classes and extend the role and power of civil society. By aligning local development initiatives (including local economic production) with local and provincial government, the party is attempting to increase the role of civil society and in the process develop conditions for alternative logics of social organization to take root. Similar to the CPI(M)'s approach, the initiation and coordination of these alternatives came from the grassroots-oriented leadership. Thus, in Gauteng and KZN grassroots party members have redirected the SACP away from the hegemonic generative politics based on mass mobilizing to a counter-hegemonic generative politics enlisting participatory organizing. The initiatives ultimately transferred some power to subaltern classes in order to increasingly shape events in the polity and economy that affect their lives.

Conclusion

For the SACP the 1994 election victory marked a turning point. After 40 years of clandestine activity the party was now at the helm of power with the ANC. The SACP recognized the need for renewal and the importance of developing transformative politics, yet there was a disjuncture between its campaigns and activities and its proclamations of society-led development. While the potential for a counter-hegemonic generative politics existed in the early years, ultimately these initiatives yielded into a new phase of its politics, one marked by hegemonic generative politics.

Thus, in the 1990s the SACP was realigning itself from a politics of protest to a generative politics in which it was a crucial actor in constructing new institutional structures for mass participation and nation building. Unlike the CPI(M), however, the SACP's shift is best characterized as a shift from protest politics to hegemonic generative politics as the party helped strengthen the ANC-led state and demobilize civil society. For the SACP the difficulties associated with shifting from armed struggle to a politics of reconstruction and development dovetailed with its organizational challenges, making a counter-hegemonic generative politics difficult to

achieve even if its ideological moorings pointed it in that direction. Over the course of the 1990s the radical aspirations of a socialist society were increasingly muted by the ANC's consolidation of capitalism in the new South Africa. The party would come to learn that holding state power is like a violin. While the left hand might hold it, the right hand will play it.[70]

The party was exceptional in its engagement in developing policy and strategies for nation building and in its contribution to advancing democratic visions of socialism. Its record sheet on implementation, however, is equivocal. What explains the party's relative failure to develop practices that engaged its base of support in a counter-hegemonic generative politics? Reflecting the statist faction's control for most of the nineties the party's practices narrowly focused on government policies in a hegemonic generative politics. After the adoption of GEAR, cracks in the Alliance began to manifest as the party found it increasingly difficult to defend ANC macroeconomic policies that were pro-capitalist in nature. These tensions filtered into the party and helped shift the balance of power in favor of the trade union faction. Thus, at the dawn of the new millennium the trade union faction was pursuing its first major campaign, the Financial Sector Reform Campaign. Similar to the statist faction, however, the trade union faction continued to pursue hegemonic generative politics with moments of protest actions. In other words, both the statist and trade union factions failed to develop counter-hegemonic generative politics that sought the extension and empowerment of civil society into both the economy and polity. Why did the SACP fail to develop counter-hegemonic generative politics and participatory organizing practices? What led the trade union faction to gain control within the party and why did it fail to shift to counter-hegemonic generative politics? The answer to these questions will be addressed in chapters five, six, and seven.

PART II

Party, Class, and State
in Historical Context

By the 1980s both South Africa and Kerala faced economic crises. In South Africa, the crisis precipitated an emerging rift between the ruling economic and political elites. The apartheid regime's repressive strategy was no longer providing the same economic benefits for capital with labor increasingly challenging the iniquitous character of the repressive labor regime. Capital, thus, demanded more influence over the state's decision-making processes and actively sought accommodation with labor. The combination of internal pressure from the economic elite, labor militancy and civil unrest within black communities, as well as international pressures ultimately led the apartheid regime into negotiations with the ANC. In Kerala, the economic crisis threatened the survival of the social welfare character of the state and, hence, the future of the redistributive gains. The Kerala state-led development approach prioritizing human and social development as a catalyzer to economic growth was not yielding the promised economic development. In the face of low economic growth, stalled industrial development, and a failure to attract investment the state was increasingly unable to support its high costs in education, health, and public employee wages. The economic crisis ultimately forced the political elites to transcend narrow party-political interests and begin thinking about development-for-development's sake as opposed to development as a political maneuver to secure the interests of its base. Thus, in both South Africa and Kerala economic crises registered in the political and social spheres and precipitated political transformation.

The economic crises in the two societies, however, were the result of two different dynamics: rapid industrialization and capitalist development in the one and low-level industrialization and rudimentary capitalist development in the other. The 1960s was a decade of intensive industrial growth (especially in manufacturing sectors) in South Africa, which transformed the country from a primary extractive and agricultural society into an industrial one (Seidman, 1994: 73). By the end of the 1960s the South African economy was gaining its entry into the world order as a "newly industrialized country" (NICs).[1] The industrial growth, however, had

internal contradictions that began to surface in the 1970s and became acute in the 1980s with shrinking internal markets (due in part to low wages for the black working class, minimal increases in employment in comparison to industrial output,[2] and a job reservation system that prevented black skilled workers from taking employment in positions reserved for white workers) and the overproduction of consumer (especially luxury) goods (Bond, 2000: 21–23; Seidman, 1994). By the mid-1980s economic growth was unsustainable and capital responded by demanding new labor relations and political reform from the apartheid regime.

Kerala's economic crisis stemmed not from the contradictions inherent in capitalist development, but from problems associated with its low level of economic development (i.e., limited capital accumulation). Unlike South Africa, Kerala is primarily an agrarian society with a poorly developed industrial base. Similar to the relatively quick transformation of the South African economy, the agrarian landscape in Kerala underwent a dramatic transformation in a relatively short period of time. The 1970 land reform transformed the precapitalist relations of a subsistence-oriented rural economy primarily based on food crops into a highly commercialized cash crop economy based primarily on rubber and coconut. Land reform, however, did not bring large-scale capitalist production as it prioritized small-scale farming. The shift from labor-intensive paddy crops to cash crops resulted in a decrease in agricultural employment with only 37.8 percent of the population earning its livelihood from agriculture in 1991 (Heller, 1999: 51). The situation was exacerbated by the fact that both the agricultural and industrial sectors performed poorly through the 1980s (agriculture had a negative growth rate while industry had an annual growth rate of 3.48 percent) (GOK, 1991a: 2; Heller, 1999: 9). The CPI(M)-led development approach offset the social impact of economic sluggishness by social welfare and entitlement programs that helped lift growing numbers of the population out of poverty (Dreze and Sen, 2002: 16, 98–99). Without economic growth, however, the social welfare and entitlement programs were unaffordable; this translated into a political crisis for the state administration.

Thus, South Africa and Kerala both faced economic and political crises. While the way in which the political crises played out in both societies varied, the potential for far-reaching transformation through these crises can represent historic turning points that allow new solutions to take root that were previously unimaginable. "Crises of hegemony" as Burawoy has noted "are historic junctures when legacies and structures lose their resilience, their obduracy, and the future has a surprising openness. These are times when alternative trajectories are indeed possible, when democracy may give rise to fascism or socialism, when state socialism may give rise to capitalism or democratic socialism" (Burawoy, 2003: 43). The way in which crises evolve, however, is linked to the balance of class forces. Thus, while crises provide moments of opportunity, the possibilities are weighted by the particular conjuncture of class forces, political initiatives, and historical legacies prevailing at the time.

The CPI(M)'s and SACP's remarkable parallel theoretical advancements in the early 1990s laid the foundation for new politics to emerge in both Kerala and South Africa. After developing broadly similar ideological orientations, however,

the SACP and CPI(M) diverged in their efforts to translate their visions of social-ist democracy into reality. The CPI(M) shifted to a counter-hegemonic generative politics and strengthened its reliance on participatory organizing, while the SACP pursued a hegemonic generative politics and continued to rely on mass mobilizing. What explains this divergence in practices? Why was the CPI(M) able to shift gears and implement its ideological advancements? And conversely, why did the SACP fall short in implementing its theoretical visions?

There are three primary sets of factors that explain the divergence: organiza-tional capacities in historical context, political factions, and economic and political contexts of each society. I deal with each factor separately for the sake of clarity, but do not see any one factor as a sufficient explanation on its own. Rather it is the par-ticular configuration of the interrelation among the factors that shape the politics of the two parties in different ways. But we must ask in what way do the different factors affect the parties?

In chapter five I look at the organizational capacities and histories of each party. I compare the organizational characteristics of the two parties against each other in an effort to determine whether the organizational structures affected the politics and practices. Based on the comparison of the two parties against each other an argument could be made that the organizational capacities determines the politics as the CPI(M) is an impressive and highly capable party, while the SACP, compared to the CPI(M), is a shadow of an organization. In other words, it could be argued that the organizational capacities determined the trajectories in the present. But when we look to internal comparisons within each party over time we see a dif-ferent dynamic. I review the histories of the two parties in order to determine the degree to which their histories influenced the politics and practices of the nineties. Comparing each party against itself over time reveals that organizational capacities and party histories are part of the story, but they are not sufficient explanations on their own. Thus, while I appreciate the potential importance of both history and the organizational structures in affecting the political trajectories of the SACP and CPI(M), they are necessary, but not sufficient, conditions in determining the political practices.

Such an argument assigns to the parties a monolithic internal character that is not borne out in reality. Indeed, both parties are internally contested battlefields with political factions vying to capture the helms of the organizations. Thus, we must ask to what extent do the different political factions affect the practices? In chapter six I look at the political factions competing for power within the parties during the 1990s. Highlighting the importance of factions begs the question of what gives rise to certain factions at particular points in time. Thus, I shift the focus to the politi-cal and economic contexts within which the parties are embedded and investigate their affects on the parties' practices. Do the political fields and economic contexts in which each party operate produce particular configurations of the balance of power among competing factions within each party, providing opportunities for the emergence of the grassroots faction in Kerala and the trade union faction in South Africa? In chapter seven I turn to explanations of the political environments and economic contexts.

In the following chapters we see that the explanation for the divergent political practices of the SACP and CPI(M) is found in the confluence of organizational capacities and histories, ideological cleavages manifested in factions, and economic and political environments that together shaped the particular political practices for each party. It is the unique, and different, confluence of these three factors that helped steer the two parties in different directions despite their similar ideological foundations.

CHAPTER 5

Party Capacities in Historical Perspective

S tudents of political parties have often pointed to the organizational characteristics as the defining moment affecting political parties' goals, practices, and trajectories, as well as the possibilities for social change (e.g., Michels, Duveger, and Gouldner). Some scholars might point to the vastly different capacities and histories of the CPI(M) and SACP in explaining the variation in their practices in the 1990s. It could be argued that the capacities and histories of the two parties contrast so starkly that there is no basis for common trajectories. This chapter explores the genealogy of each party to assess the influence of their unique histories and capacities on their politics in the nineties. To what extent do the capacities and histories *explain* the present? Are the parties' destinies locked into a path-dependent dynamic in which historical capacity determines the present? Are there particular aspects of either party's history or organizational capacities that led it to emphasize either counter-hegemonic or hegemonic generative politics? Do their organizational characteristics encourage the parties to enlist one practice over another?

In this chapter I argue that the organizational capacities and histories are *not sufficient* in explaining the variation in practices, but are part of the story. The CPI(M) is, by all accounts, an efficacious and formidable organization with far more capacity than the SACP. While we might be tempted to conclude that the organizational capacities explain the divergence in their practices, when we look at each party over time we find a surprisingly different picture. Comparing each party against itself diachronically reveals that the CPI(M)'s capacities are not the determining factor explaining the shift to counter-hegemonic generative politics. Indeed, for most of the CPI(M)'s history it has tended to emphasize protest and hegemonic generative politics enlisting mass mobilizing with the same high-level capacity found in the 1990s. Similarly, the SACP's emphasis on hegemonic generative politics enlisting mass mobilizing is not the result of its capacities as its history demonstrates a vibrant organization able to pursue a range of practices in periods with much less capacity. I thus argue that the capacities and histories of the two

parties certainly played important roles in shaping the direction of their activities, but in themselves do not explain the shift to counter-hegemonic or hegemonic generative politics. Indeed, the historical trajectories and capacities of each party helped lay the foundation for *both* counter-hegemonic and hegemonic projects.

The CPI(M)'s Capacity in Historical Perspective

The Communist Party of India (CPI) formed in 1939 in Kerala under the leadership of A.K. Gopalan and E.M.S. Namboodiripad. While the Communist Party in Kerala is part of a national organization, from the beginning it enjoyed a great deal of autonomy to accommodate local conditions.[1] Indeed, the Communist Party grew out of practical experiences with popular causes rather than widespread knowledge of Marxism (Nossiter, 1988: 47). It was through the work of early Congress socialists turned communists that Kerala's CPI developed its mass-based appeal as activists worked in communities and took great effort to educate and activate subordinate classes. For example, efforts were made to establish committees in most villages throughout the region, to set up reading rooms where political education was taught through literacy classes, and to stage socialist dramas as a form of mass media. Through the party's energetic involvement with local developments such as food relief committees and social reforms against caste indignities the party gradually embedded itself in the lives of ordinary people (Nossiter, 1982: 47).

Activists also turned their attention to radicalizing workers and peasants by developing a trade union movement during the 1930s in factories and British plantations and by working in the rural areas among the peasants and agricultural laborers.[2] Communists succeeded in forming a peasant union in 1938 and by 1946 had organized urban trade unions and led 17,000 Alleppey coir[3] workers on strike. The initial demands (bonus pay as a right) were quickly accepted (Nair, 1973) and its success led the CPI to broaden the strike to the demand for responsible government.[4] The strike escalated into a full-blown revolt, the Punnapra-Vayalar[5] revolt as it came to be called, against the constitution of the government. Though the uprising was ruthlessly repressed and met immediate defeat, it nevertheless established the Communist Party as the leading political force at the forefront of the growing anti-absolutist struggle targeting princely states and introduced the trade union movement to the politics of mass democracy. In short, it radicalized and mobilized residents and workers throughout the region.

Throughout the 1940s and 1950s the Kerala CPI was actively involved in local issues such as the Unite Kerala Campaign, the library movement (by 1947 most villages had reading rooms), a cultural renaissance, the Indian People's Theater Association as a form of popular media, and labor organizing efforts in the factories and the countryside. For example, by 1952 there were 555 registered unions in Kerala most of which were affiliated to the CPI. The popularity of communist activists also stemmed from their daily experience among subaltern classes where they were seen to live honest, sincere, and ascetic lives. Communists lived among the people breaking down social and cultural taboos in their daily lives. For example, high-caste comrades slept and ate among low-caste villagers, endearing themselves and the party to many along the way (Nossiter, 1988: 54). In this early period the party

was a small cadre-based organization, but despite its small numbers it was the most efficacious and vibrant political formation in Kerala and helped build civil society.

The Ascendance of the Communist Party: Popular Struggles for Transformation

In 1957 the CPI in Kerala adopted the resolution, "the Communist Proposal for Building a Democratic and Prosperous Kerala," which promised to build not merely participatory democracy but also prosperity, political stability, social justice, and economic reconstruction. It was a unique document that came out of the Kerala CPI's broad-based approach and involvement in popular grievances rather than the recommendations from the CPSU and reflected the belief that social transformation could be achieved through democratic administration (Nossiter, 1988: 65). To appreciate the shift this entailed, we must understand its previous position. In the early 1950s the CPI in Kerala used elections as a propaganda machine to popularize the party and mobilize the masses (CPI, 1953: 283–300; Nossiter, 1982: 107). It did not see the state as a vehicle for peaceful social transformation. After 1957, the CPI began viewing the state as an instrument of change.

With the highest voter turnout in India, in 1957 the Communist Party in Kerala became the first democratically elected communist party. The 1957 Communist Ministry was informed by three central concerns: it was committed to working within the Indian Constitution, it understood that Congress was in power at the national level, and it took the decision to implement progressive policies of Congress (Namboodiripad, 1957: 59–69). Thus, armed with its new perspective on the state as an instrument for social transformation, in 1957 the CPI government set out to implement the progressive policies of the national government.

The CPI's tenure in government, under the leadership of E.M.S. Namboodiripad, initiated a number of efforts to help shift the balance of power in favor of subalterns and extend the role of civil society in the polity and economy. It established advisory committees to monitor and assist the administration, which were elected bodies that elicited popular participation. It mobilized popular participation in local government and party committees, recruited officials into the communist movement as well as the cooperative movement, and transformed the education system by increasing expenditure to 30 percent of state funds. It organized many popular associations such as the press, student, youth, and women's organizations, and art and culture clubs. Communists spent a great deal of energy politically galvanizing rural residents through participatory organizing, and spearheaded initiatives for popular participation in rural development. For example, the Communist Ministry organized large-scale voluntary labor efforts "throughout the state for rural electrification, constructing roads, desilting ponds, and creating minor irrigation channels. A mass movement was launched to propagate the use of organic manure. As part of this movement, millions of sheemakonna cuttings were planted as live fences around garden plots" (Isaac and Franke, 2001: 32–33). The Communist Party also participated in local government institutions and allowed lower-tier party structures a great deal of autonomy to address local conditions. These efforts politicized and educated subaltern classes, strengthened the party's presence in civil society,

and facilitated mobilization efforts around a range of issues. The initiatives and emphases of this Ministry bear resemblance with the practices of the grassroots faction of the 1990s in which civil society is strengthened and expanded into political and economic spheres.

In addition to these popular efforts, the CPI's 1957 program in office threatened vested interests as it immediately began formulating land reform (and implemented a stay of eviction disallowing landlords from evicting anyone from the land in the interim) and an education reform bill that took control of education out of private hands (namely churches) and vested it in the state. This attack on two strongly entrenched pillars of power, wealthy landlords and the Christian community,[6] led the landlord and "bourgeois" sectors to form a "liberation movement" under the umbrella of the Congress Party (Surjeet, 1997: xii–iii). Despite the flouting of parliamentary norms by Congress, the CPI continued to adhere to the rules of the system and fought through parliamentary means. Both reforms were passed by the Kerala parliament, but the land reform failed to gain presidential assent. Instead, facing widespread unrest instigated by the "liberation movement," the CPI was dismissed from government by the central government in December 1959. Before it was dismissed, however, the CPI implemented the local government system of Panchayats (rural municipalities), marking its first attempt to decentralize power to lower tiers of government and indicating its commitment to expanding the role of popular involvement in the political system.

Tensions within the Party: The Communist Party Splits in Two

The failure in 1959 to implement agrarian reform led many within the party to believe that

> "the electoral process" as Ronald Herring has noted "could not bring fundamental change or real relief for the propertyless masses because the organs of state power at the Center were in the hands of a bourgeois-landlord coalition. The purpose of electoral office was to use the limited resources and power of the government to relieve the immediate oppression of the people as much as possible and to utilize the public arena for mobilizing and politicizing them." (Herring, 1983: 172)

This marked a return to the earlier understanding of the state as an instrument of struggle rather than a means for change. This fissure exacerbated the already acute tensions within the Communist Party with some members more convinced than ever that Congress was the principal enemy and that there were very real limitations to working within constitutionalism (Namboodiripad, 1961: 913–33).

After a period of intense turmoil, in 1964 the Communist Party of India split into two parties: the CPI and CPI(M).[7] The split reflected differences in the party's relation to the Congress Party and about the nature of, and possibilities for, social transformation within constitutionalism and parliamentarianism with the CPI advocating change through parliamentary means and the CPI(M) arguing that parliamentary means needed to be buttressed with extra-parliamentary activities[8]

(CPI(M), 1964b: 77–88 and 1964d; Surjeet, 1997a: xii–iii; Nossiter, 1982). The CPI emphasized national identity and saw the proletariat as the principal force of revolutionary change, while the CPI(M) prioritized regional identity and saw the peasantry (with the working class) as the agent of revolutionary change and left open the possibility for revolutionary ruptures that would introduce a postcapitalist era (CPI(M), 1964b; Nossiter, 1988: 21).

In Kerala, attitudes toward Congress were especially critical after Nehru's government dismissed the first Communist Ministry in December 1959, making the CPI(M)'s position especially popular in Kerala (CPI(M), 1964e: 231–34). After the split the CPI in Kerala enjoyed a two-to-one majority among party functionaries, while the CPI(M) enjoyed a majority among the organized peasantry and agricultural laborers (Nossiter, 1988: 82). The CPI, on the other hand, succeeded in keeping the urban constituents of Travancore, Quilon, Cochin, and Trichur.[9] The CPI(M) favored local party development over national-level development (Nossiter, 1982: 204–10). For example, the CPI(M) specified in its 1964 "Resolution on the Tasks of the Party" that the party's activity must "be oriented towards taking up the problem of the basic classes" (CPI(M), 1964c: 188). In comparison with the CPI, the CPI(M) had more organizational flexibility that translated into a larger mass base, as the CPI(M) was better able to respond to local-level concerns in a manner that was appropriate to the peculiarities of each particular region (Nossiter, 1982: 187–89). Thus, after the split the CPI(M) continued to work among subaltern classes and further rooted itself in civil society.

Consolidating the CPI(M): Activism in Civil Society and Mass Mobilizing

Widespread support for the CPI(M) was demonstrated in the 1965 elections in Kerala, in which the CPI(M) won the largest share of any party with 20 percent of the vote while the CPI only received 8 percent and Congress also lost significantly (Nossiter, 1988: 22). The party's popular support at elections reflected its emphasis on local developments emphasizing issues germane to subaltern classes.[10] The opposition, however, joined forces and formed a coalition preventing the CPI(M) from forming the government. After the CPI's dismal performance at the polls the CPSU wanted to avoid further humiliation and recommended that the CPI forge relations with the CPI(M) for the 1967 elections, an approach that paid off as the joint effort won control of government and formed a United Front government with the CPI(M) the dominant party (Nossiter, 1988: 85–86). The 1967 victory further committed the CPI(M) to immediately begin formulating land reform.[11]

Learning from its past experience, the party was careful to draft a hermetically sealed bill in order to withstand court scrutiny and ensure national-level assent. The CPI(M)'s objective was to "legislate benefits for as many of the rural poor as possible within the limits of the federal structure and constitution" (Herring, 1983: 192). In the auspicious climate of Indira Gandhi's pro-poor populism, the Kerala Land Reform Amendment Act (KLRAA) received presidential assent shortly after the CPI(M)-led coalition government disintegrated in 1969, with the CPI changing sides and forming a mini-front government with Congress. This meant that the

CPI and Congress were responsible for implementing a contentious bill they did not draft (Herring, 1983: 193).

While the CPI(M) did not explicitly legislate popular participation during implementation of land reform, in practice it pursued exactly that. The legislative efforts were buttressed by extra-parliamentary, political activities (e.g., strikes, land occupations, demonstrations, literacy campaigns, and mass education) as well as efforts to ensure the democratization of local institutions by securing informed popular participation and exerting pressure on local officials to identify excess land, fill out petitions, and follow up on implementation. For example, in the 1970s the CPI(M) jettisoned its strict adherence to constitutional means, urged popular action that went beyond the technical provisions of legislation, and launched an agrarian agitation campaign intended to force the implementation of the new legislation. The agrarian agitation advised *kudiyirrippu* (hut dwellers who lease a house-site and some land from landowners) to not pay rent to owners and to forcibly occupy excess land.[12] The movement attracted mass participation and ultimately forced the successful implementation of the reform (Heller, 1999: 79–80).[13] Over 200,000 laborers took control of their land in this manner (Oommen, 1985: 127). By 1983–1984, 93.3 percent of rural workers' households owned land compared to 66.8 percent in 1964–1965 (Heller, 1999: 132). The legacy of the "excess land agitation" was not so much in the land recovered, though it did make a significant difference for those who benefited, but in the tremendous mobilization and politicization of the agrarian community. Thus, land reform not only redistributed property to subaltern classes, it also realigned agrarian class forces and undermined the last vestiges of the old order.

In the 1970s the CPI(M) led agricultural laborers in agitations,[14] which led to the 1974 protective legislation.[15] In the 1970s conditions worsened on the land as crop prices fell due to the Green Revolution and the deregulation of interstate sales. In response, farmers shifted from the rice production to more lucrative tree crops (Narayana, 1990). Between 1975 and 1995, paddy production decreased by 46 percent (from 884,020 hectares under paddy cultivation to 404,870 hectares), while coconut rose by 42 percent (to 982,100 hectares) and rubber by 119 percent (to 449,000 hectares) (Heller, 1999: 124). Unlike paddy production, however, tree crops are less labor intensive and resulted in a significant drop in the labor-absorbing capacity of the agricultural sector. For example, in 1964–1965 male agricultural laborers worked an average of 198 days a year and females 164 days, while in 1983–1984 males only worked an average of 147 days and females 112 days (Heller, 1999: 131). Despite the net loss in employment, the higher wages paid for these cash crops resulted in an increase in total income; similarly, increases in real wages in paddy cultivation helped compensate for the loss of employment. The result has been a rapid decline in rural poverty from 10.2 million in 1973–1974 to 5.5 million in 1987–1988 (only matched by a few other states in India) (Datt and Ravallion, 1996: 30; Heller, 1999: 135).

In addition to reconfiguring power relations, the party also instituted a system of social welfare programs (e.g., subsidized universal food distribution system) and investment in education and health, raising the human and social indicators (e.g., literacy, life expectancy, and infant mortality) to developed country levels (see table 5.1). For example, Kerala has one of the most extensive and comprehensive public distribution systems with a network of 13,028 ration shops that provide subsidized

Table 5.1 Comparison of basic socioeconomic indicators (2002 unless otherwise noted)

Indicator	Kerala	India	USA	South Africa
Population (in millions)	32	1,027,5	263	44
Per capita GDP (in PPP US dollars)	292 (GNP 1995)	2,840	34,320	11,290
Adult literacy (percentage)	91 (1995–1996)	61	99	86
Life expectancy	73 (1992–1996)	63	77	48.8*
Infant mortality (per 1,000 live births)	13	62 (2005)	8	52
Fertility rate (number of births per woman)	1.8 (1995–1997)	3.4 (1994)	2.1	2.6

* Life expectancy has dropped dramatically over the past decade due to large numbers of young people dying of AIDS.

Sources: Kerala figures are from the GOK (2000). All other figures are from United Nations (2004) and World Bank (2004 and 2007).

staple foods to virtually all households (it is one of the few programs that provides to all households and does not just target below-poverty-line households). It accounts for more than 50 percent of rural poor households' consumption of rice and 90 percent of wheat (Ramachandran, 1996: 249; Heller, 1999: 134).

Subaltern mobilization has also yielded impressive achievements in countering child labor[16] and in increasing the percentage of children who complete the fifth grade. For poor households, it makes more sense to send their children to school than to work as the noon-meal scheme provides primary schoolchildren basic nutrition, ultimately raising the percentage of children completing primary education. The percentage of children who complete the fifth grade is 26 percent for India as compared to 82 percent for Kerala (Weiner, 1991: 174). Through the 1980–1981 CPI(M)-led Ministry's labor policy, pensions were secured for agricultural laborers, old people, and widows (CPI(M), 1981: 385–86). Pensioners receive a basic pension of 60 rupees, which helps offset basic monthly expenditures (in 1993 the central planning commission report estimated the poverty line per capita monthly expenditure at 113 rupees) (Figures are for 1987–1988 in Heller, 1999: 134). The achievements in literacy are no less impressive. In the early 1930s only about one in five Malayalis (i.e., 20 percent) was literate (Jeffrey, 1992: 128), which rose to a striking 91 percent by 1991 where it has remained. Again, these achievements were at the behest of subaltern classes organized and mobilized by the CPI(M).

Organizational Capacities in the 1980s and 1990s

As its history attests, the CPI(M) is by all accounts a formidable organization with tremendous capacity both in terms of the quality of its members and the sheer

number of its supporters. This capacity has been built over its long history of popular participation in local politics. During much of its history, the party complexion resembled an elite vanguard of mostly middle-class (and upper-caste) individuals with superior theoretical understanding of the social conditions, yet integrally linked to subaltern classes. It was this party that can claim a great deal of success as it spearheaded the social reform movements, consolidated the disparate rural- and urban-class elements into an organized, efficacious working class, and successfully implemented agrarian reform.

In 1978, however, the party took the decision at its Salkia Plenum to grow the organization both in its internal membership as well as its presence in civil society (CPI(M), 1978: 341–42). In order to effectively implement the Salkia Plenum decision the party's strict membership requirements had to be relaxed. Before 1978 it was incredibly difficult to become a party member as both commitment to the movement as well as theoretical sophistication and a high level of consciousness were required. The effect of such stringent membership entry was that the party consisted mostly of middle-class, educated members. The Salkia Plenum specifically sought to open the party to members from affiliated organizations such as the trade unions and women's, youth, and student associations. It was felt that the commitment of these members should be rewarded as they offered impressive strengths in their agitational capacities. It was further argued that it was the party's responsibility to ensure all members were given the appropriate theoretical and political education to raise consciousness (CPI(M), 1978). Thus, the Salkia Plenum decision to open the party to activists from affiliated organizations changed the complexion of the party as the ratio of lower-class members grew relative to middle-class members. It is important to note, however, that the party continues to attract large numbers of middle-class members to its ranks. For example, at the 2002 Congress the largest number of delegates came from the middle-class/peasant strata or higher (459 delegates) and those with tertiary education (396 delegates) (CPI(M), 2002b: 37).

After the Salkia Plenum decision Kerala's membership exploded partly reflecting the level of class- and mass-based organizing as well as the party's presence in civil society. All-India membership increased from 161,000 in 1978 to 579,000 in 1991 and further to 796,073 in 2001 with total membership in mass organizations over 40 million (CPI(M), 2002a). But the growth was uneven in the country with West Bengal and Kerala accounting for the majority of new members.[17] The majority of Kerala's top-level leadership hails primarily from middle- and upper-class backgrounds (which often corresponded to higher caste), while the lower-level leaders and the mass base have tended to be from lower-class backgrounds (working class, poor peasants, and agricultural laborers). For example, in 2001, 80.1 percent of party members in Kerala were from the working class, poor peasants, and agricultural laborers,[18] while only 218 out of 742 delegates to the 17th Congress were from these lower-class groups[19] (CPI(M), 2002b: 36 and 2002c: 2). In Kerala, synergies between leaders and base were originally forged through a common Malayali background and the leadership's commitment to breaking down cultural and caste taboos, all of which helped gain the party popular support. With ballooning numbers the ratio of subaltern to middle classes tilted further in favor of subaltern

classes. The 80.1 percent of members from lower-class backgrounds coincided with the ascendance of the trade union faction into the leadership.

The Kerala CPI(M) is a cadre party with strict membership requirements (e.g., a one-year probation period for new members) and claimed a membership of 301,562 in 2001,[20] which translates into approximately one party member for every 106 people in the state.[21] Its affiliated organizations bring the number of active sympathizers to over 10 million (see table 5.2). To become a member, new candidates must have written recommendations from two members. If the application is accepted, the candidate is admitted on a probationary status for at least one year after which time his/her membership is reviewed. In addition to following codes of discipline and adhering to the party Constitution, the party defines the duties of members both in terms of their practice and theoretical development (e.g., participate in activities, read and popularize party publications, and place the interests of the people and the party above personal interests). In order for members to remain involved in civil society, the party requires members to work in at least one mass organization. Clearly the party represents a highly organized structure that exacts a firm commitment from its members.

The CPI(M) has a vast network of full-time activists (there are 4,697 full-time paid activists in Kerala) and almost all of its leadership are full-time party members (CPI(M), 2002b: 38). The party has developed infrastructure at every level of the organization, including apartments for its 14 state secretariat members and dormitory-style rooms for other leaders and activists. The salaries of leaders and rank-and-file activists are not very high, reducing the chances that the party becomes a conduit for self-enrichment.[22] The majority of the leaders have been in the party for more than 20 years. For example, out of 742 delegates at the 2002 National Congress only 5 delegates joined the party after 1991 and the majority (510) delegates were in the party for 30 or more years.

The all-India 79-member Central Committee[23] is based on proportional representation of the number of members in each state. Therefore, Kerala and West Bengal have the highest number of central committee members as their states make up the vast majority of CPI(M) members. In Kerala the highest structure of the party is the 14-member state secretariat (which is similar to the national-level Polit Bureau), which is drawn from the 78-member state committee (equivalent to the Central Committee). One area the party has not achieved much success is in recruiting women to its ranks. For example, out of the 78-member state committee only 6 are women. Below the state committee is the district secretariat and district committee, which is followed by the area committee and then the local committee. The branch is the primary unit of the party and may not exceed 15 members.

The central committee decides national-level issues and policies, while the state committee enjoys a great deal of autonomy in dealing with state-level issues. The state committee has the authority to set agendas and policies for the party in the state (as long as they do not contravene national policies). Thus, within the party there is a great deal of decentralization and autonomy of state structures especially in terms of policies and practices in relation to the mass base. The high degree of decentralization is partly a result of the split with the CPI as the CPI(M) prioritized

regional developments over national, arguing that the diversity of India requires a flexible party able to appropriately respond to regional and local issues.

The Kerala CPI(M)'s strength lies in its long tradition of political education, which led it to establish the AKG Center for Research and Study in Thiruvananthapuram and in 2001 it inaugurated the EMS Academy.[24] The EMS Academy offers the 20,000 branch secretaries yearly week-long political education courses as well as a number of other shorter courses to a range of party members and nonmembers. The EMS Academy is set up as an informal university for study and research as well as a permanent teaching center for party cadres.[25] The party tries to ensure that a uniform system of education for its members is developed every year by a state-level political education committee. The political education committee draws up a yearly syllabus with study notes used to train state-level and district-level political education officers who are then deployed to districts to teach the year's syllabus. The newly trained district leaders are then sent back to teach their branch and unit members. In addition to the formal training, committees at all levels of the organization are expected to have ongoing discussions and seminars about a range of topics that go beyond the syllabus. The party also offers classes to members of mass organizations and sympathizers.[26]

The CPI(M) has developed a mass communication system with newspapers, theoretical journals, popular magazines, radio slots, people's theater, and two television channels reaching millions of people. With the state's high literacy rate the party has immensely benefited from a strong readership, which has continuously grown since the 1940s.[27] For example, in 1957 the Communist Party's paper circulation was 40,000, which grew to 60,000 by 1960. By 2001 the party's daily newspaper *Deshabhimani* was published simultaneously in six locations across the state with a readership of over 2 million people (approximately 500,000 copies sold a day with the average copy read by four people).[28] The paper plays a crucial role in the movement as a teacher, galvanizer, and popularizer of issues. The role of a daily newspaper is especially relevant for Kerala, which has the highest newspaper readership rate in the country with an average of one paper for every 10 people. Despite accounting for only 3.5 percent of India's population, 8.5 percent of all daily newspapers are in Malayalam (the language of Kerala) (Jeffrey, 1992: 3). In 1981, there were more than 50 daily newspapers for every 1,000 Malayali speakers (more than three times as many than for Hindi speakers). This avid newspaper readership, it must be appreciated, was built over time. For example, in the early 1930s, daily circulations rarely sold more than 1,000 copies (Jeffrey, 1992: 128).

The central organ of the party is *People's Democracy*, which targets its cadres at all levels. The party also has a theoretical journal, *The Marxist*, covering a wide range of questions facing the movement and providing space for elaborating new ideas.[29] The party also runs a successful publishing house, Chinta Publishers, which publishes left-wing scholarship on a range of topics. In addition to print media, the party began a television channel, Kairali TV, at the end of the millennium in an effort to challenge the mainstream television coverage of news and events and by 2005 it had a second TV channel that plays popular shows with a progressive inflection. By the first years of the new millennium the party had succeeded in growing its membership, while retaining a high level of education and political consciousness

of its members. It has remained apace with the aspirations of the populace through its various forms of media.

CPI(M) Affiliated Organizations

While the party is strong in its own right, it also benefits tremendously from the vast network of organizations in civil society. The party's mass-based affiliated organizations include AIDWA (women's movement), Democratic Youth Federation of India (DYFI), Student Federation of India (SFI), Kisan Movement (farmers movement), and CITU (trade union federation). Taken together the estimated membership of the affiliated organizations is approximately 10 million. Table 5.2 provides a breakdown of membership by organization. The relation of the party to these organizations is complicated and dynamic. The affiliated organizations enjoy a great deal of autonomy as long as their agendas do not come into direct conflict with the party. Most of the affiliates are cognizant of the party's attitude on many issues and prefer to avoid direct confrontation if possible. For example, the women's movement has been criticized from within its own ranks for kowtowing to party interests rather than pursuing its own agenda.[30]

The organizations are affiliated with the party, but the connections run much deeper as all party members participate in affiliated organizations. One of the responsibilities of party members in their roles in affiliated organizations is to communicate the party positions on various issues. Obviously, most members of affiliated organizations are

Table 5.2 Membership numbers of CPI(M) and affiliated organizations in Kerala

Name	1998	1999	2000	2001
CPI(M) membership	268,183	287,088	293,141	301,562
		1995		*1999*
Trade union membership		731,096		973,102
		1996–1997		*2000–2001*
Kisan membership		1,323,562		1,796,520
Agricultural workers' union		1,274,044		1,549,233
		1997		*2000–2001*
Youth federation		3,530,535		4,403,081
Student federation		632,270		815,896
Women's federation		1,100,000		1,737,240 (2001)
				2000–2001
Total membership affiliated organizations				10,302,943
Total Party and affiliated organization membership				10,604,505

Source: *Political-Organizational Report*, 17th Congress, Hyderabad, March 19–24, 2002b: 54–61.

not party members, but all party members are members of at least one mass organization. Despite conscious efforts to attract more women to the party, it has performed abysmally in this regard. For example, AIDWA, the women's organization, has 1.7 million members, yet the party has less than 25,000 women in its ranks.[31]

Clearly the CPI(M) is a formidable organization with a dedicated base of members from whom to draw support. As this accounting of the party's characteristics throughout its history demonstrates, the CPI(M) is a force with exceptional organizational capacities. With its sheer numbers and density in civil society, it is hardly surprising that the party was able to successfully pursue counter-hegemonic generative politics enlisting participatory organizing. With its affiliated organizations, it had over 10 million people (one-third of the population) on whom to draw. The strength of the organization also helped instill a confidence in the members to develop the imagination to introduce a counter-hegemonic generative politics. Clearly its organizational capacities and long history of organizing subaltern classes offer at least part of the explanation for its ability to pursue counter-hegemonic generative politics. Let us now turn to the SACP to see whether its history and organizational capacities shed light on its political practices.

The SACP Capacity in Historical Perspective

The Communist Party of South Africa (CPSA)[32] officially formed in 1921 by uniting a number of splinter groups under a common banner committed to an integrated society regardless of color or sex. Though the CPSA's 1921 Manifesto claimed commitment to an integrated nonracial society, in the first three years of its existence the party focused its attention on the white working class, because of the belief that the white working class was the most class-conscious and developed sector and, therefore, the most able to fulfill the vanguard role. The party believed interracial solidarity would grow out of class struggle (Simons and Simons, 1983: 276). In addition, despite the Comintern's recommendation to assist emergent colonial liberation movements, the CPSA saw African nationalism as bourgeois ideology and did not attempt to build ties with nationalist organizations until the second half of the decade (Simons and Simons, 1983: 260). Instead, the CPSA translated the CPSU's call for a united front into an alliance with conservative white groups, which led the party to support the National Party and Labour Party. By 1924 the alliance proved disastrous, leaving the trade union movement virtually moribund and alienating the few blacks the CPSA had succeeded in recruiting (Simons and Simons, 1983: 309, 321).

Under the leadership of S.P. Bunting and E. Roux the CPSA began organizing black workers in 1924 after a Central Committee decision to "Africanize" the party. The decision was partially a response to white workers' inability to transcend racial categories, a point made painfully clear during the Rand Revolt[33] (Lerumo, 1987: 52). In addition to building the trade union movement among blacks, the CPSA also developed its night school movement where it taught political education through literacy classes (Bundy, 1991: 15). In 1928–1929 the party adopted the Native Republic thesis for an independent black republic. During this time, many blacks were recruited to the party such as Moses Kotane, J.B. Marks,

E.T. Mofutsanyana, Johannes Nkosi, Gana Makabeni, and Josie Mpama. By 1928 the vast majority of members were African (1,600) out of a total membership of 1,750 and by its annual conference in 1929 the party represented almost 3,000 members (Bundy, 1991: 25). Thus, the CPSA closed the decade as a vibrant political force with a growing base of support among blacks.

Reflecting shifts in Comintern policy, between 1930 and 1933 the CPSA purged its ranks of some of the most loyal and committed members in a particularly intolerant and sad phase of its history (Simons and Simons, 1983: 448).[34] African trade unionism declined with the expulsion of many crucial leaders in 1931[35] and most party branches closed, with Johannesburg and Cape Town among the few to survive (Bundy, 1991: 25–26). The party refused to work with nationalist bourgeois groups, claiming instead to be a united front from below. This was an especially ironic claim considering that while it professed to organize from below the CPSA was increasingly out of touch with the mass base and made no headway into organizing workers in either mining or secondary industry during this period (Simons and Simons, 1983: 446). After a few unsuccessful efforts to recover, by 1938 the CPSA had run itself into the ground with the party virtually lapsing into inactivity and its total membership dwindling to between 150 and 300 people, most of whom were white (Simons and Simons, 1983: 483–85).[36]

The Rebirth of the CPSA: Popular Struggles for Transformation

In 1939 the Comintern jettisoned its 1935–1936 International Communist United Front policy forcing the CPSA to make new allies once again. The CPSA rekindled its earlier spirit of inclusiveness and participatory organizing. It elected a new Political Bureau and moved its headquarters from Johannesburg to Cape Town in January 1939, where it remained until it disbanded in 1950. The move from the country's industrial center marked the beginning of a new phase in its history, one in which it grew tremendously and proved to be one of the most active and responsive organizations to subaltern interests in the country.

With a new spirit of unity under the leadership of Moses Kotane and Bill Andrews, by the end of World War II the CPSA grew dramatically and spent a great deal of energy organizing labor, which translated into the growth of the trade union movement (Lodge, 1983: 28). Indeed, as the industrial base grew so too did the black trade union movement, which was responsible for the "record number of 304 strikes, involving 58,000 Africans, Coloureds and Indians and 6,000 whites [...] in 1939–1945, as compared with 197 strikes in the fifteen years from 1924 to 1938" (Simons and Simons, 1983: 555). Inroads were also made into the mining industry with the formation of the African Mine Workers' Union (AMWU), which went on strike in 1946 with 70,000 strikers (Brooks, 1967: 27). The most important African trade unions in the 1940s and early 1950s were affiliated with the Council of Non-European Trade Unions (CNETU, formed in 1941), which allied with the CPSA and had a predominance of communists in its leadership.

Similar to the Communist Party in Kerala, the CPSA simultaneously tried to link local concerns with the broader struggle against oppression and exploitation. Both parties emphasized grassroots activity that spoke to the everyday concerns

of residents and subaltern classes and extrapolated from these experiences broader lessons that linked to systemic issues. While the CPSA was very active in grassroots activities, it was also a crucial source of information and knowledge dissemination and placed a great deal of importance on educating its cadres and the populace. For example, two of the premier bookshops in Johannesburg had links to the party.[37] The best and largest bookshop in Johannesburg, People's Bookshop,[38] grew out of a hole-in-the-wall place into a top bookseller that included a range of topics (Bernstein, 1999: 119). Thus, among its many activities the party can also claim to have participated in the cultural and literary life of the Johannesburg metropolis.

Organizing residents around immediate concerns, the CPSA developed branches and grassroots voluntary associations in a number of townships on the East Rand of Johannesburg. For example, in the 1940s Brakpan, Benoni, Sophiatown, Newclare, and Boksburg all had very active groups engaging participatory organizing practices around an eclectic range of issues (Delius, 1996: 147–48; Sapire, 1993; Lodge, 1983: 97–99, 131–32). It was involved in the squatter movements from 1944 to 1947, food raids, contested advisory board elections in townships, held regular public meetings, mobilized residents around bread-and-butter issues such as the right to brew beer and rent and bus boycotts, and opened night schools (where it taught political education) (Lodge, 1983: 12). It also used elected positions (e.g., Hilda Watts Johannesburg city counselor) to defend local interests (Delius, 1996: 98; Lerumo, 1987: 80–82). It was this participation in local concerns and the efforts to empower ordinary residents that helped secure the party widespread support (Lodge, 1983: 131).

While the party strengthened its moorings in civil society, it also consolidated its relations with opposition organizations. In the 1948 national election in which the National Party (NP) won the majority of votes, the party entered the election contest in order to challenge the legitimacy of a white-only vote and argued for equal rights for all. Together with its allies (trade unions, the ANC, and SAIC) the party organized a mass nonracial conference under the slogan "Votes for All!" to defy the whites-only election and white control of parliament. Between 300 and 400 delegates from all races attended the conference in Gandhi Hall, Fordsburg (Johannesburg), the weekend before the election. The conference marks one of the very first nonracial political events in South African history and demonstrated that a loose coalition of the Congresses, the Communist Party, and trade unions could jointly mount a broad popular campaign that served as a model for later nonracial political campaigns (Bernstein, 1999: 109). Its significance lies not only in the fact that it marked one of the earliest nonracial events, but also it transformed the "Right to Vote" from a long-term aspiration into an immediate demand. Its radical message lay in the fact that it shifted the opposition's terrain from "reform and betterment" to a demand for an equal share in political power (Bernstein, 1999: 109). This increase in political organization among urban blacks threatened white minority rule, and, therefore, caused a great deal of anxiety within white power structures.

In response, the government both intensified its repression and expanded the range of those affected. The decade began with the Suppression of Communism Act of 1950 (which gave the state draconian powers of arrest over anyone promoting economic, political, social, or industrial change) and legislation further prohibiting

black unions and making strikes involving African workers illegal (Lodge, 1983: 33; Seidman, 1993: 25). In 1950, together with the ANC, the ANC Youth League, and the South African Indian Congress, the party called for a May Day stay-away in protest against the Suppression of Communism Act as well as low African wages. By this time all the organizations were using the tactic of "civil disobedience, non-cooperation, boycotts, and politically directed strikes" (Posel, 1991: 97; Bernstein, 1999: 118). The protest received significant support especially among Africans, but had little effect in preventing the draft legislation from becoming law. Instead, the state intensified its onslaught. The pass laws were extended to include African women and influx control laws were tightened to prevent an increase in permanent urban residents in 1952 (Posel, 1991: 102–3). In 1956 a law was enacted segregating unions, making it illegal for unions to have mixed-race membership. Virtually all the opposition leadership was detained in some way or another (e.g., Treason Trial from 1956 to 1960) (Clingman, 1998).

Illegality and Exile: Mass-Mobilizing Practices

Learning of the Suppression of Communism Act early, the CPSA disbanded in June 1950[39] and was officially reformed clandestinely as the South African Communist Party in 1953, relocating its headquarters once again to Johannesburg.[40] Though operating underground the party continued to organize and mobilize the black population in much the same way as it did during the 1940s. For example, among the many campaigns in which communists participated were the widespread mobilization in the 1952 Defiance Campaign, resistance to removal schemes (e.g., the government's demolition of Sophiatown in 1955 was met with large-scale resistance), the school boycott in Brakpan, and the bus boycotts in Alexander and Eaton in 1955 through 1957. Moreover, despite state repression it strengthened its alliance with other liberation organizations. For example, in 1953 the ANC, South African Indian Congress (SAIC), Congress of Democrats (COD), and the South African Coloured People's Organization (SACPO) launched the Congress Alliance under the formidable triumvirate of Oliver Tambo, Walter Sisulu, and Nelson Mandela (Bundy, 1991: 44; Bernstein, 1999: 145). In 1954 the Congress Alliance launched the "Congress of the People" to draft the Freedom Charter. Similar to the CPI(M)'s attempts to elicit feedback on land reform, in an effort to politicize and mobilize the black population the Congress Alliance led a two-year campaign eliciting popular opinion about the content of the Freedom Charter. The range of organizations (e.g., COD, SAIC, ANC, and SACTU) participating in the Congress Alliance allowed communists to help shape the overall development of the Congress movement as well as have a hand in drafting the Freedom Charter,[41] which the ANC and SACP later adopted (Lodge, 1983: 69, 72). Thus, if the 1940s witnessed the organizational flowering of the Communist Party, the 1950s saw not so much a decline in grassroots activism, but rather a shift in the political terrain on which the party operated.

The 1960s saw considerable economic growth, especially in the manufacturing sector, with the formidable tripartite alliance between foreign, domestic, and state capital ensuring economic growth for the country (Seidman, 1993: 69). In order to

secure economic elites' passive support of the regime, the authoritarian state used repression to glean economic profits by supplying docile cheap labor. Thus, as long as the state secured high economic growth rates, there was a great deal of overlapping interests between political and economic elites (Seidman, 1993: 45). In other words, South African business was willing to cooperate with the state's authoritarian means as long as profits were good.

The 1960s began, however, with two events that threatened to destroy the NP government's promises of economic growth through the policies of apartheid. The 1960 Sharpville massacre[42] and the NP government's withdrawal from the British Commonwealth in 1961 led international capital to pack its bags. It did not take long, however, for international corporations to be wooed back and with their return South Africa experienced an economic boom that won it a privileged position as a "newly industrializing country" in the world order. During this time South Africa had evolved from a "primarily extractive and agricultural society into an urbanized industrial one" (Seidman, 1993: 73). South Africa's impressive growth, however, was not felt by the majority of the people as income stratification and inequality worsened between 1954 and 1970 (Seidman, 1993: 83).

In the 1960s the terrain for political opposition further changed. The ANC and Pan Africanist Congress (PAC) were banned in 1960 as well as any meetings that could be deemed a threat to the state and the police was granted unlimited powers of arrest (Lodge, 1983: 321). The Rivonia Trial[43] (1963–1964) and many other less famous trials locked up most of the opposition leadership still in the country. Unable to withstand the intense state repression, by the mid-1960s internal opposition organizations (including trade unions) were virtually destroyed. Though Umkhonto we Sizwe (MK), the military wing of the SACP and ANC, was only established in 1961 by the mid-1960s its internal structures were also destroyed, forcing it to regroup in exile with the ANC and SACP.

While the apartheid state was solidifying itself through repression within South Africa, the liberation movement was consolidating itself in exile. Between the late 1960s and early 1970s there were a number of foiled attempts by MK to penetrate South African borders. This was an especially difficult period for the movement as organizational structures and democratic practices withered as military activity eclipsed political activity. In 1968 MK rank and filers in training camps expressed widespread dissatisfaction with their leadership and the external movement in general. The morale was particularly low due to MK's inability to access South African borders after 1965, leaving many rank-and-file members feeling a sense of purposelessness as they withered away time in training camps in faraway countries.[44] The membership complained that the leadership had failed to develop political structures in South Africa and leaders were criticized for isolating themselves from the membership. After rank-and-file charges against an unresponsive leadership and threats of mutiny at the end of the 1960s, the ANC called the 1969 Morogoro Consultative Conference (Karis and Gerhardt, 1997: 34–36).

After Morogoro, and partly responding to the membership's demands, the SACP and ANC leadership saw the need to establish an underground political presence in South Africa prior to military combat. In 1978 the SACP/ANC set up a commission to review MK strategy, tactics, and structures, out of which emerged a newfound

commitment to antiapartheid political activities of a legal and semilegal nature; military activity was to develop out of political activity (ANC Politico-Military Strategy Commission, 1979). This signaled a return to its previous commitment of political mobilization with the recognition that political structures had to be in place before guerrilla warfare could succeed.

With the shift of the party headquarters from London to Luanda (1981) and eventually to Lusaka and the influx of new recruits in the late 1970s, units grew in Africa, making the 1979 augmented meeting of the Central Committee the first meeting in which the party was anchored on African soil (Maloka, 2002: 40). During the 1980s the party's strategy focused on building an underground movement in South Africa, especially among the working class (Maloka, 2002: 41–42). Thus, in 1984 the Polit Bureau deployed stalwarts to help rebuild internal structures and allocated regions to particular leaders (e.g., Ray Simons and Chris Hani were in charge of the Western Cape, John Nkadimeng and Dan Thloome the Transvaal, Josiah Jele and Chris Hani the Eastern Cape, and Mac Maharaj Natal) (Maloka, 2002: 42). Over the course of the 1980s the SACP stabilized its internal workings: it held regular Polit Bureau meetings, had members released from other responsibilities in the ANC and MK in order to conduct full-time party work, and strengthened communications between the different regions. During the 1980s propaganda work inside the country also stabilized resulting in a tremendous increase in the circulation of party documents.

Renewal within South Africa, 1970s and 1980s: Intensification of Popular Participation

While these developments were brewing in exile, the situation within South Africa was also changing. Labor and community activism flourished in the 1970s and 1980s, merging into "social movement unionism" by the end of the decade (Seidman, 1993: 232–33). As these developments were threatening to eclipse the SACP's and ANC's hegemonic role in the liberation movement, a tragic event provided the crucial spark that thrust them once again into the heart of the struggle. On June 26, 1976, students in Soweto organized a peaceful demonstration protesting the use of Afrikaans in their schools which turned into a bloody civil war leaving a number of children dead and many more injured. This event shocked the nation and the world and led many to get involved in the liberation movement, which they did by joining MK. Throughout the rest of the 1970s and 1980s the SACP/ANC reclaimed their position as leaders of the liberation movement and actively engaged in community and labor struggles within South Africa (Lodge, 1983: 339; Marais, 2001). The SACP and ANC's hegemony stemmed less from their successes in leading the mass movement and guerilla warfare than from their successes in international diplomacy and the symbolic struggle. At the center of the symbolic struggle was the Freedom Charter, which became the unifying document of the various groups in the mass movement and trade unions in the 1980s.

The labor movement that emerged in the 1970s began by focusing primarily on factory-based issues and union-member interests, consciously steering clear of political movements and issues (Hindson, 1987: 209). As the movement grew in size and

strength, however, members increasingly pressured unions to address community issues as the connection between community deprivation and workplace issues was patently clear (Seidman, 1993: 202; Hindson, 1987: 214). State-led authoritarian capitalism, where a small elite enjoyed most of the benefits while the majority of the population was denied access to state resources and economic profit, spurred many into action (Seidman, 1993: 203, 217). The union movement continued to grow,[45] first with strikes within individual industries and then with general strikes across the country and by 1979 political unionism had reemerged (Lodge, 1983: 347–48). By the mid-1980s, the trade union movement was a national movement, representing the working class as a whole. Furthermore, as communities came out in support of labor strikes (helping to feed strikers and refusing to replace workers as scabs) the shared interests of the trade unions and community groups became increasingly clear. By late 1984 South African labor unions were forming a broad-based labor movement fighting for factory-based issues as well as political (e.g., political rights) and social (e.g., housing, education, health care) issues (Seidman, 1993: 232–33; Eidelberg, 2000: 132–33). Thus, the SACP's broad vision of political democracy with economic and social justice was once again taking root in the movements within the country.

In August 1983 the disparate movements that emerged in the 1970s and early 1980s were coordinated under the organizational umbrella of the United Democratic Front (UDF). The UDF brought together individuals and organizations from a broad range of experiences and social locations and provided organizational structure, leadership, and direction to the popular forces exploding on the scene. It played a crucial role in organizing and mobilizing the internal movement that spanned from the local to the national levels. It coordinated a panoply of mass actions, protests, and campaigns and reinforced the underground structures of the SACP and ANC (Seekings, 2000: 3). The ANC and SACP's ability to regain symbolic hegemony of the internal movement during the 1980s is partly thanks to the UDF's link with the exile structures and its efforts to promote the profiles of the ANC and SACP, while also making clear that it was not a replacement for the exiled liberation movement. For example, the Freedom Charter became a crucial unifying document for the UDF and its affiliates, with both the Congress of South African Trade Unions (COSATU) and the UDF adopting the Freedom Charter.

The UDF originally formed with the specific objective of opposing the Tricameral parliament elections and the Black Local Authorities,[46] but quickly grew to include school and rent boycotts that yielded into urban uprisings and insurrectionary tactics (Von Holdt, 2003: 22–23; Seekings, 2000: 3). The state responded with an intensification of repression through the state of emergencies in 1985 and 1986, which eventually led to the banning of the UDF in 1988. In 1988 the Mass Democratic Movement (MDM) emerged largely made up of former UDF activists and organizations, which included trade unions (most notably COSATU), progressive churches, student associations, and community groups. Almost immediately the MDM carried on in the oppositional tradition of the UDF and launched the immensely popular 1989 Defiance Campaign calling on people to defy apartheid laws and demanding the unbanning of the ANC and SACP (Lodge, 2002: 20).

One of the most significant developments of the 1980s was the reemergence of political trade unionism and the party's rapprochement with COSATU, the largest federation in the country (Macun, 2000: 60). COSATU formed in November 1985 after nearly four years of negotiations in which SACTU played a fundamental role in getting the different traditions[47] in the labor movement into discussions. In exile the party closely allied with SACTU and focused on SACTU's role in developing the trade union movement, but after the formation of COSATU and as it grew in prominence and adopted the Freedom Charter in 1987, the party began to question the role of SACTU. SACTU's role in exile had largely focused on "encouraging the revival and development of progressive unionism in South Africa, in building international solidarity, and in encouraging the unity talks which led to the setting up of COSATU" (Kiloh and Sibeko, 2000: 178). Representatives of SACTU met with COSATU representatives in March 1990, where the SACTU NEC proposed to phase itself out in favor of COSATU (which included transferring SACTU's resources to COSATU) (Kiloh and Sibeko, 2000: 178). Reflecting the growing ties between COSATU and the party, they began meeting formally shortly after COSATU's official formation.

Just one year before it returned to South African soil the SACP held its 7th Congress in April 1989 in Cuba. One of the most notable developments of this Congress was the adoption of a new Program, *Path to Power*, which replaced the 1962 Program, *Road to South African Freedom*. In the *Path to Power* the conception of guerilla warfare was refined and more suitably adapted to South African conditions with the political and military struggles culminating in insurrectionary seizure of power, while simultaneously entertaining the possibility for a negotiated transfer of power[48] (SACP, 1989a: 56–58).

When in February 1990 the ban on the SACP and ANC was lifted, allowing the two organizations to legally return to South African soil after 30 years in exile, the SACP was well poised to shift gears and begin addressing the demands of a negotiated transition. In addition, the party enjoyed immense popularity and strength among subaltern classes and had a long history of pursuing alternative politics and participatory organizing around local concerns. That the SACP would pursue a hegemonic project in which civil society is subordinated to the state and economy does not follow inevitably from its history. Indeed, in the early 1990s there was widespread optimism that South Africa was entering an era of radically new politics in which the role of civil society would be extended and popular democracy realized.

Organizational Capacities in the 1990s

While few parties can claim the organizational capacities of the CPI(M), the SACP has had a long history of efficacious involvement in the political and economic struggles of South Africa. Though the 1990s brought profound changes to its internal structure, the SACP managed to set up functioning structures throughout the country, absorb thousands of new recruits in a very short period of time, command more financial and personnel resources than at any time on South African soil, and has participated in both government as well as mass actions.

When the SACP returned to South Africa in 1990 it immediately began rebuilding itself. The simultaneous collapse of the Soviet Union and its return to a legal party operating in South Africa led to a sea change in the SACP's organizational structure. The demands of clandestine and exile existence required a particular type of organization. For one, the party was very elusive and secretive about its membership, its relations with the ANC and MK, and its activities in South Africa. For another, it operated as an elite vanguard with highly restrictive requirements to membership. For the SACP the collapse of the Soviet Union was especially bitter as it implicated weaknesses in its own *modus operandi*. After going into exile the SACP had increasingly allied with and depended on the Soviet Union for financial, military, and ideological support. As a result, many SACP members were trained and educated in the Soviet Union and were well schooled in the Soviet style of organization.

Thus, as the SACP returned to South African soil, it faced tremendous challenges, which ultimately led the party on a journey of renewal in which it asked fundamental questions about the nature and form of the party organization. One of the most immediate challenges was the need to establish itself as a legal organization that could absorb the hordes of new recruits joining its ranks as well as cohesively negotiate with the apartheid regime. Within three months of its return the party convened a Consultative Conference to discuss organizational challenges and deliberate on issues of membership and recruitment policy (e.g., it jettisoned its probation policy for new recruits), democratic centralism and party democracy, the relevance of *The Path to Power* in the new conditions, and a Program of Action for the public launch.

Perhaps one of the most dramatic challenges was in terms of new members flocking to its ranks precisely when the party was trying to establish internal structures. After 40 years of furtive existence, the SACP's internal structures were weak with the emphasis on highly secretive underground units with links to structures in exile. Thus, the party had to rebuild its organizational structures virtually from scratch (SACP, 1994b: 8). Having been a tightly knit vanguard party during exile, the SACP suddenly faced a situation in which vast numbers of people were joining the now-legal, mass-based Communist Party. As new members flocked to its ranks, old members (and many top leaders) allowed their membership to lapse. For example, approximately half the Central Committee (including President Thabo Mbeki) elected at the 1989 Congress allowed their membership to lapse. While it was losing much of its leadership, within a few months the party's membership grew from 2,000[49] to 25,000 and by its public launch in July 1990 there were over 45,000 supporters (members and sympathizers) present at the stadium in Soweto. Thus, at a time in which the party could have benefited from a continuity of leadership, it was facing a situation in which every level of the organization had new leaders. In stark contrast to the length of membership of CPI(M) leaders, the 1991 SACP Congress was represented by an almost entirely new membership from top to bottom as over 90 percent of delegates were new members[50] (SACP, 1995a: 4).

At its 8th party Congress in 1991 the question of organization dominated debates. The party opened its membership and became what is known as a "mass-vanguard" party, indicating its commitment to lead but anchoring this in a mass base. Indicating the fluidity within the organization, the 8th Congress was fraught

with tensions, and everything was up for debate. For example, the 1991 Congress rejected the slogan "Forward to Democratic Socialism" with a small, but vociferous faction led by Harry Gwala arguing that socialism was inherently democratic and, therefore, it was superfluous to add democratic in front of the word socialism[51] (SACP, 1995a: 4). At the heart of this debate lay the analysis of Soviet socialism and the importance of democracy for the emerging strategy and vision. The 1991 Congress adopted a new manifesto, *Manifesto of the South African Communist Party: Building Workers' Power for Democratic Change,* that elaborated the process of negotiations, the importance of maintaining "strategic initiative" as well as issues of governance (and a growth strategy) (Maloka, 2002: 66). In 1995 the party reached its peak with 600 delegates representing 75,603 members at the 9th Congress in which the party consolidated its internal strategic unity. After this period, the party began a process of numerical decline as the rapid growth was impossible to sustain and placed tremendous burdens on the organization.

In addition to these challenges, the loss of luminaries such as Chris Hani[52] (in 1993) and Joe Slovo[53] (in 1995) stripped the SACP of continuity and strategic leadership at a time when it was most needed. Both leaders were firmly anchored in Alliance politics[54] and commanded respect both within the Alliance and among subalterns that translated into qualitative engagements within the Alliance. This period also saw many leaders go into government or be co-opted to business ventures depleting the movement of many of its best cadres and weakening the Left within the Alliance generally (SACP, 1994b: 9). Thus, by the mid-1990s there was a leadership vacuum in the party with few qualified leaders that could claim the stature and experience of the previous generation of leaders, especially in terms of relating to the ANC.

It is clear that the SACP's organizational characteristics differ from the CPI(M) in a number of ways. While both parties are Marxist-Leninist parties organized on principles of democratic centralism and share broadly similar ideological visions, they have chosen different membership forms. The CPI(M) is a 360,000 member-strong cadre party with strict membership requirements. The SACP, by contrast, is a mass-vanguard party with no restrictions on membership[55] and has a membership ranging from 25,000 to 75,000 in the 1990s.[56] At its 2002 Congress, 750 voting branch delegates represented 19,385 active, paid-up members.[57] While the party is clearly in a state of flux, it has recovered from its period of decline (it reached its nadir in 1999) and continues to grow yearly, claiming a membership of 25,998 in October 2003. Thus, in just over one year the party grew its membership by over 20 percent. While the party abandoned its strict membership requirements, members are not only meant to be active in civil society, but are expected to know the documents and programs of the party and be familiar with all party decisions and journals. Like in Kerala, members are expected to attend political education classes, though the SACP has not adequately provided ongoing classes at any level of the organization and the quality of members has not been maintained.

Obviously the density of membership in the population is much greater in Kerala than in South Africa. There is approximately one party member for every 106 people in Kerala, while in South Africa there is approximately one party member for every 1,692 people.[58] The size of branches also contrasts. The SACP has a 25-member

minimum requirement to constitute a branch, while the CPI(M) has a maximum of 15 members per branch of which two should be women. Unlike the CPI(M), which has thousands of full-time paid activists, the SACP has about 25 full-time paid officials (in the national and provincial offices combined) and the only full-time paid elected leaders are the general secretary and three out of nine provincial secretaries.[59] In both parties the salaries are not very high with the notable exception of most of the top leaders in the SACP in their various locations in government, state administration, and various private sector institutions. The leadership's salaries are disproportionately high compared to its base.[60]

Unlike the CPI(M), which has a steady source of funds from its vast base of support, the SACP struggles to remain solvent with the main source of funds coming from debit orders from party and COSATU members, fund raisers, individual donations, and particular arrangements with COSATU (e.g., the SACP's head office is in COSATU's building, which allows it to pay a reasonable rent). Similar to the CPI(M), all SACP members who earn above a certain amount are constitutionally mandated to pay a levy determined by the Central Committee.

Under the leadership of the trade union faction finances have been increasingly centralized with all debit orders going through the national office, which then distributes a percentage of the funds back to provinces based on their contribution. There is, however, discrepancy across provinces and the actual formula for financial distribution is murky. For example, in 2003 the KwaZulu Natal provincial office had four full-time officials (including the provincial secretary position) and is considerably better funded than the Gauteng office, which had only one full-time official (and the provincial secretary is not paid by the party). This tends to lead to the impression (either real or illusory) among many members that a sort of nepotism exists in the party with those provinces overtly allying with the trade union faction at the national office faring better than other provinces. Whether or not this is the case is difficult to determine, but the relevant point is that there is enough secrecy around such issues that members are not clear as to the procedures.

The SACP's 30-member[61] Central Committee is not based on proportional representation (unlike the CPI(M)'s) and has tended to have a high number of members from Gauteng, Western Cape, and KwaZulu Natal. This is largely owing to the fact that a high proportion of national-level leaders are located in these three provinces. The Central Committee meets quarterly for three days. The eight-member Polit Bureau is constituted from Central Committee members and meets fortnightly.[62] Under the Central Committee, the next tier of leadership is the provincial executive committee,[63] which is headed by a seven-member provincial working committee. The district executive committees[64] (also led by a district working committee) directly report to the provincial structures. The basic structure of the party is the branch, which is either residentially based or is in an industrial location and directly liaises with both the provincial and district structures. Branches have a minimum requirement of 25 members and a maximum of 100 members. Guiding the branch is a branch executive committee consisting of five ordinary members and the five elected office bearers. Units are formed with no less than six members in circumstances where a branch cannot be formed (e.g., less than 25 members) and may only

function for one year before converting into a branch. The units are linked with the nearest branch.

In an effort to coordinate the activities of lower tiers (and centralize control!) in recent years the party has centralized certain aspects of its functioning. For example, provincial structures experience pressure to overtly agree with the head office. In 2006 a series of critical articles of the general secretary were published and provincial structures were instructed by the head office to issue statements of support for the general secretary. Some provinces felt this was highly irregular and that the Central Committee should issue a statement based on proper information. The provinces that did not issue statements were then threatened with disciplinary action. The head office has also increasingly monitored activities of lower structures. All structures are required to provide regular progress reports to the national organizer, who selectively draws from them for the Central Committee report.

The SACP has a long history of producing print media. *Umsebenzi* is the party's monthly periodical targeting the mass base and acts as the voice of the party. Its sister publication, *Umsebenzi Online*, is a fortnightly publication, targeting the educated, middle class.[65] *Bua Komanisi* is the Central Committee's official publication that comes out after Central Committee meetings (started in 2001). *The African Communist*, started in 1959, is the party's quarterly theoretical journal—there were a number of predecessors that were consecutively banned—and offers a critical avenue through which new ideas get tabled and debates launched.[66]

Affiliated Organizations of the SACP

Unlike the CPI(M), the SACP does not have a network of affiliated organizations.[67] Rather the SACP is in a formal strategic alliance with COSATU, the ANC, and SANCO with each organization officially maintaining its organizational independence.[68] The Alliance is based on a shared commitment to governing and transforming South Africa. While the party has consistently grappled with the difficulties of building its own organization, it has done so within the framework of the Alliance. Thus, it has had to find the space to both develop its own independent political formation, while not threatening the ANC's role. While the Alliance partners are ostensibly equal, in reality the ANC's ascendance to state power shifted the balance of power among the organizations strongly in the ANC's favor. It is, by all accounts, the dominant partner and increasingly wields its power indiscriminately.

COSATU and the SACP enjoy important ideological and strategic convergences though they remain independent of each other.[69] The party places special emphasis on working closely with the organized working class and envisions its responsibility to include developing class confidence as well as the political, strategic, and leadership skills of workers to ensure that the working class develops beyond narrow workerist and sectoral politics into transformative unionism that seeks the long-term transformation and democratization of the economy (SACP, 1999). Thus, the party has established industrial units, extended its joint program of political education with trade unions, convened socialist forums, and worked toward a production system geared at meeting basic needs. Indicating a shift to working more broadly with a range of organizations at the grassroots, in its 2003 Program of Action, the SACP

acknowledged the importance of working with working-class and poor communities in conjunction with the ANC, COSATU locals, community-based organizations, and progressive NGOs (SACP, 2003: 8). Linked to this is the SACP's Dora Tamana Cooperative Center (founded in 2003), which conducts research on and training of cooperatives, and the Chris Hani Institute, which is meant to offer political education for party cadres, shop stewards, and the movement more generally. Both institutions are meant to broaden the party's ties to the panoply of organizations and institutions in civil society, but neither has adequately fulfilled its role.

Coming out of 40 years of clandestine existence required a makeover of the organizational culture including the ways in which the party communicates with its structures, alliance partners, and subaltern classes. It had to shed itself of its secretive methods and limited forms of discussion and debate. Thus, in the language of the party, it "destalinized" its internal methods of communication and encouraged open democratic debate. Despite these efforts it still uses strong-arm tactics when necessary. For example, at the 2002 National Congress two commissions I attended the debate was significantly curtailed through the chairpersons' summaries. Sadly, under the leadership of the trade union faction the culture of debate is eroding as intolerance and dogmatism reemerge

As this accounting demonstrates, the SACP did a remarkable job at rebuilding its organizational structures within a short period of time. While it is a party in transition, it has established a national structure with functioning branches, districts, and provincial bodies in every province of the country. Moreover, it has been an important actor in the Alliance and ANC-led government.

Conclusion

Clearly the organizational capacities of the CPI(M) and SACP vary significantly. The CPI(M) is a formidable political organization firmly anchored in civil society. Compared to the CPI(M), the SACP is a shell of an organization with neither the membership numbers nor the quality of cadres or leadership. Based on this comparative analysis we might conclude, then, that the capacities of each party accounts for the variation in practices. It could be argued that the CPI(M) was simply more capable of rolling out a counter-hegemonic generative politics enlisting participatory organizing. The SACP, one could argue, was simply unable to advance counter-hegemonic generative projects enlisting participatory organizing due to its organizational deficiencies. But can we explain the divergence in their politics through these organizational differences alone? Does such an argument tell us why the parties pursued the different political projects?

Clearly the capacities vary across the two cases. One must be careful, however, in assigning causal claims as the organizational capacities do not explain what *led* to the shifts in the balance of power among factions within each party. Looking at each case over time we find an unexpected outcome. The CPI(M)'s capacity did not change dramatically in the 1990s, yet its politics shifted to counter-hegemonic generative politics. Despite its growth due to the Salkia Plenum decision, the party's capacities have not improved since its earlier organizational history. Indeed, some of its most innovative and successful periods were before the massive growth in the

party. Thus, at most we can argue that the organizational capacities help account for how the CPI(M) was able to successfully pull off such a widespread campaign. It does not tell us why it turned to these practices. Similarly, the SACP experienced some of its most efficacious activism at times when it was at its smallest. In the 1940s and 1950s communists only numbered in the couple thousands, yet the party was one of the most dynamic organizations on the scene. Similarly, in exile the party was a small elite vanguard with tremendous ability to influence the direction of the liberation movement. Over its 80-year history, the SACP has thus been a remarkably dynamic organization with varying capacities throughout its history. The SACP was both larger and better resourced in the 1990s than at any time in its history on South African soil. Thus, looking at the SACP over time we see the party has a long history of activism in civil society and participatory organizing practices.

The genealogy of each party reveals (1) that comparing each party against itself over time uncovers different dynamics than the synchronic comparison against each other and (2) that behind the idiosyncratic histories lie extraordinary parallels. Thus, while the histories are unique and specific to each party, there are remarkable and salient parallels that laid the basis for similar politics and practices to emerge. Both parties have long histories anchored in popular politics enlisting both mass mobilizing and participatory organizing around local concerns. Neither party is a sectarian fringe party on the margins of politics. Rather both are popular, mass-based parties that have been at the center of politics in the second half of the twentieth century.

Both parties further share in their links to formidable labor movements that have helped shape the contours of each society. The links to labor find their roots in the parties' mobilizing and organizing efforts of the 1940s and 1950s, which helped the labor movements transcend narrow workerist orientations to adopt broader social and political issues. In addition, both Kerala and South Africa have vibrant and densely organized civil societies in which a range of community-based organizations have played important roles in the struggles against oppression and exploitation. Indeed, the robust civil societies did not simply arise from indigenous civic traditions; rather the emergence of dynamic civil societies is rooted in the histories of social conflict and mobilization much of which has been assisted by the parties.

We thus must be circumspect in ascribing to explanations based on organizational capacities. Clearly, the capacities are part of the story—the CPI(M)'s ambitious counter-hegemonic generative project required a capable organization that could provide the organizational support and political will for the implementation of such a project, while the SACP's emphasis on hegemonic generative politics required less organizational capacity as the emphasis was on state-led initiatives. But this alone does not provide an adequate explanation as to why the parties pursued the particular politics that they did. Let us now shift comparative lenses and look specifically at political factions within the parties. Do factions vying for power within the organizations explain the variation?

CHAPTER 6

Organizational Faultlines

There have been both sympathetic and critical studies of the importance of political organization. For Lenin, the organizational apparatus played a fundamental role in organizing subordinate classes in order to effect social transformation. He envisioned communist parties consisting of enlightened individuals who helped elevate and radicalize the working class to become a political class.[1] Building on Lenin, Gramsci (between 1930 and 1935) developed his notion of the importance of the communist party to be in synergistic relation to its base of support. Rather than bringing superior ideology and consciousness to the working class, the Modern Prince (as Gramsci called the Communist Party) articulated and refined the common sense ideology of subaltern classes (1992 [1971]: 125–33).

From the critical perspective, Michels (1999 [1910]) suggests that political parties inherently tend toward oligarchy with the leaders at the summit wielding power over the organization, ultimately leading political parties to abandon radical goals in favor of organizational stability (335–38). Similarly, Selznick (1952) conceives of communist parties as organizational weapons seeking organizational power to gain social and political control in order to undermine the liberal democratic world (97). Less polemical yet still emphasizing the role of organization, Duverger (1972) analyzes the internal organization of political parties to develop an outline of what makes a political party (5). Similarly, Roberts (1998) explains there are two ideal types of political organization, highly structured and less highly structured, with highly structured and disciplined parties able to weather environmental disruptions better than decentralized fluid parties (46). Differences aside, these perspectives challenge the late twentieth-century disillusionment with political parties by drawing attention to the fact that political parties play an important role in shaping societal transformation, some, as history has shown, in devastating directions and others in more positive directions. The common denominator in all of the accounts is the belief that the possibilities for social transformation are integrally linked to the role of political parties.

What these scholars neglect is that political parties are not monolithic organisms mechanically engaging the social world. Organizations have different capacities,

which impact on the opportunities and limitations faced by parties. However, organizational capacities are not the only internal dynamic affecting a party. Political parties are internally contested battlefields with vying factions seeking to control them. Indeed, who controls a political party profoundly affects its political engagements. Factional cleavages, as Schorske has shown, can define the trajectory of political organizations for many years to come. Like Schorske's turn-of-the-century German Social Democratic Party, the CPI(M) and SACP, too, have political factions competing for the helm of the organization.

A note about terminology is in order since faction is a loaded word often referring to firmly entrenched cleavages of a dogmatic character. For lack of a better alternative I have chosen to use faction to refer to the different ideological tendencies in the two parties, but I want to highlight that the factions in the SACP and CPI(M) in the 1990s were fluid and specifically refer to different visions of change and understandings of who the crucial agents are.

In this chapter I look at the political factions within the CPI(M) and SACP. Understanding which faction controls the party brings us closer to unraveling the puzzle of the divergent political practices.

Political Factions in the CPI(M)

Ushering in the CPI(M)'s counter-hegemonic generative politics was a grassroots faction firmly moored in civil society with a clear vision of social transformation based on expanding the role of civil society in political and economic domains. In the early 1990s this grassroots faction shifted the balance of power away from the trade union faction enough to nudge the party to adopt a new type of politics. To appreciate what this shift entailed we must take a closer look at the different factions.

Within the CPI(M) there are two main factions vying for power: a trade union faction and a grassroots faction.[2] The trade union faction sees the organized working class (including the unorganized sector as the informal sector is called in India) as the primary agent of change and holds an orthodox vision of modernization based on increased industrialization. The trade union faction also adheres to a traditional vanguard understanding of the party with a particular emphasis on state power. The grassroots faction, by contrast, has a broader understanding of the agent of change to include the poor, unemployed, and working class (again including the unorganized sector) and has a skeptical approach to modernization, arguing that industrial development must be accompanied by alternative forms of local-level development that are deliberated, formulated, and implemented by ordinary citizens. Related to this, the grassroots faction promotes a synergistic relation to the base and an appreciation of multiple sites of power within society in addition to state power.

During the 1950s the party's efforts to build class consciousness and organize subaltern classes around issues arising from local conditions helped keep the party unified and minimized the entrenchment of competing factions. In time, however, factions began to emerge out of the ideological debates around the Communist Party's relation to the Congress Party and issues of parliamentarianism (Nossiter, 1988: 21). The tensions culminated in the 1964 split in the Communist Party with the

majority of members from a statist faction remaining with the Communist Party of India (CPI). The statist faction argued for the importance of working through parliamentary means and allying with the Congress. Another group (the majority of whom joined the CPI(M)) argued for a middle road that advocated the use of extra-parliamentary means when necessary and qualified support of the Congress on particular progressive acts. While a few important leaders such E.M.S. Namboodiripad and A.K. Gopalan joined the CPI(M), its defining characteristic was its mass appeal. Over 80 percent of the rank and file joined the CPI(M), while the majority of ministers remained with the CPI (Nossiter, 1988: 82, 1982: 187–89). The CPI(M) has partly defined itself in opposition to the statist-dominated CPI and, therefore, a statist faction has not found much resonance within the CPI(M). Rather the two principal factions—trade union and grassroots—are both firmly anchored in mass politics and mass and class organizations in civil society.

The current configuration of factions vying for power, thus, has its roots in the 1964 split. During the 1960s and 1970s struggles intensified on the land resulting in further growth of the trade union movement. The labor movement in Kerala was borne out of the social and political struggles of the 1930s and firmly linked labor to traditions of community-based organizing and a more encompassing project of social transformation. Under the auspices of the Communist Party, the early labor movement rapidly grew and built firm links to the agrarian movement. For example, between 1957 and 1959 over 80 percent of all unions affiliated with the CPI-led All-Indian Trade Union Congress (AITUC) (Nossiter, 1982: 159). After the split, the CPI retained control of AITUC, leading the CPI(M) to form the Center of Indian Trade Unions (CITU) in May 1970 (Basu, 1998: ix). Reflecting the CPI(M)'s popularity with rank and filers, CITU quickly eclipsed AITUC and became the largest federation of trade unions in the state.[3] Thus, by the 1970s the CPI(M) had further consolidated a strong working-class movement out of the disparate class elements and strengthened the role of the trade union faction.

The Rise of the Trade Union Faction

As trade union issues came to dominate the CPI(M) in the 1970s, a trade union faction slowly gained ascent within the party. Reflecting the trade union faction's influence within the party, throughout the 1970s and early 1980s trade union issues and practices dominated party politics, which argued for a "revitalized policy of centralized and state-led modernization" (Tornquist, 2000: 121). The tremendous efforts to organize the agrarian and urban laborers into a coherent working class led to a predominance of trade union leaders in the party throughout the 1970s and 1980s. For example, a number of the state committee members and district leaders are also trade union leaders. To take one prominent example, the CITU state president K.N. Raveendranath is a CPI(M) State Committee member (the state's equivalent of a central committee).

Under the leadership of the trade union faction the Communist Party effectively used the state to help limit labor's vulnerability to market forces and curtailed the prerogatives of capital through various measures. The party also promoted labor cooperatives for toddy tappers, beedi workers, coir- and cashew-processing workers,

fishermen, and handloom weavers. When capital fled, as in the cashew-processing industry, the state intervened and combined 34 factories with 34,000 workers into a state cooperative (Heller, 1999: 178). It further consolidated and institutionalized collective bargaining, effectively providing labor and capital an effective process through which to hammer out negotiated settlements. Under the leadership of the trade union faction the party helped secure the passage of various labor laws such as regulation of mechanization, unemployment allowance, minimum wages, and pension schemes (CPI(M), 1981: 385–86). Until the 1980s the trade union faction was virtually uncontested as the politics of protest were successful in raising the quality of life for the majority of Kerala's people.

While the CPI(M)'s achievements on the social front were impressive, the lingering sluggishness in the economy led to the realization that redistributive policies were unsustainable without economic growth.[4] Because the trade union faction sees the organized working class as the primary agent of change, it promotes a vision of labor-absorbing industrialization and enlists typical trade union tactics such as the strike and negotiations with state and capital. Under the leadership of the trade union faction in the 1980s the government began focusing on industrial development to encourage economic growth. The state played an active role through state-owned enterprises and a variety of service agencies as Kerala suffered from low levels of capital formation, a failure to attract private investment, and an absence of indigenous industrial enterprise (Nossiter, 1982: 284). Despite Kerala's high labor productivity[5] and one of the most developed infrastructures in the country (e.g., power supply, transportation, and communications), its perceived labor militancy has kept investors away (Heller, 1999: 213). As a result the CPI(M) has tried to woo private capital to invest in industrial development. In 1987–1991 the CPI(M) Ministry assigned K.R. Gouri (the architect of the land reforms) minister of industry, making her responsible for breathing new life into industrial development, while using her political credentials among the working class to ensure union restraint (Heller, 1995: 661). These efforts signaled an attempt by the trade union faction to promote growth through industrial development. When the trade union faction lost the election in 1991, however, its grip on power began to loosen as the grassroots faction made its bid for control.

The Grassroots Faction Eclipses the Trade Union Faction

The shift to counter-hegemonic generative politics reflected a shift in the balance of power as the old-style politics increasingly lost credibility and its main advocates in the trade union faction struggled to formulate alternatives that addressed the problems facing the state. As the trade union faction struggled to find answers, the grassroots faction was actively pursuing a range of possible alternatives through pilot projects, action research, education classes, and local-level activism. The international and national challenges made the party leadership more receptive to the grassroots faction's vision as it was well aware of the failures of the Soviet Union's statism and the urgent need to develop alternatives that alleviated the deteriorating conditions of Kerala's populace. Thus, the trade union faction's grip on power within the party was eroding, and the grassroots faction was able to capture the imagination of

key leaders[6] who supported a new type of politics and a new emphasis in practice. One indication of this shift was EMS Namboodiripad's public announcements in the early 1990s that a new approach to economic development was necessary and that it should not be party-political, but should unite people around a common vision (Namboodiripad, 1991, 1994). Further reflecting the shift in the balance of power within the party, a few innovative thinkers from the grassroots faction (e.g., T.M. Thomas Isaac, E.M. Sreedharan, M.A. Baby, Gulati) made their way into the state leadership in the 1980s and 1990s. Prior to this, the grassroots faction had been largely working through institutions in civil society, primarily the Kerala Sastra Sahitya Parishad.[7]

The Kerala Sastra Sahitya Parishad (KSSP or the "People's Science Movement" as it is known in English) formed in 1962 by a group of scientists who wanted to popularize science and combine the revolutionary potential of science for the realization of social revolution. Informed by a Marxist-Gandhian perspective that seeks social revolution through ecologically sensitive and sustainable local-level initiatives, it is a volunteer-based mass movement that brings together a high-caliber cadre of volunteers to present ecologically informed perspectives of development and plays a major role in conscientizing the mass base. In contrast to many social movements and grassroots organizations that emerged during this period, the KSSP did not shy away from working with and complementing efforts of political parties. Indeed it has quite self-consciously remained an autonomous grassroots organization that works in close alliance with political parties by supporting and complementing political initiatives and campaigns. It also offers a space for innovating and incubating novel ideas about development by running pilot projects and action research as well as scrutinizing legislation and development policies for their progressive potential.[8]

While many early KSSP members were CPI(M) members, the link to the CPI(M) intensified during the state of emergency in 1975–1977[9] (Zachariah and Sooryamoorthy, 1994). Up to this time the KSSP was a relatively small organization made up of largely middle-class professionals (especially scientists and teachers). During the state of emergency, its membership grew with most of the new recruits coming from CPI(M) structures (Zachariah and Sooryamoorthy, 1994). Unlike the CPI(M), which was ruthlessly persecuted, KSSP was not targeted during the state of emergency thus providing a relatively safe avenue for party members to continue their work. While this period radicalized the KSSP, it also broadened and deepened the outlook of a significant number of party members. Many members went through a "greening" of their Marxism and developed a deep appreciation for participatory development in which people are empowered to direct and control the development of their communities.[10] The traditional vanguard party was, for many members, adapted from a party directing from above to a party guiding and implementing from below. Thus, the KSSP played a critical role in shaping a number of party activists during this period, many of whom became significant voices in the grassroots faction. In addition, the KSSP's involvement in all the campaigns helped the grassroots party activists mainstream the new orientation into party thinking. When the balance of power within the party had shifted enough to provide the grassroots faction a window of opportunity to initiate a new politics in the early 1990s, the grassroots faction was thus well prepared and ready to grasp the

opportunity. It wasted no time and immediately began busying itself with steering the party toward a new type of politics.

The grassroots faction finds its strength in various institutions of civil society, such as the KSSP, the women's movement, and local-level development organizations as well as trade unions. It is thus more widely grounded in civil society than the trade union faction and seeks change through local-level initiatives that construct alternatives in and through the current conditions. Its vision of alternative forms of development based on local resources, capacities, and needs finds resonance with a wide range of citizens, which has further strengthened its position in the party.

The struggle between the two factions often leads to Machiavellian politics with each faction doing what it needs to capture power within the leadership. In the 1990s, for example, the grassroots faction successfully expelled important trade union leaders from the state secretariat (though the Central Committee later overturned the expulsions), which gave it a window of opportunity to initiate a new and radical project. For its part, in 2004 the trade union faction expelled key grassroots faction leaders in its attempt to reclaim power.[11] However, the grassroots faction has managed to maintain enough control to continue to influence the party's direction. The point is that the faction able to control the party also shapes the politics at any given time.

Let us turn to the SACP to look at the role of factions within its structures.

Political Factions in the SACP

For the SACP the 1980s were marked by its strengthening ties to the ANC. With Moses Mabhida as the general secretary of the party and his firm moorings in the ANC together with the relocation of the party's headquarters to Lusaka where the ANC's headquarters were, the two organizations consolidated their relations. The 1979 Politico-Military Commission's recommendations in the *Green Book* were also beginning to bear fruit. At the SACP's 6th Congress in 1984 and the ANC's 1985 Kabwe Conference the importance of grounding military struggle in political structures within the country was highlighted and a shift to "people's war" and a focus on urban struggle was instituted (SACP, 1985a, 1986a). The SACP also elaborated its vanguard role as the leading political force of the working class and in the national liberation struggle, which it qualified by explaining that it was to do this through "participating in and strengthening the liberation alliance of all classes and strata […] headed by the ANC" (Maloka, 2002: 48). By the mid-1980s the regularized meetings between the ANC and SACP further helped solidify relations and the concept of a "tripartite alliance" between the ANC, SACP, and SACTU emerged. The party, however, was careful not to appear as though it was pushing itself to the fore and maintained the necessary balance to ensure both the ANC and SACP were strengthened (Maloka, 2002: 59).

A significant outcome at the 6th Congress was that it consolidated and formalized party structures and procedures (e.g., a Constitution was adopted and a Congress was to be held every four years), which was necessitated by the growth in party membership.[12] Underground structures within the country were also taking root with functioning structures in the Western Cape, Transvaal, the Border region

in the Eastern Cape, and Natal (Maloka, 2002: 57). The party also lifted its cloak of secrecy and allowed a handful of names to be revealed as SACP leaders, which helped maintain the profile of the party as well as facilitated contact between the leadership and the units.

Similar to the CPI(M), the SACP has factions vying for power within the party. During exile, however, the party (like the ANC) seems to have not tolerated factional cleavages. To be sure, there were ideological differences, but these differences did not evolve into irreconcilable tactical cleavages among factions as the party marginalized or, in the extreme cases, expelled "dissident" voices.[13] The demands of exile did not nurture open and democratic debate, though there was effort made to ensure cadre input on major party documents. For example, a draft of the Program *Path to Power* was first disseminated for comments from units around the world in the early 1980s. It took the better part of the decade before a final draft was formulated and adopted. These efforts notwithstanding, there was not a great deal of space for dissenting views that challenged the party's fundamental premises, which included its relation to the ANC as well as the Soviet Union. For example, the party ignored blatant transgressions in the Soviet Union as it did not want to believe that important aspects of socialism were being debased (Slovo, 1990: 34). Whether this was simply due to Machiavellian calculations based on conditions of dependence or blindness is difficult to determine, but it does seem clear that it did not countenance dissenting views. Shortly before his death, Joe Slovo, apparently contrite and regretful about his unwavering support for the Soviet Union during the period of exile, acknowledged he had his doubts much earlier: "His own doubts began in the mid-1960s but he chose to remain silent because he had seen the alternative at close hand. His wife, the fiercely unorthodox and independent author and academic Ruth First, was, he said, sidelined by the movement" (van Niekerk, 1997: 221). As a result, the emergence of factions vying for power within the party was kept at bay with a firmly entrenched leadership core.

After its return to South Africa the SACP faced its history of silence and encouraged vigorous debate and a plurality of visions.[14] For example, in 1993 the SACP convened a national strategy conference with the objective to deepen strategic debate and consolidate the party around a broad strategic orientation. While this culture of debate was certainly welcomed and helps explain the party's theoretical advancements, it also led to a culture of ideological debate rather than practice. Many branches spent a tremendous amount of energy studying and debating the current conditions and appropriate responses, but did not spend a great deal of effort on branch activities that linked with a base of support nor implemented new policies. In these conditions ideological and tactical cleavages began to manifest.

The shift to generative politics coincided with the ascendance of a statist faction within the SACP. While the old-style protest politics increasingly lost legitimacy in the new conditions a new politics had to be forged. As the party struggled to find answers, key leaders (many of whom eventually formed the statist faction) were actively involved in the negotiations, policy formulation process, and the strategic thinking of the Alliance. In this process different perspectives emerged, eventually coalescing into three factions—a statist faction, a trade union faction, and a

grassroots faction—each anchoring its vision of change in a different societal agent (i.e., the state, the organized working class, and subaltern classes respectively).

The dominant faction for most of the decade was the statist faction closely allied to the ANC, which distinguishes itself by its emphasis on state-led industrial development and its allegiance to the ANC (rather than a more qualified support for progressive policies of the ANC). There is an additional faultline that characterizes the statist faction and its overlap with the ANC. The leading cadre of the statist faction and many in the ANC leadership were in exile. The majority of the SACP's base (and the grassroots and trade union factions), on the other hand, are largely drawn from UDF and COSATU activists. The trade union faction sees the organized working class as the primary agent of change and holds an orthodox vision of modernization based on increased industrialization.[15] While the working class is always the important agent of change for a communist party, the trade union faction adopted a more explicitly trade union orientation that sees the working class as the party's main constituency. Rather than its functional role in revolutionary struggle, the working class is the party's primary interest. The grassroots faction understands the agent of change more broadly to include the poor, unemployed, and working class (including the informal sector and the rural population) and has a skeptical approach to modernization, arguing instead that industrialization has to be complemented by alternative forms of local-level development initiatives deliberated, formulated, and implemented from below.

The Rise of the Statist Faction

To appreciate the power of the statist faction in the early 1990s one must understand what it meant to be a party member in the movement at this time. During exile it was difficult to become a party member with potential recruits individually (and furtively) invited to join the party on a strict probation basis, keeping its cadre membership at an exceptionally high caliber. Hence, to be a party member was a prestigious honor and guaranteed the party a special place within the movement. Moreover, before 1990 there was immense leadership overlap between the party and the ANC (with the exception of Oliver Tambo[16]). The SACP and ANC had developed a strong alliance that reflected 40 years of working together in joint struggle against the apartheid regime. Thus, in the early 1990s the dominant trend within the party was strongly allied to the ANC with little factional activity tolerated. After returning to South Africa and opening itself to mass membership, however, factions began to emerge within the organization.

The factions within the party are complicated, and reinforced, by the dynamics of its alliance with the ANC and COSATU. The Tripartite Alliance between the ANC, SACP, and COSATU formed in May 1990 out of a common commitment to governing and building a new South Africa (Baskin, 1991: 430–34; Eidelberg, 2000: 139). In its original guise, the three partners complemented one another with each adding value to the arrangement.[17] While the SACP supported the arrangement, COSATU showed reluctance from the beginning. It did not want to become a trade union wing to the ANC and was very critical of too much conciliation (Lodge, 2002: 21; Götz, 2000: 167). And given its 1994 membership of 1.2 million

it was a formidable ally that the ANC could not afford to alienate. There were elements in COSATU that favored establishing a separate workers' party with the SACP. The argument that gained wider currency, however, favored the Tripartite Alliance so as to prevent the ANC from abandoning its leftist commitments[18] (Eidelberg, 2000: 130). COSATU's support was only consolidated in 1993 when senior COSATU leaders invested their political efforts in elaborating what would eventually become the *Reconstruction and Development Program* (RDP). Similar to the Freedom Charter's symbolic role in unifying the movement in the 1980s, the RDP became the basis of widespread support for the ANC (Götz, 2000: 163). The party's alliance with the ANC and COSATU thus provided strong allies for the statist and trade union factions respectively.[19]

Moreover, when the SACP and ANC returned to South Africa the two organizations enjoyed a great deal of continuity in terms of membership (indeed, most SACP members were also ANC members), but also the two organizations shared programmatic and strategic visions with the ultimate goal of a democratic and socialist South Africa. In concrete terms this vision informed the debates and thinking around the RDP (Götz, 2000: 168–69). In these early days, the SACP enjoyed a significant degree of influence within the ANC and, thus, over the direction and content of the transition to a nonracial democratic South Africa. The ANC's election victory, however, consolidated ANC dominance and represented a realignment in the balance of power within the Alliance.

One indication of the degree to which the statist faction controlled the party is the number of leaders in key positions of government. By 1998, 28 out of 30 Central Committee members were employed in top positions of government either as elected representatives or bureaucratic officials. These numbers slightly shifted in favor of the trade union faction in the 2002 Congress when the number of Central Committee members who were employed in government slid to 25 out of 30. Three were employed in trade unions, one in a grassroots development organization, and the general secretary was employed by the party.

Access to state power and the euphoric optimism in the ANC-led Alliance's capacity to administer a new development trajectory added to the statist faction's credibility among the populace as well as within the movement. The statist faction was well positioned to pursue a range of possible alternatives through its integral role in the transformation process. Reflecting its dominant position, the statist faction emphasized ideological and strategic developments within the Alliance as it saw this as the party's primary role. Moreover, its focus on state-led development led to an emphasis on policy issues relating to nation building enlisting mass-mobilizing practices. For example, during the first half of the 1990s the SACP emphasized mass actions and demonstrations to strengthen the ANC/SACP's position in the negotiations with the apartheid regime. After the 1994 ANC-led Alliance election victory, the mass actions continued in order to build solidarity around the new nation. With its position firmly entrenched within the SACP, the statist faction was able to direct the trajectory of the party for a significant period of the 1990s with its dominance only seriously challenged in 1998. At this time the balance of power within the party began to shift with the trade union faction making inroads into the leadership of the party.

The Trade Union Faction Eclipses the Statist Faction

By the late 1990s a trade union faction had firmly coalesced and allied with COSATU. This faction distinguished itself by the priority given to the organized working class as the driving force of change and its orthodox view of development through increased industrialization. From the beginning of the Tripartite Alliance COSATU's relation with the ANC was fragile and internally contested. Unlike the SACP, which had a long history of working closely and interdependently with the ANC, COSATU was very reluctant to give up its autonomy. Despite the accord between COSATU and the ANC,[20] tensions persisted between the two organizations. For example, the ANC's unilateral decisions (e.g., the decision to end guerilla war in August 1990 and its support for an all-party congress to negotiate the route to a constituent assembly) were viewed suspiciously by COSATU. In response, COSATU demanded its own delegation and introduced its own set of constitutional provisions (e.g., proportional representation and a two-term limit for the office of presidency) (Lodge, 2002: 21). By the middle of the decade COSATU's hesitations resonated with many in the SACP, especially as the ANC was shifting to a more pro-capitalist position and increasingly wielding its power within the Alliance. While the party was struggling to come to terms with the changing nature of its relationship with the ANC through the 1990s, the statist faction continued to stay the course of hegemonic generative politics focusing on issues of governing.

At the party's 10th Congress in 1998 the trade union faction gained a significant presence on the Central Committee and won the position of general secretary. Further reflecting the shift in favor of the trade union faction a subtle but consistent shift can be seen in the 1998 party Program that emphasized a more class-on-class analysis, which led the party to further prioritize the need to establish working-class hegemony, but also lost some of its nonracial inflection. Related to this, the party affirmed the organized working class in the formal sector as its principal constituent and the crucial social force. The party argued that "the working class [...] has the collective numbers, and the strategic economic location, as well as the revolutionary organizational traditions, to provide effective social weight to any progressive agenda" (SACP, 1998: 17). The party further argued that the working class "must dare to assume power, to engage with, transform and hegemonize the state, the legislatures, and key institutions (economic, cultural, and social) of society" (SACP, 1998: 18). Along these lines the trade union faction advocated working with people in key sites of power and influence in society (SACP, 2003: 7). While the trade union faction contested the hegemonic generative politics of the statist faction, it did not launch an alternative (and counter-hegemonic) politics. Rather it has fluctuated between hegemonic generative politics (e.g., the Financial Sector Reform Campaign) and emotive protest politics (e.g., strikes and anti-privatization demonstrations), and relies on mass mobilizing. Indeed, its practices bear strong resemblance to trade union tactics that prioritize corporatist negotiations and formal bargaining processes buttressed by mass actions. Further indicating a top-down turn, the general secretary has centralized power and has shifted the focus more explicitly to the importance of state power. Indeed under the leadership of the trade union faction

the culture of intra-party debate nurturing a plurality of views is eroding in favor of a centralized line given from above.

The increasing control of the trade union faction is captured in the configuration of the Polit Bureau. In 2002 six out of eight Polit Bureau members were employed in government, while in 2007 six out of 12 Polit Bureau members are employed in government. In the 2002 Congress the number of members in the Central Committee employed in government only marginally went down to 25 (from 28). However, three out of six ministers were purged from the party at this Congress, indicating the increasing power of the trade union faction. In 2007 the Central Committee was increased to 35 members with 7 employed by trade unions and the party, and the Polit Bureau is stacked in favor of the trade union faction. A worrying trend is the growing control of the head office, which manifested in 2007 with two head office functionaries (one past, one present) elected to the Central Committee rather than coming up through party structures. These two members are also members of the Polit Bureau.

The Grassroots Faction Emerges at the Local Level

A third, and the smallest, faction is a grassroots faction, which sees the informal sector, unemployed *and* working class as the primary agents of change and views the state as a key institution to effect radical transformation, but must be subordinated to civil society. Many activists in the grassroots faction were former activists from the UDF and thus well schooled in participatory organizing and grassroots activism. It is important to note that the grassroots faction has not coalesced like the trade union and statist factions. While there are a growing number of grassroots activists, many activists do not see themselves as part of any group, faction, or tendency in the party (some even loosely identify with the statist or trade union factions). I have characterized the existence of a grassroots faction based on practices and people's understanding of who are the agents of change, not how they see themselves within the party. For example, one group of activists involved in community issues and building cooperatives did not view themselves representing a particular type of development politics. They saw themselves as working with their communities to develop livelihood strategies. In my framework, the activists represent a grassroots faction.

The grassroots faction seeks to establish a responsive state with reduced coercive power, and unlike the trade union and statist factions it does not believe industrialization will bring the type of development South Africa needs (i.e., labor-producing jobs, increased standards of living, and ecologically sensitive development) and advocates building elements of socialism through local-level initiatives. The grassroots faction argues that the transformation to socialism consists of local experiments, new institutional forms, and real alternatives in township economies that allow the state and economy to be progressively subordinated to civil society. Despite the numerical minority of the grassroots faction it has spent the most effort in putting the party's vision into practice.

Conclusion

Clearly, the CPI(M) has a long history of popular politics anchored in civil society. For most of its history, however, it has primarily focused on protest and hegemonic

generative politics, defending and championing the interests of subaltern classes through extending the state. By the mid-1980s the CPI(M) was forced to address the limits of redistributive politics without economic growth, which ultimately challenged it to rethink its approach to development. That the party would choose a counter-hegemonic generative politics attempting to enlist novel forms of development, based on local initiatives and alternative logics of accumulation and governance, was not inevitable. The counter-hegemonic generative project was largely championed by the grassroots faction that came to the fore in the 1990s. Clearly the role of competing factions represents an important part of the story as the grassroots faction's control of the party fundamentally shifted emphasis.

Similarly, the SACP has a long history of popular activism grounded in civil society. For most of its history its politics have focused on protest politics. During the 1990s the SACP was forced to shift to generative politics and focus on nation building. That the party would choose hegemonic generative politics was also not inevitable. The hegemonic generative politics was largely operationalized by first the statist faction and later the trade union faction. Hence, like the CPI(M), competing factions have played an important role in determining the practices of the SACP.

It would seem, then, that the role of factions is a crucial part of the explanation. While the existence of and battles between factions helps us understand the shift in political practices, it also begs the question of what gives rise to different factions. Why did the grassroots faction come to the fore in the 1990s in the CPI(M) and similarly why did the statist and trade union factions dominate the scene in the SACP? To understand what gives rise to particular configurations of the balance of power among factions we must place the parties in their larger environments. It is to the political fields and economic contexts that I now turn.

CHAPTER 7

Party and Class under Electoral Politics

In Kerala and South Africa, the nature of the economic systems and the electoral arenas shaped the conditions for generative politics to emerge. In South Africa, industrial development created a strong capitalist class and an organized working class both with links to the state, while in Kerala the relatively low industrial development and the particular nature of agrarian capitalism reflected a weak capitalist class and strong subaltern classes with firm links to the state. In South Africa, capital responded to economic crisis by courting carefully selected cadres within the ANC and labor movement in order to shape the post-apartheid economic dispensation. In Kerala, the absence of a strong capitalist class and the presence of powerful subaltern classes led the CPI(M) to respond to stalled economic growth by pursuing radically new forms of economic development.

In chapters five and six we saw the relative importance of the parties' organizational capacities and competing political factions in shaping practices. It became clear, however, that focusing on the internal character of the parties does not capture the whole picture. Indeed, looking at political factions, while certainly important in understanding the practices of the 1990s, begs the question of what gives rise to different factions. In this chapter I investigate the wider political and economic environments in order to draw a fuller picture of their effects on the parties. More specifically, I look at the electoral arenas, the balance of class forces, and the particular nature of party-class alliances. On the one hand, the different degrees of capitalist development in South Africa and Kerala produced unique configurations of class forces, which registered in the political realm through party-class alignments. On the other hand, the different degrees of electoral competition affected the parties' relations with their bases of support.

The State, Classes, and Political Parties

Both Kerala and South Africa can rightfully claim a relatively unique combination among developing countries of progressive developmental states with high state

capacity and vibrant civil societies. The states in Kerala and South Africa enjoy widespread legitimacy among the citizenry with highly developed and bureaucratic administrative state apparatuses and regular competitive elections. At century's end, democracy was firmly established in Kerala with subaltern classes' (especially the urban and rural working classes) demands regularly and effectively expressed in the state. In South Africa, while the fledgling democratic political system was successfully finding its moorings, working-class demands had not yet found a strong and consistent presence in the state. Nevertheless, both Kerala and South Africa share the basic foundations of what characterizes a state as democratic and efficacious. The most general, and limited, understanding of democracy is "a regime in which those who govern [the executive and legislature] are selected through contested elections" (Przeworski et al., 2000: 15). Both are multiparty parliamentary systems with free and fair elections. There is a strong sense of constitutionalism and rule of law in each society, which is supported by a myriad of institutions. There are established mechanisms of accountability (e.g., access to information) and both societies can claim professional civil services functioning on the basis of constitutional values such as impartiality, dedicated service delivery, and fiscal accountability. Both systems provide for extensive mechanisms for citizen participation in government. And, finally, both societies share integrated and highly developed infrastructural systems. Thus, democratic structures with legitimate electoral systems and high state capacity are similarly defining features of the states in Kerala and South Africa.

The nature of the electoral system can vary along the dimension of high and low contestation. In a parliamentary democracy the degree to which the system is considered democratic depends, in part, on the existence of electoral contestation, which lies on a continuum from high to very low competition (Przeworski et al., 2000: 16–17). Contestation exists when an opposition has at least a chance of winning the election. Thus, the existence of at least two or more parties competing against each other is a sine qua non of contestation. The electoral field has high contestation if the outcome of every election is uncertain (i.e., there is a high probability of the incumbent losing the election). An electoral field with low contestation is one in which the outcome of elections is certain (i.e., high improbability of the incumbent being voted out of office). Thus, electoral competition among political parties is a defining feature of representative democracy. Parties are, however, organizational entities that represent different ideological and political beliefs often linked to particular classes.

How economic actors translate their interests into political action and state policy is hotly contested. A vulgar Marxist view holds the idea that states are simply instruments of capital. Yet, as history as shown, this view is too simplistic. A unitary class rarely enjoys direct influence over monolithic states. This is for a variety of reasons: classes consist of fractions with varying demands and interests rather than one class with uniform interests (e.g., Poulantzas); similarly, states are not monolithic, but are complex and heterogeneous institutions (e.g., Miliband; Evans); and finally class interests often take political form through the vehicle of political parties (e.g., Przeworski). It is this last point, the relation between classes and parties, that is most relevant for our discussion. Classes ally with political parties, which in turn pursue class interests through various state institutions.

Indeed, political parties act as one of the primary vehicles through which economic actors influence and engage state power. The basis of party-class relationships, however, is not uniform as different classes hold different forms of power. Given the numerically small number of the economic elite, it is not through the ballot box that the capitalist class finds its source of influence over political parties. Rather capital's leverage vis-à-vis political parties stems from its location in the economy—providing financial contributions either directly to the party or indirectly through supporting programs, think-tanks, and studies, or by threatening to withhold investment or exit the economy—and its ability to shape the ideological realm through influencing the media, education, economic studies, and linkages with international capital and institutions such as the World Bank.

Subaltern classes, by contrast, find their political leverage primarily through their numerical majority, which gives them power in both the electoral arena and civil society. The degree of contestation in the electoral field, thus, affects a party's relation to the base of support. A highly competitive field provides subaltern classes more leverage as the threat of withdrawing support carries more weight since the possibility of losing the election is omnipresent and thus can make parties more likely to incorporate demands emanating from civil society as a means of shoring up support. In a field with low contestation the necessity of shoring up support in civil society is significantly diminished as withdrawing electoral support does not affect the outcome of the election. Thus, since one primary point of leverage for subaltern classes is their numerical majority, in an electoral field with low contestation subaltern classes have less power vis-à-vis the political system.[1] Conversely, capital's power is often enhanced through low contestation and diminished in electoral fields with high contestation.[2]

In addition, the political configuration of interparty relations within a competitive representative electoral system affects the terrain on which parties act. Political parties are always in dynamic relation with other political organizations, economic elite, trade unions, and social movements in civil society. Beyond these informal relations, political parties often enter formal arrangements with other organizations such as coalitions and alliances. A coalition is an agreement between independent parties who join forces to secure as many votes and ensure a particular electoral outcome. Very often a coalition is based on a very broad agreement of principles, but not common ideological or programmatic perspectives. Thus, parties with very different political programs can still jointly contest elections. While one party might be the dominant party, smaller parties tend to have a substantial amount of power due to the fact that their participation is necessary for an electoral victory for the dominant party. Coalition members normally agree to allocate electoral regions in order to not compete against each other. An alliance, by contrast, is a more encompassing relationship that assumes a broad strategic and ideological commonality, and thus, transcends the electoral process. Because the degree of interdependence in an alliance is much deeper than in a coalition, the distribution of power among alliance members and the internal political culture of an alliance affects the functioning of each organization. In general, there is less space for autonomous action (at least for the nondominant members) and members are more beholden to their partners in an alliance than a coalition.

While the SACP and CPI(M) compete in electoral systems for access to legitimate and capable states, the degree of contestation as well as the class character of the two political landscapes contrast markedly with varying effects on the SACP and CPI(M). It is commonly accepted that political environments affect the external conditions for action (they both limit and create opportunities for social actors) (Ray, 1999; Fligstein, 2001). Less commonly acknowledged, however, is the effect political environments have on the internal workings of political parties. How do the electoral fields and class contexts affect the CPI(M) and SACP? More specifically, how do the economic and political environments together with the nature of party-class alliances affect the internal struggles among competing factions within parties?

Kerala's Economy and Electoral Field

While labor is highly organized and has a history of militancy organized by the Communist Party in Kerala, capitalist development is relatively underdeveloped and a strong and cohesive business class has yet to emerge. The poorly developed industrial base and capital's penchant to avoid the state led to sluggish economic growth in the industrial sector.[3] Kerala's agricultural sector has not produced a tenacious capitalist class asserting its interests in the political arena. The peculiar nature of agrarian development in favor of small-scale holdings and agricultural laborers has similarly skewed the power dynamic in favor of subaltern classes on the land. In other words, the capitalist class, in both the industrial or agricultural sectors, has been too weak to assert its interests as hegemonic and has been unable to direct state policy.

Kerala is predominantly an agrarian society with over 50 percent of the population depending on agriculture and, in 1998–1999, approximately 58.10 percent of total land under cultivation (16.90 percent of which is sown more than once) and 27.80 percent forested land. While Kerala's agricultural sector is undoubtedly capitalist, it is not one of large- or even medium-sized capitalist farms. Rather small-scale farming predominates Kerala's agricultural sector with the rural areas peppered with marginal and small holdings. For example, in 1991 92 percent of the 5.4 million operational holdings were less than one hectare in size (Heller, 1999: 118; GOK, 1993). For many, the size shrunk as the average agricultural holding dropped from 0.36 hectares in 1985–1986 to 0.27 in 1995–1996 (GOK, 2004: 1). For many farmers, agricultural production has become a secondary occupation as many have been forced to pursue alternative forms of employment (e.g., teachers, shopkeepers, civil servants, agricultural laborers). In the 1991 census, only 12.4 percent of full-time workers reported agriculture as their chief source of work, well below the 38.7 percent national average (Heller, 1999: 118).

While farming as a primary occupation decreased dramatically, agricultural labor remained high with 27 percent of the workforce engaged in agricultural work (the third highest percentage in India). This means that Kerala's agrarian landscape is skewed heavily in favor of part-time or seasonal agricultural laborers with a marginal number of full-time farmers. The agricultural sector managed to generate higher income per hectare of land than the national average. For example,

agricultural income per hectare of land was Rs. 1,993 (crore)[4] in 1972–1973 and grew to Rs. 17,865 (crore) in 1992–1993, which is considerably higher than the national average of Rs. 1,034 (crore) in 1972–1973 and Rs. 9,001 (crore) in 1992–1993 (GOK, 2004: 3). The high wages, however, came under threat in the 1990s with the national government's liberalization polices resulting in increasing difficulties in the agrarian sector and growing pressure for nonagricultural uses of the land (GOK, 2004: 5, table 4.4). Thus, agricultural production is best characterized as a system of small-scale producers with an increasing proportion of part-time farmers. Clearly, with such a small number of farmers relying primarily on cultivation, it is hardly surprising that while Kerala's agrarian system is capitalist, it has not produced an agrarian capitalist class with enough economic or political clout to assert its interests in the political arena.

While Kerala only accounts for a small percentage of the national economy, it is well integrated into the world economy with many of its products (e.g., rubber and coconut) produced for export markets. The shift to cash crops in the 1970s transformed Kerala's economy toward external markets. In the 1970s farmers increasingly shifted away from the high-volume low-value crops such as tapioca and rice to low-volume high-value crops such as pepper and coconut. For example, the total area under paddy production dropped by 60 percent by 1998–1999 and tapioca dropped by 65 percent during the same period. As food-crop production decreased, the total area under cash-crop production rose: coconut, pepper, and rubber increased by approximately 27 percent, 68 percent, and 127 percent between 1995–1996 and 1998–1999, respectively (GOK, 2004). By the 1990s a number of Kerala's cash crops such as tea, cashew nuts, coir products, marine products, coffee, and curry powder constituted a significant percentage of national consumption and the state had become the largest producer in the country of natural rubber, coconut, pepper, and cardamom and the second largest producer of tapioca, cashew nuts, and coffee (GOK, 2004a). For example, the production of pepper shot up—giving the state a near-monopoly in pepper production with 97 percent of the country's pepper production—as did rubber and cardamom; Kerala produces 85 percent of rubber in the country and 70 percent of the country's share in cardamom (GOK, 2003: 3–4). While the shift to cash crops had negative implications for food security in the state, it promised solid economic growth for agricultural sectors. Indeed, the agricultural sector showed positive signs of growth during the late 1980s and early 1990s (with a steady annual growth rate of 3.6 percent in agriculture, well above its 2.5 percent target, and an overall annual growth rate of 5.6 percent (GOK, 2003: 3, 5). However, the shift ultimately made the economy acutely vulnerable to international fluctuations in commodity prices and the increased competition resulting from the neoliberal macroeconomic reforms implemented by the central government.

Faced with an unprecedented balance of payments crisis in 1991 the Indian government launched a package of economic policy reforms in order to stabilize the macroeconomy and restore economic growth. The government sought to stabilize the economy (balance aggregate demand and supply) by decreasing budget deficits. It looked to restructuring the economy in order to make industry internationally competitive through industrial and foreign trade policies, allowing free flow of foreign capital, opening the service sector to foreign capital, devaluing the currency (the

Rupee), and allowing a phased convertibility of the Rupee. The economic rationale behind these reforms was to strengthen market forces and allow the market to function freely (Prakash, 1999b: 27). Kerala's economy was heavily affected as a major cash-crop producing state reliant on export earnings. By the late 1990s the central government's liberalization policies and the steep fall in prices of many agricultural commodities had wreaked havoc on sectors of Kerala's economy. With pressures increasing on the land, the percentage of agricultural income as a contribution to state income diminished over the course of the 1990s from 26.23 percent in 1993–1994 to 21.38 percent in 2000–2001 (GOK, 2003: 5). Many people were forced to move to urban areas in search of more sustainable livelihoods. The urban areas, however, struggled to absorb the influx of new jobseekers and as a result, while rural poverty decreased, urban poverty registered an increase in the 1990s.[5]

The industrial sector was, however, showing hopeful signs. After three decades of slow growth, in the early 1990s the state's efforts to attract investment in the industrial sector seemed to pay off.[6] Industrial development had a brief recovery before it slipped into a deep recession in 1996–1997, but recovered again by century's end when industrial sector growth jumped to 7.18 percent. The majority of industries continue to be located in the small-scale industrial sector (including the informal sector), which grew by 397 percent between 1987–1988 and 2000–2001, which is over double the 145 percent growth registered at the national level (Muraleedharan, 2005: 185). The tertiary sector (especially banking services, transportation and communications, and tourism) registered the most growth in the late 1990s and first years of the new millennium, over doubling the secondary industries' contribution to the Net State Domestic Product (Subrahmanian, 2005: 38–41). While the growth in the tertiary sector has accounted for 44.69 percent of Kerala's Net State Domestic Product in 2001, a great deal of this growth is linked to remittances from overseas Keralites.[7] In the late 1990s remittances accounted for 22 percent of the State Domestic Product (compared to 11 percent in the early 1980s) and significantly increased the per capita income (Harilal, 2005: 101–2). However, the increase in disposable income has not led to a growth in producer services for commodity production, but rather has led to an increase in consumption services (Subrahamanian, 2005: 39).

Nevertheless, while industry has shown hopeful signs of improvement it continues to be a relatively small sector of the economy. For example, there are only 18,602 registered working factories and 12,334 small-scale enterprises (employing 180,000 workers) and only 511 medium and large industrial enterprises in the state (GOK, 2003: 2, 8). Another indicator of the industrial sector's small contribution to the economy is its contribution to the national industrial output. Kerala factories only contribute 2.5 percent to the national industrial output from factories though its population accounts for 3.86 percent of total population (Thampi, 1999: 247).

One of the state's areas of strength is in traditional industries such as coir, cashew, handlooms, handicrafts, and bamboo, which constitute one of the major sectors in the economy and employ over 1 million people. The traditional industries are, however, increasingly under threat from international competition as they suffer from high production costs, low quality, lack diversified products, and have failed to professionally market for export. In addition, mechanization, large-scale

production, and global competition in quality and price threaten to destroy the survival of the industry (GOK, 2004a: 5). Thus, in comparison to agriculture, Kerala's industrial and traditional sectors do not constitute a major contribution to the state's economy and, therefore, only marginally mitigate the negative developments in the agricultural sectors.

The particular character of Kerala's economy has produced a configuration of class forces that strongly favor subaltern classes. Neither the industrial nor agricultural sectors have produced strong and coherent capitalist classes able to assert their interests in the political arena. Rather the working classes and small-scale producers have been successfully organized and are able to assert their interests in the political domain. For example, working-class interests have been successfully championed through state policy both through labor market interventions as well as through the advancements of social welfare entitlements pursued by the state (e.g., minimum wage standards, pensions, and social security).[8]

In addition to the problems in the economy, and partly reflecting the ability of subaltern classes to assert their interests, the state government faced a financial crisis due to the combination of low economic growth and high state spending with the majority of the state's plan money locked into fixed costs in health and education sectors and public employee wages. Kerala has a high number of (total of 110) large-scale public sector industries, making the state an important economic actor. Thus, the redistributive capacities of the state were increasingly difficult to sustain and the quality of public services consistently deteriorating. Popular discontent with the poor quality in public services (e.g., those who could afford it were choosing private health care and private schools over public services) made defending such services a political liability and disingenuous for a political party committed to improving the conditions of subaltern classes. A new approach to public services and a new mode of governance was desperately needed to address issues of quality and not just quantity.

Clearly, political parties in Kerala faced significant and daunting challenges in both the economic and political domains. The particular way in which agricultural capitalism developed did not produce a strong capitalist class on the land, while low industrial development prevented a fledgling industrial capitalist class from wielding a great deal of power in either the economic or political arenas. Kerala's unique feature, however, is not simply the absence of a strong capitalist class able to assert its interests. Rather the presence of strong and well-organized subaltern classes able to assert their interests in the political domain is a defining feature of Kerala. One of the ways subaltern interests registered in the political arena was through the CPI(M)'s regular access to state power.

Electoral competition is especially fierce in Kerala with the CPI(M) and Congress dominating the scene, but neither party commanding an absolute majority. The CPI(M) has enjoyed a slight margin of votes for a number of years, but has not been able to significantly increase its electoral support in relation to Congress (CPI(M), 2001). Nevertheless, the CPI(M) is in a constant struggle to broaden its mass-based appeal and thus consistently looks to new ways in which it speaks to new sectors of subaltern and middle classes.[9] The high voter turnout places additional pressure on the party to try to directly speak to the demands of the citizenry. While people

generally look favorably on elected officials and government,[10] political parties are expected to act on behalf of the interests of the people. The high expectation of its populace together with the absence of a strong and organized capitalist class has strengthened the CPI(M)'s linkages with subaltern classes. In the 1990s the party extended its reach to include the unemployed and poor, and shifted to counter-hegemonic generative politics.

In the face of economic stagnation, the impetus to look to other segments of subaltern classes and the middle class partly stemmed from its inability to increase its electoral fortunes over the previous 20 years. The grassroots faction's alternative practices were presented as one possible way to expand the support base, which the trade union faction had failed to do.[11] Since the 1960s neither the CPI(M) nor the Congress Party has been able to enter government without forming a coalition (Nossiter, 1988: 84). Partly due to splits in the political parties in the 1960s, the electoral field is highly fractured with 26 parties contesting elections. Many of these smaller parties vie for the same subaltern base as the Communist Party. Moreover, the Communist Party's success in organizing mass and class organizations has translated into rival parties copying the Communist Party by starting their own mass and class organizations. In addition, Christian and Muslim communities each constitute approximately 20 percent of the population making them numerically significant minorities. The large number of parties has further encouraged a coalition dynamic, which has often led to volatile political arrangements. It has, however, afforded minority parties significant leverage in the political system. Indeed, many governments have internally disintegrated with the withdrawal of a minor coalition partner.

Without being able to win a clear majority, both the CPI(M) and the Congress have been forced to form coalitions with smaller parties. After a period in the 1970s of mercenary-like coalition arrangements, since the 1980s the CPI(M)-led coalition has only included progressive parties and is referred to as the Left Democratic Front (LDF).[12] The Congress Party has also formed a coalition, the United Democratic Front (UDF). With the narrow margin of votes, the opposition still has a strong presence in government with a large contingent of elected representatives in the Legislative Assembly. For example, in 2001 the CPI(M)-led LDF lost the election, but still won 40 Legislative Assembly seats (the UDF won 99 seats). Since 1980, control of state government has fluctuated between the CPI(M)-led coalition and the Congress-led coalition with every other election won by the other coalition.[13] Clearly, electoral contestation is extremely high in Kerala.

For the CPI(M), one important implication of the highly contested electoral field is the need to develop synergies with civil society. Kerala is relatively unique in the particular character of its class-based social mobilization that has epitomized post-Independence political life. Organizing along class lines has nurtured synergies between the Communist Party and civil society. Thus, the regular exclusion from state power and the contested electoral environment has led the CPI(M) to strengthen its mobilizational and organizational capacities and consolidate its moorings in civil society. With over half of the population in either mass or class organizations (e.g., trade unions, peasant associations, employee's organizations, student, youth, and women's organizations) active participation in civil society is one of the means through which the party attempts to secure electoral support.

The Effects on Factions within the CPI(M)

The particular character of Kerala's economy and the highly contested electoral arena have colored the political domain in fundamental ways. But less recognized are their effects on competition among factions within the party. Electoral stagnation between two political fronts and low economic growth came to a head in the late 1980s registering within the CPI(M) by opening a window of opportunity for the grassroots faction. In the absence of a cohesive capitalist class asserting its interests and the presence of politicized subaltern classes, the grassroots faction within the party sought to widen its links to the unemployed and poor by tapping this reservoir of potential support by initiating counter-hegemonic generative politics in which the role of civil society increasingly intersects with institutions of governing and production. In its efforts to expand its allies and gain wider electoral support, the politics of the grassroots faction was gaining currency as it directly called on the active support of the middle class (e.g., teachers in the literacy efforts) to assist in its developmental efforts aimed at the unemployed and poor, and especially women.

The party's constant search for greater electoral support in a highly contested political arena has translated into competition within the party among competing factions vying to control the trajectory of the party. Thus, innovations and changes in party practices result from shifts in the balance of power among competing factions, which result from the constant need for the party to remain apace with the aspirations of the populace and to translate this into electoral support. In other words, the strength of subaltern classes and the competitive electoral arena led to a window of opportunity for the grassroots faction.

The competitive electoral field thus reinforced the efficacy of subaltern classes in the political domain as it led the party to constantly shore up electoral support. In this effort, the competing factions are constantly trying to expand the range of people under the party's fold, which in turn lends credibility to different political projects. During the 1970s the trade union faction firmly established its dominance within the party and emphasized a politics of advancing working-class interests. In the late 1980s Kerala's economy was at a crossroads, placing tremendous pressure on political parties to think of viable alternatives that would steer the state out of its economic troubles. At the helm of the 1987–1991 LDF government, the trade union faction was unable to steer the party in new directions that addressed the economic crisis as it continued to rely primarily on its traditional working-class base. After the CPI(M) lost the 1991 election to the UDF, the grassroots faction turned the trade union faction's electoral defeat into an opportunity to shift the balance of power enough to allow it to push its new vision that spoke to a broader section of subaltern classes and sectors of the middle class. It offered the party a novel approach to development and, given the constant need for innovation in order to widen its electoral base, a new form of politics that would appeal to a wide range of constituents in civil society. The grassroots faction garnered support in civil society for its alternative vision and used this to challenge the trade union faction's hold on power. Thus, the competitive electoral field translated into an opportunity for the grassroots faction, while the party-subaltern class alliance provided the conditions to develop counter-hegemonic generative politics.

Both the highly competitive electoral field and the party's relation to subaltern classes provided an opportunity for the grassroots faction within the party. The absence of a strong capitalist class has allowed the party to moor itself in subaltern classes and seek development alternatives that contest the logic of capitalism by expanding the role of civil society into the institutions of state and economy. Thus, the particular class context of Kerala created conditions that together with the competitive electoral field helped shift the balance of power within the party in favor of the grassroots faction in the early 1990s.

South Africa's Economy and Electoral Field

Broadly speaking, the SACP operates within a multiparty parliamentary democratic system that requires on the one hand strategic and tactical alliances, which entail compromise and negotiation, and on the other hand, the need to generate a popular base of support.[14] Unlike the electoral field in Kerala, electoral competition has not been fierce in South Africa with the ANC garnering well over 60 percent of the national vote since its first election in 1994.[15] Thus, while the new South Africa inaugurated a competitive electoral system, it has not developed a system in which there are a number of relatively equal parties vying for power in a contested environment. Rather, electoral contestation is low with the ANC only challenged in local elections in a few metropolitan regions, but not seriously threatened. Thus, at the national level and in a number of provinces the ANC with the support of the SACP and COSATU enjoys majority seats in government institutions as well as hegemony in civil society. For most of the 1990s the statist faction enjoyed unrivaled dominance within the SACP, but in 1998 the trade union faction made its claim on power within the party. In what way does the broader political and economic environment help account for the rise of the trade union faction's control within the party?

In the 1960s South Africa experienced an economic boom that secured it a privileged place as a "newly industrialized country" in the world order. During this period the economy transformed from an agrarian and primarily extractive economy into a modern industrialized one. In the early 1970s, however, an economic crisis, triggered by the international oil crisis, threatened to undermine the alliance among the state, local capital, and international capital. While South Africa was able to eke its way out of severe crisis, the economy continued to struggle into the 1990s. Thus, while South Africa made an impressive entry into the industrialized world order, its industrial development ultimately stalled in the "semi-industrialized" phase, which is marked by "low productivity, limited skills base, aging plants and, hence, large surplus capacity, [and] a preponderant dependency on capital goods imports" (Marais, 2001: 105). For example, the capital goods sector had performed relatively well during the 1960s, but had slowed dramatically by the early 1970s (Kaplan, 1991: 176), and by the late 1980s there was a firm reliance on imported capital goods, making the economy especially vulnerable to balance of payments difficulties (World Bank, 2004a).

By the early 1990s the balance of payments difficulties seemed a constant feature of the economy. While the country had managed to keep its external debt to GDP ratio low (in 1990 it was 27.3 percent and by 1994 it had dropped to 22.9 percent,

well below that of similar middle-income countries), which allowed some latitude for developing economic alternatives, the increasing reliance on imports (especially new machinery and technology) prevented it from tackling its balance of payments problems. Many economic analysts erroneously assumed that the disinvestment of the 1980s was purely political and, hence, the country could expect massive increases in foreign capital inflows with the dismantling of the apartheid government. While there was an increase in inflows of capital in the mid-1990s,[16] it was primarily in terms of equity capital and bonds issues which represented volatile, short-term investments that could easily be sold off (Gelb, 2005: 377–78; UNDP, 2004). Foreign direct investment, by contrast, was disappointing between 1995 and 2002 and represented only 3.3 percent of gross market-based capital flows to developing countries comparing unfavorably to South Africa's high rate of 22 percent net portfolio equity flows to developing countries (Gelb, 2005: 387).

Thus, after two decades of increasing difficulties, by the time the SACP and ANC entered the transition period the economy was in the doldrums: economic growth trickled into the negative range, investment dropped, capital fled the country, unemployment soared, and the economy suffered from chronic balance of payments problems. The crisis in the economy reflected the country's accumulation strategy that relied heavily on primary product exports and inward industrialization based on stringent labor supply. Growth of domestic demand was limited and productivity inhibited, and there were acute shortages of skilled labor. Thus, the particular range of problems reflected the particular nature of the South African economy.

The South African economy has been predominantly industrial with mining and manufacturing comprising the two dominant sectors of the economy. Owing to its place in the world order and the fact that it is rich in natural resources, the economy has developed a heavy dependence on commodity exports, especially raw materials such as minerals, which are especially vulnerable to exchange rate fluctuations and changing commodity prices. South Africa failed to shift from primary products to manufactured goods (in 1988 raw materials made up 88 percent of exports), which perpetuated its acute vulnerability to external forces. By 1993, 63.7 percent of exports were primary or primary processed products (Marais, 2001: 101, 107, 119). There was also a shift from labor-intensive sectors to capital-intensive sectors, diminishing the labor-absorbing capacity of industry. Between 1990 and 2002 there was a significant shift from minerals (which are labor intensive) to basic processed goods and to capital-intensive machinery and equipment (especially vehicle components) (Gelb, 2005: 396).

While the 1960s growth and development in the manufacturing sector launched South Africa on a course of rapid industrialization and economic growth that was impressive by any measure, manufacturing's growth was ephemeral as the last quarter of the twentieth century saw the structure of the economy shift increasingly toward services, which grew from 51.1 percent of GDP in 1983 to 60.3 percent in 1993 and still further to 63.7 percent by 2002 (World Bank, 2004a). While services experienced tremendous growth, industry (mining and manufacturing) dropped from 44.5 percent of GDP in 1983 to 35.5 percent in 1993 and by 2002 only accounted for 32.2 percent of GDP.[17] Thus, while the labor-intensive sectors of mining and

manufacturing shares in output declined, transport and communications and financial services grew particularly strong (Gelb, 2005: 396). While these shifts were taking place in the industrial and service sectors, agriculture remained relatively stable only registering a slight decline from 4.4 percent of GDP in 1983 to 4.2 percent in 1993 and 4.1 percent in 2002 (World Bank, 2004a).

The changes in the structure of the economy precipitated changes in the labor-absorbing capacity of the economy, which fell from 97 percent in the 1960s to 22 percent in the 1980s and to a meager 7 percent between 1985 and 1990. More than 400,000 formal sector jobs were lost between 1985 and 1993 (excluding agriculture, which shed 30 percent of the sector's jobs) (SAIRR, 1992:39; Marais, 2001: 103).[18] In the 1990s there was a marked shift to capital-intensive sectors with their share of exports rising from 56.1 percent in 1993 to 60.8 percent in 1997, while labor-intensive sectors—such as food and beverages, textiles and clothing, and footwear—suffered from increasing import penetration, which rose from 55.5 percent to 67.5 percent in the same period (Gelb, 2005: 395–96). The effect of such shifts exacerbated the already low growth in employment levels and skills composition of the labor market. South Africa's job seekers were facing difficult conditions with high unemployment and the economy's inability to create enough new jobs to absorb new entrants into the labor market, which was exacerbated by underinvestment in labor-intensive sectors. For example, during the economic boom of the 1960s, 74 percent of new jobseekers found jobs in the formal sectors, which dropped to 12.5 percent by the late 1980s and slid to 7 percent by the early 1990s (Marais, 2001: 119; Gelb, 1991: 6 and 1994: 3–4). Thus, while the number of people in employment increased from 9.6 million to 11.2 million—an increase of 1.6 million jobs—between 1995 and 2002, the number of unemployed grew by 2.3 million due to the large number of new entrants into the labor market (Roberts, 2005: 488). Compounding the high unemployment was the steady flow of people from the rural areas to urban areas. By 1995 the urban population registered 52.6 percent and grew to 58.4 percent by 2002 (World Bank, 2003a).

The situation was compounded by the fact that there was a shortage of skilled labor and a surplus of unskilled and poorly educated labor. By the 1980s industrial decay had set in with ageing capital stock, limited capital goods production, and failure to develop exports by expanding the scope of the manufacturing sector. Linked to this was the lack of investment in research and development with the overwhelming majority of investment channeled into the armaments and telecommunications industries. Moreover, there was a strong bias against small- and medium-sized businesses with an industrial climate firmly in favor of large corporations. For example, capital has been highly concentrated and centralized with six corporations controlling 71.26 percent of total assets on non-state corporations in 1985 (Davies, 1988: 177; Southall, 2005: 460).

The weaknesses of the apartheid-era accumulation strategy bequeathed the transition a struggling economy. Seeing the end of apartheid on the horizon, in the late 1980s, the NP government and sectors of big business shifted to a neoliberal accumulation strategy that sought to restrict state involvement in the economy—withdrawing the state from providing goods and services and limiting its role to creating broad economic parameters that facilitate market forces. Thus, the new

democratic state inherited limited capacity to shape economic strategy (Gelb, 2005: 368 and 1991: 29–30; Marais, 2001: 105). In addition, in the midst of political uncertainty important sectors of capital were able to consolidate their economic locations. During the negotiations the economy sunk into a recession between 1989 and 1993 in which it registered negative real economic growth. Painting a particularly ominous picture of the situation, the economic elite was united in the potential deleterious effects of a sluggish economy on the future of South Africa. For example, the Reserve Bank governor, Chris Stals, warned that "the country would plunge into ungovernability by 1996 if the annual growth rate remained at around 1 percent while the population grew at 2.5 percent" (quoted in Marais, 2001: 102). The macroeconomic indicators seemed to corroborate the millenarian scenarios. Real fixed investment growth remained negative showing only slight improvement from –7.4 percent in 1991 to –3.1 percent in 1993. Private (nonhousing) investment was 10 percent of GDP, well below the 16 percent required for sustainable positive economic growth. Domestic savings slipped to 16 percent of GDP in mid-1994 well below its 1980s record of 24 percent (which the Reserve Bank deemed necessary for an annual economic growth rate of 3.5 percent). Per capita disposable income fell by –11 percent in real terms between 1980 and 1993 (Marais, 2001: 102). The economy seemed to lurch from poor performance in one sector to another with prospects for a positive change left in the balance. While the economy's future growth was unclear, what was certain was that South Africa's economic development had produced a strong and efficacious capitalist class with moorings in the state as well as a robust and militant—if threatened—working class with close ties to the ANC and SACP.

The economy's poor performance led pundits, supported by different class actors, to advocate diverse solutions. One thing was beyond doubt: something had to be done. What was contested was the question of what was to be done: increased state intervention advocating redistribution as a chief catalyzer to economic growth or minimal state intervention ensuring a propitious environment for market forces. Ultimately the ANC opted for the latter choice, significantly curtailing the post-apartheid political project of national reconstruction from its earlier more expansive vision. It was within this class context of capital's ability to ensure its preference for a neoliberal macroeconomic strategy that the SACP faced the daunting tasks of constructing elements of socialism in the 1990s.

As the dominant partner in the Alliance between the ANC, SACP, and COSATU, the class alliances of the ANC have a tremendous bearing on the SACP's politics and practices. The SACP found itself in a situation fraught with contradictions. On the one hand, the party had achieved significant access via the ANC to state power. The sheer presence of a number of party members in the legislature, the Presidential Cabinet, and all levels of government (national, provincial, and local) corroborated claims that the party had access to power and could help drive the direction of development. In addition, many SACP leaders held positions in ANC leadership structures and the Alliance convenes regular forums, summits, meetings, and workshops that provide the SACP another avenue to access power. On the other hand, the party is under increasing pressure to accommodate its ideological aspirations of socialist democracy with the ANC's vision of a capitalist state. One example of

this is Thabo Mbeki's (then deputy President to Mandela) reprimand at the SACP's 10th Congress in 1998 for its vociferous protestations against the government's 1996 neoliberal macroeconomic policy *Growth, Employment, and Redistribution Strategy* (GEAR) (Satgar, 2002: 163–64).

The new emphasis in economic policy articulated in GEAR betrayed a shift in the ANC, which was affected by both international forces such as the turbulent financial markets and capitalist globalization as well as the South African economy's poor performance. The ideological hegemony of neoliberalism in the international arena lent further credibility to capital's vision of an extended role of the market and minimal role for the state in South Africa. A 1996 COSATU discussion document succinctly summarizes the difficult conditions under which the ANC assumed power:

> The power of the apartheid-era ruling class remains largely entrenched in critical areas: the security forces, the media, the bureaucracy, and above all the commanding heights of the economy [...] The new democratic government, while fully legitimate, popular and apparently in full control, neither has its hand decisively on all tillers of state power (the security forces, bureaucracy, parastatals, reserve bank, judiciary, etc.) nor has it been able to strategically direct the economy of the country based on our own agenda. (COSATU, 1996: 3)

These pressures were compounded by the movement's historical neglect to develop an economic policy, making the ANC especially susceptible to heed counsel from business and mainstream foreign experts. Because neither the ANC nor SACP had devised a coherent economic program before 1990 that could serve as a platform from which to engage the economic elite and shape the contours of the future economic dispensation, the movement was especially vulnerable to capital's efforts to adumbrate the economic discourse. For its part, South African business was well prepared as part of its interests in securing a negotiated transition stemmed from its desire to create the conditions for future economic growth. South African capital was patently aware that economic growth partly depended on peace and stability in the country and, therefore, sought a political settlement that was inclusive and managed by political forces that could garner widespread compliance and at the same time pursue a development path that would bring economic growth.

The ANC's thinking was further influenced by capital's efforts to court and befriend leading cadres within the ANC.[19] For example, leading sectors of capital (assisted by the World Bank) ran a number of studies[20] and scenario-planning exercises in which carefully selected leaders from the liberation movement were invited. The country's economic elite had also begun making inroads into labor. By the 1990s capital had succeeded in truncating the economic debate to such a degree that labor slowly came to accept certain demands of capital. For example, in 1992 COSATU agreed to support an export-oriented modernization strategy "under the guise of their own 'post-Fordist' rubric linking democracy and development," which led big business to "find itself allied with the Democratic Movement on behalf of more rapid political and economic liberalization" (Bond, 2000: 24). COSATU

leaders such as Alec Erwin[21] conceded on a number of issues such as the World Bank's proposals for trade policy and failed to develop radical alternatives to counter capital's proposals (Bond, 2000: 66).

Despite the economic elite's rapprochement with the ANC and its influence over policy, the ANC is not a monolithic organization, but rather has contesting factions vying to push the organization in various directions. It is with the left-leaning faction in the ANC that the SACP finds resonance with its vision of transformation. While capital has successfully gained formidable allies within the ANC, the SACP (and COSATU) continues to have influence as well. For example, in 2002 six cabinet ministers in President Mbeki's cabinet maintained public membership of the SACP and served on its Central Committee (three were not reelected to the Central Committee at the SACP's 11th Congress in 2002[22]), two provinces (Gauteng and the Eastern Cape) were considered "red" with their Premiers and a number of provincial cabinet ministers and members of legislative assemblies publicly maintaining membership to the SACP. In addition, 65 members of parliament were SACP members in 2002. The majority of SACP members in leadership positions in the ANC and government, however, come from the statist faction, which is increasingly losing its base of support among rank-and-file party members.[23] Thus, the ANC has come to represent both capital and subaltern classes, which leads to tensions within the Alliance and within the SACP.

With the majority of South Africa's residents falling in low-income indicator levels, a great deal of the ANC's appeal is its claim to represent the interests of subaltern classes. Part of its success at promoting this image has been its alliance with the SACP and COSATU. The links to subaltern classes trace back to its earlier period of activism and were reinforced in the 1980s when the ANC and SACP successfully regained hegemony over the liberation movement. The apartheid regime facilitated this process by focusing on the ANC as its main negotiating partner. As discussed in previous chapters, the SACP and ANC returned to South African soil more popular than ever and immediately began consolidating this popularity into concrete structures under their control. While the SACP continues to look to the working class and poor for its support base, the quiet ANC rapprochement with leading sectors of capital affects the SACP's politics.

The ANC's dominant electoral position helped to create a particular dynamic for the SACP. As the smaller and more ideologically oriented partner, some suggest that the SACP has more access to political power than it would if it were not in such an alliance. At the same time, the SACP's position in power is mediated by the nature of its alliance with the ANC. The original *modus operandi* of the Alliance saw the three organizations playing complimentary roles and based on mutual respect.[24] Curiously, the SACP seems to have had little misgivings about the nature of the Alliance even though it was giving up its ability to directly contest elections (usually a defining feature for a political party). Even more curious, and reflecting its trust in the ANC, it did not insist on a formal arrangement with the ANC guaranteeing it a certain number of seats in parliament and direct access to state power.[25]

After 40 years of working together in close alliance in the national liberation struggle a particular culture of engagement had emerged between the SACP and ANC. Though there were tensions throughout their history, the two organizations

recognized their mutual complimentarity and developed a culture of cooperation and consultation. The ANC needed the SACP as much as the SACP needed the ANC.[26] Moreover, when the SACP and ANC returned to South Africa the two organizations enjoyed a great deal of continuity in terms of membership (indeed, most SACP members were also ANC members), but also the two organizations shared programmatic and strategic visions with the ultimate goal of a democratic and socialist South Africa.[27] After their return to South Africa, the balance of power between them shifted in favor of the ANC, a fact that did not go unnoticed by the ANC.[28] As the nation-building project was underway, new rules of intra-Alliance engagement were forged. While the ANC was well aware of the shift in the balance of power in its favor, the SACP, perhaps with little choice, continued to work under the old rules of the game. The ANC, on the other hand, was redefining the culture of engagement to suit its interests.

The relation between the party and the ANC went from healthy respect and engagement to a strained relationship carefully managed by both sides. During the first half of the 1990s the Alliance was relatively strong and unified around a common commitment to a clearly defined shared project: the democratic breakthrough and the Reconstruction and Development Program. After the ANC adopted GEAR in 1996 relations began to strain. Historically both organizations had focused on their shared strategic and ideological commitments, but by the mid-1990s the focus had shifted to their differences.[29] By the time the 1998 SACP Program was adopted, tensions with the ANC reached a new low and the two organizations seemed set for a collision path.[30]

Effects on Factions in the SACP

The ANC's ascent to power shifted the balance of power within the Alliance strongly in favor of the ANC, while both the SACP's and COSATU's influence steadily eroded. This shift also coincided with the ANC's rapprochement with capital. The SACP had envisioned an Alliance in which the ANC would support SACP positions.[31] Much to the SACP's chagrin, the opposite is more often the case: the SACP is often cajoled into supporting the ANC-led state in capitalist development. To ensure the SACP's passive consent (or at least to restrict its opposition) to macroeconomic policy, the party has been given influence over particular aspects of development (e.g., labor legislation and local economic development). At the same time, the ANC is seen to be drifting away from subaltern class interests, the natural base for the SACP, and as a result tensions within the Alliance have increasingly manifested and have begun translating into battles among factions within the party. While in the first half of the 1990s the statist faction's grip on power was strengthened through its close relations with the ANC, after the adoption of GEAR, which for many was the most palpable sign of the rapprochement between the ANC and sectors of capital, the trade union faction was able to challenge the statist faction.

The adoption of GEAR marked an important turning point both for Alliance relations and intra-SACP developments. The SACP was thrown into a tailspin, uncertain of how to respond. The terrain of engagement within the Alliance was shifting and required adroit maneuvering to salvage the SACP's preeminent place.

Though a few party members responded immediately with a trenchant critique of GEAR (Zita et al., 1996), it took the SACP well over a year before it was able to mount a coherent response against the macroeconomic policies. In its 1998 Program the party launched a critique of GEAR and argued that it was essentially a neoliberal approach that is at variance with the objectives embodied in the RDP (SACP, 1998: 10).

Thus, the statist faction was originally strengthened through its close relations with the ANC as it advocated state-led development that broadly resonated with progressive ANC policies. As tensions began to emerge between the SACP and ANC after the adoption of GEAR, the statist faction's authority began to erode as discontented rank-and-file members challenged the statist faction's leadership. The trade union faction was strengthened through the ANC's adoption of GEAR as the statist faction was implicated for not challenging the ANC's rightward shift. Thus, the ANC-capital's rapprochement, manifested in the adoption of GEAR, changed the nature of intra-Alliance relations and affected the internal balance of power within the party. The tensions within the Alliance have reverberated into the SACP's own structure, ultimately realigning the balance of power among competing factions.

Thus, the ANC's dominant electoral position combined with its rapprochement with sectors of a strong and well-organized capitalist class to shape the political terrain on which the SACP operates. As tensions within the Alliance increasingly emerged after 1996, battles within the SACP among competing factions helped shift the balance of power in favor of the trade union faction. The battles were primarily between the trade union and statist factions, but the grassroots faction was able to carve out a contested and fragile space at the local level in some provinces.

Conclusion

The nature of politics is directly linked to the balance of power among factions in the two parties. But which faction comes to dominate is linked to the class context—which class actors are able to push their interests to the fore—as well as the nature of the electoral field. In South Africa a strong capitalist class allied with the electorally dominant ANC, ultimately influenced the political choices of the statist faction in the SACP, and also helped bring the trade union faction to the helm in the late 1990s. In other words, a strong and efficacious capitalist class succeeded in making its interests (or at least a particular fraction of the capitalist class's interests) dominant in the post-apartheid transition by nurturing and consolidating firm links to important cadres within the ANC, which was quickly becoming the dominant political organization in the country. Capital's efforts quickly paid off and within a year of its return to South African soil the ANC was shifting its emphasis in which it used its dominant position in the state to extend the role of the market. These shifts resulted in acute tensions within the Alliance and ultimately opened up space for the trade union faction to eclipse the statist faction.

In Kerala, by contrast, the strong subaltern classes allied to the CPI(M) in a highly competitive electoral system ultimately created space for the grassroots faction to

Table 7.1   Electoral fields, class context and political factions

South Africa	*Kerala*
Electoral field • ANC dominant in Alliance with SACP • Low electoral contestation	Electoral field • CPI(M) dominant partner in coalition • High electoral contestation
Class context • Capital strong and able to assert its interests • ANC-Capital links override SACP-subaltern links	Class context • Subaltern classes strong and able to assert interests • CPI(M)-subaltern strong links
Effects on party • ANC electoral dominance strengthens statist faction in first half of 1990s • ANC pro-capital approach opens space for trade union faction	Effects on party • Electoral competition erodes trade union faction's control because not able to increase electoral support • Grassroots faction innovates by reaching broader sector of society

come to the fore within the CPI(M). Moreover, capital (and capitalist development) was relatively weak and unable to make its interests hegemonic or exert significant pressure on the CPI(M) in its efforts to revitalize Kerala's lagging economy and political impasse. While secondary and tertiary industrial development has grown since the 1990s (Subrahmanian, 2005: 37–38), the industrial capitalist class has not cohered into a class asserting its interests through state policy. Instead of strong links to capital the CPI(M) developed strong relations to the working class; by the late 1980s, it was expanding to include subaltern classes as well as progressive sectors of the middle class within a highly contested electoral field. While the SACP had to contend with a strong capitalist class making inroads into ANC thinking within an electoral environment of low contestation, the CPI(M) had strong links to a broad section of vibrant subaltern classes in a highly contested electoral field. The subaltern-CPI(M) alliance allowed the party to use the state to expand the role of civil society and challenge the role of the market (see table 7.1).

Thus, the SACP's and CPI(M)'s political projects—hegemonic versus counter-hegemonic generative politics—are shaped by the class context (i.e., the balance of power among class actors) and the degree of competition in the electoral field. For the CPI(M) subaltern dominance, a weak capitalist class, and a competitive electoral field combined with the party's capacities and history to provide the grassroots faction enough power to challenge the trade union faction's position within the party. The particular conjuncture of the balance of class forces, the electoral field, and the crisis in the economy translated into propitious conditions for the birth of counter-hegemonic generative politics in which the state and economy have been increasingly subordinated to civil society. For the SACP, the ANC's dominance in the Alliance in the context of low electoral competition together with the strength of capital and its ability to assert its interests within the ANC combined with the

party's history and capacities to strengthen the statist faction in the SACP. As friction in the Alliance increasingly manifested with the ANC's rightward turn, spaces opened within the party for the trade union faction to challenge the statist faction's power. The trade union faction, however, has largely sought a hegemonic generative politics punctuated by moments of protest politics that ultimately extend the role of the state over civil society.

CHAPTER 8

Conclusion

In 1994 the Marxist utopian Andre Gorz proclaimed: "As a system, socialism is dead. As a movement and an organized political force, it is on its last legs. All the goals it once proclaimed are out of date. The social forces which bore it along are disappearing. It has lost its prophetic dimension" (vii). In these brief words Andre Gorz eloquently captured the death of socialism. But his words also belie a more fundamental demise. With the Soviet Union's collapse *visions* of alternatives to capitalism seemed to also die. All alternatives were rolled up in the failures of twentieth-century socialism, and as a result discussions of socialism were silenced by the belief that socialist alternatives were a utopian impossibility. In some places, however, out of the rubble a renewed appreciation for democratic socialist alternatives was found. Surprisingly, this renewal has not come from the Global North. Instead, some parties in the Global South have found in these difficult times an opportunity for the rejuvenation of radically democratic socialist visions grounded in local conditions and practices. It is in this context that the novel experiments in South Africa and Kerala take on particular relevance.

Protest and Generative Politics Revisited

It is quite extraordinary that the SACP and CPI(M), located in different places and spaces, responded to the challenges of the late twentieth century by theorizing broadly similar visions of socialist democracy around four common themes. First, both parties expressed a deepened and extended notion of democracy in which ordinary citizens are empowered to play a decisive role in all sectors of society. Second, the parties shifted their views of the state and its role in development. They envisioned a state that plays an affirmative role in responding to the demands of its citizenry in combination with real and meaningful participation. A primary role of the state is to create institutions for popular participation and ensure that the citizenry is well prepared to participate in these new institutional spaces. Third, the parties envisioned a transition in which capitalism and socialism would coexist for an indeterminate period of time. They similarly argued that the conditions

for and transition to socialist democracy would have to be created on and through the terrain of capitalism by developing socialist logics alongside the predominant capitalist logic. Finally, the SACP and CPI(M) envisioned an expanded role for civil society in the economy and argued that markets had to serve the needs of the populace. The parties argued that decommodification of certain services, the promotion of cooperatives, and a degree of state intervention in the economy were the primary tools through which markets could be reorganized to serve societal needs and not simply the profit motive.

The SACP's and CPI(M)'s experiences teach us that different combinations of the four themes result in fundamentally different political projects. In the case of the CPI(M), the party attempted to pursue all four themes resulting in a politics that shifts the vector of power from the state and economy to civil society. For the SACP, the party focused primarily on state-led development initiatives resulting in a politics that subordinates civil society to the state and economy. Thus, despite having developed similar ideological visions, the CPI(M) and SACP pursued two very different political projects.

Broadly speaking, there are two types of politics: protest and generative. Protest politics seeks to transform political and economic relations by primarily focusing on claims against the state through mass-mobilizing practices. Generative politics, by contrast, seeks to transform the state and economy by developing new institutions. Transforming the political and economic arenas can be initiated from above by the state or below by civil society. Thus, protest politics can be either state led or civil society led, while generative politics is either hegemonic or counter-hegemonic. By state-led protest politics I mean mass-mobilizing events organized by the state to garner support for state projects. They are primarily symbolic events that reassure the state of its support and give citizens the sense that they are part of a nation-building project. Civil society-led protest politics, on the other hand, are organized by groups in civil society and target the state (and often key economic actors) around particular grievances. They too are campaign based, but rather than showing support for the state they demonstrate challenges to the state. Generative politics is also state led or civil society led. Drawing on Gramsci's classic understanding of hegemony as the production of consent of the majority through the institutions of civil society, hegemonic generative politics seeks to build new institutions that extend the state's control over civil society, while counter-hegemonic generative politics builds new institutions to extend the role of civil society into the political and economic realms.

Ideally in practice, there is a combination of all four. A closer look at how the SACP and CPI(M) transformed their politics in the 1990s shows that both the SACP and CPI(M) pursued protest and generative politics in the 1990s, giving a great deal of attention to building new institutions and channels for mass participation. The nature of their protest and generative politics, however, differed. Before 1990 the SACP focused on civil society-led protest politics without attention to generative politics. With the end of apartheid, the SACP shifted to hegemonic generative politics in support of the nation-building project. At the same time, it also shifted to state-led protest politics. The CPI(M), on the other hand, shifted from hegemonic to counter-hegemonic generative politics, but maintained civil society-led protest politics (see table 8.1).

Table 8.1 Political orientation of the SACP and CPI(M)

	Initiative from above (state)	Initiative from below (civil society)
Protest politics	State-led protest SACP 1990s	Civil society-led protest SACP pre-1990s CPI(M) pre-1990s, CPI(M) 1990s
Generative politics	Hegemonic SACP 1990s CPI(M) pre-1990s	Counter-hegemonic CPI(M) 1990s

The CPI(M)'s experience suggests that noisy and demanding civil society-led protest politics married to a hegemonic generative politics can help keep the state's objectives in line with mass-based interests and lay the basis for a counter-hegemonic generative politics to emerge. The SACP, on the other hand, demonstrates that when state-led protest politics complement hegemonic generative politics civil society is demobilized, allowing the state to not only define civil society's interests, but also giving the state little incentive to incorporate demands that it has not determined. Thus, the existence of and relation between protest and generative politics has far-reaching implications for the nature of the state and its willingness to incorporate subaltern demands.

The Eclipse of Political Parties?

There has been a great deal of recent scholarship celebrating the arrival of a new politics based on global social movements (e.g., de Sousa Santos, 2007; Holloway, 2002). The old political party model of the twentieth century has been discredited for its failures to achieve robust, democratic socialist alternatives. Indeed, the twentieth-century political party model is replete with tales of failed experiments resulting in authoritarianism and low economic growth. Dismissing political parties as anachronistic forms of organizing, however, represents a failure to understand the continued importance of political parties in shaping the contours of political and economic development. Political parties are fundamental to achieving patterns of democratic, egalitarian development for two primary reasons. One has to do with the state and the other with civil society.

The importance of political parties is directly related to the continued relevance of the state. As many scholars have shown, efficacious developmental states are crucial actors in developing countries in achieving economic and social development (Evans, 1995; Kohli, 2004; Chang, 2004). States, however, are not simply populated by lone individuals. Political parties are crucial actors in shaping the policies and strategies of developmental states. As crucial actors in state institutions, political parties are, thus, the vehicle through which different groups access state power and thus influence the direction of development. As we saw in this study, a sine qua non condition of generative politics is efficacious political parties with access to sites of state power in order to build new institutions.

In Kerala, the CPI(M) took advantage of its access to state power by initiating a democratic decentralization campaign that devolved financial and decision-making authority to lower tiers of government and extended democratic institutions in civil society. Central to these efforts was the creation of new institutional spaces for ordinary citizens' involvement in both the polity and economy. The CPI(M) used the state to deepen and extend democratic state institutions on behalf of subaltern classes. In South Africa, the SACP's relation to state power is mediated through the ANC, which has pursued a particular vision of development. While the ANC-led state has implemented many progressive policies and legislation to deepen democratic institutions in society, many of these have withered with increasing pressure to show quantitative results in service delivery. Nevertheless, the SACP's experience highlights the importance of political parties as actors in state institutions. Indeed, the ANC has been the vehicle through which capital has been able to assert its interest in the state and influence South Africa's post-apartheid political and economic development.

In addition to political parties' relevance with regard to states, they are also crucial actors in civil society. Civil society is an arena of voluntary associational activity in which ordinary citizens link up with various organizations around a range of interests and identities. There is no primacy given to class in civil society. Yet, class is central to a counter-hegemonic generative politics. How, then, does civil society become organized around the centrality of class? Political parties—especially political parties linked to subaltern classes—are a crucial player in infusing civil society with a class project by organizing the myriad associations around the centrality of subaltern class interests.

The CPI(M) developed extensive linkages to civil society over the course of the twentieth century by mobilizing disparate rural and urban economic groups into highly efficacious agrarian and industrial working classes. Its organizing efforts have infused civil society with the centrality of subaltern class interests. One of the many positive effects of this is the difficulty religious fundamentalist groups have had in penetrating Kerala's civil society. Unlike many places in India that have been torn apart by communal violence, Kerala's religious diversity has not degenerated into communal violence. The centrality of subaltern class interests in civil society has also forced the Congress Party to speak to issues relevant to subaltern classes. Thus, politics in Kerala are far to the Left of politics in the rest of India. Moreover, the deep connection between the party and civil society not only ensures that the CPI(M) remains loyal to the interests of subaltern classes, it also empowered the CPI(M) to use the state to initiate its counter-hegemonic generative project. Party-civil society synergy thus helped push politics in Kerala in radically new directions.

In South Africa, the SACP has not focused on developing its links with civil society, but rather has channeled its energies in the direction of intra-Alliance politics. As a result, the SACP has not consistently advanced the interests of subaltern classes nor has it challenged the diminishing salience of subaltern class interests in civil society, which had developed in the 1980s social movement unionism. In contrast, the SACP's history shows that its strong links to civil society in the 1940s and 1950s helped radicalize the liberation movement and reframe the antiapartheid struggle into a liberation struggle in which economic and political freedom were seen as two

sides of the same coin. The SACP's recent failure to deepen its relations with civil society and organize the panoply of interests around the centrality of subaltern class interests helps account for its relative impotence in pursuing a counter-hegemonic generative politics.

In Kerala, the CPI(M)'s moorings in subaltern classes within an electoral environment of high contestation produced the conditions for counter-hegemonic generative politics. In South Africa, the SACP's reliance on the ANC and the ANC's rapprochement with sectors of capital within an electoral field of low contestation led to hegemonic generative politics that subordinates civil society to the state and economy. The divergent experiences of the CPI(M) and SACP suggest that institutional and vibrant connections between political parties and subaltern classes are essential for a democratic, egalitarian politics. Their experiences also suggest that a new type of political party is needed, one that is capable of developing synergies with civil society.

Beyond Kerala and South Africa

The conceptual framework of hegemonic and counter-hegemonic generative politics and the relation to protest politics is potentially useful in understanding political projects beyond South Africa and Kerala. There are a number of interesting experiments in democratic renewal happening in various places of the world such as Brazil, Venezuela, Mauritius, and Chile to name just a few. This is an exciting area for further research.

To take one very preliminary example, the Brazilian Worker's Party (PT as it is popularly called) won the national elections in 2002 on its strength in civil society and had clearly identified itself with socialist ideals (Baiocchi, 2005; Bruce, 2004). Within a short period of time after taking office, the PT was criticized for abandoning its redistributive agenda and participatory democratic commitments. Instead of a counter-hegemonic generative politics that many expected from the PT after its success at civil society-led transformation in Porto Alegre, the PT has pursued a hegemonic generative politics of state-led development.

The PT had successfully launched a counter-hegemonic politics in the city of Porto Alegre through a participatory budgeting process. By democratizing the allocation of part of the city's budget, civil society was transformed into a robust arena of citizen participation. For example, neighborhood associations increased from 240 in 1986 to 600 in 2000 and district-level popular councils increased from 2 to 12 in the same period, while housing cooperatives jumped from 11 to 71 between 1994 and 2000 (Baiocchi, 2005: 42). Thus, the participatory budgeting process not only gave civil society voice to determine the investment of some of the city's funds, but also engendered a vibrant civil society (Goldfrank, 2003). The PT had shifted to counter-hegemonic generative politics.

Despite the PT's highly successful participatory budgeting process, in 2004 it lost the Porto Alegre elections. One could argue its success in empowering civil society partly accounts for its electoral failure. Participatory budgeting may have been initiated by the PT, but as the opposition party made clear, it ultimately belongs to civil society and its citizens (Baiocchi, 2005: 151). Indeed, the electoral defeat

for the PT did not mean a defeat of counter-hegemonic generative politics as the city's politics had shifted to the Left. The PT in Porto Alegre, like the CPI(M), lost elections after having initiated a popular and highly successful counter-hegemonic generative politics. Yet the political projects they initiated continued. What this suggests is that empowering civil society transforms state-civil society relations. It makes the state and political parties more accountable to the interests and demands of citizens, but does not necessarily translate into electoral support for a political party. Indeed, it suggests that the dynamic of counter-hegemonic generative politics shifts the terrain of politics to civil society.

Another interesting point from the PT's experience is the different types of politics pursued at different levels of government. While the PT's participatory budgeting was highly successful in Porto Alegre, it found it more difficult to maintain the quality of democracy in the state-level participatory budgeting process in Rio Grande do Sul (Goldfrank and Schneider, 2003). Similarly, the PT's national campaign was partially won due to the party's popularity from participatory budgeting experiments in local governments across the country. Many expected that a PT national government would expand counter-hegemonic generative politics across the country. However, once in office the PT has pursued hegemonic generative politics much to the disappointment of social movements and civil society organizations. Does this suggest something about the conditions under which counter-hegemonic generative politics flourish? Is participatory democracy more viable at the local level than at the state or national level? Does this suggest that building democratic socialist alternatives can only be built from the ground up? These are exciting areas for further research.

Drawing on Kerala's experiences, it is clear that a counter-hegemonic generative political project is indeed possible. For such an alternative project to take root, however, a synergistic relation between political parties and civil society must be forged in order to ensure that the necessary institutional spaces are created and the capacity for civil society participation is developed. Moreover, it takes a new type of political party, one that is not afraid to empower civil society. A traditional party controlling civil society from above would not have created the vibrant institutions that allowed for civil society to engage political and economic arenas in Kerala. It would not have created the conditions for counter-hegemonic generative politics and hence new forms of participatory democracy.

Methodological Appendix

This study is based on materials collected over two and a half years of fieldwork. I spent three months in 2000 and all of 2002 and one month in 2005 in Kerala doing fieldwork. In South Africa I spent 2001 and three months in 2003 conducting fieldwork. In both places it took a significant period of time to gain access to the parties, but I ultimately gained entry to key party structures and events in both places. My access to both parties came through what often seemed like an interminable process of making contacts with people and allowing enough time to pass to establish a degree of familiarity (and, I later learned, to prove my commitment and trustworthiness). In South Africa it took about six months to get access and in Kerala it took about five months. While South Africa took slightly longer, once I finally gained the trust of people the floodgates opened and I was able to attend the whole gamut of events from branch meetings to the National Congress. In Kerala my access was facilitated by the fact that I had already done my fieldwork in South Africa and had managed to win the trust of the SACP—if another communist party trusted me then I must not be that bad.

Once I gained access, a major portion of my research consisted of participant observation of the parties and the communities in which they are active. Because conditions are so politicized in Kerala, I never pushed for access to internal party meetings as I feared pushing too hard would have ruined what little credibility I had managed to accrue over the many months of attending events, visiting party offices, going to the party's public meetings, interviewing leaders and rank-and-file members, and chatting informally with members and supporters.[1] Because the thrust of the CPI(M)'s activities focused on the decentralization campaign, I focused my research on communities in which the CPI(M) was actively participating in the Campaign. I attended meetings with activists, neighborhood and women's groups, and local government officials and elected representatives. For example, I met with 47 micro-production units and participated in 2 mass events organized by women's groups. I also attended 42 neighborhood group meetings, 7 mass-mobilizing events, 2 village assemblies, and numerous community meetings. I also attended four CPI(M) conferences: one on decentralization in 2000, two conferences in 2002 (one on decentralization and the other on the CPI(M)'s assessment of how it fared in its efforts to implement decentralization), and one conference in 2005 on lessons from the decentralization process.

In South Africa I went to a range of party activities (e.g., the 2002 National Congress, 2 provincial Congresses, 21 branch meetings, 8 district and provincial-level councils, numerous provincial and district meetings, 11 political education schools, 2 conferences, 7 workshops, 15 marches and demonstrations, and numerous public meetings) as well as nonparty activities (e.g., 4 ward meetings, 14 community meetings, and numerous workshops and visits to communities). While I spent time in communities, the locus of party activity was

more concentrated within the party structures, which led me to spend a great deal of time attending party events (e.g., meetings, councils, and seminars). At every event I attended in both places I took the opportunity to informally speak to rank-and-file members and ordinary citizens about their views of the parties and their politics. Many of these events were as much cultural experiences as academic field sites—SACP meetings are vibrant, boisterous events punctuated by liberation-era songs of solidarity and struggle whereas CPI(M) meetings are somber, efficient events that rarely diverge from the task under discussion. However, in both cases meetings often seemed to drag on endlessly debating issues from every possible angle before coming to consensus (or at least closure). On more than one occasion, scheduled two-hour meetings turned into eight-hour uninterrupted events—I quickly learned to carry food and water with me to everything I attended.

When not attending party events, I also spent a great deal of time in townships (South Africa) and rural communities (Kerala) in order to get a feel for the ways in which the SACP and CPI(M) are viewed by ordinary people. In South Africa, I focused my research in the provinces of Gauteng and KwaZulu Natal where I visited development projects, local economic ventures (e.g., cooperatives) and community centers, attended community events and meetings (including ward meetings), participated in demonstrations and marches, and simply chatted with people. I chose these two provinces because these are two of the strongest provinces of the party. In Kerala I did fieldwork across the state (from the north in Kannur and Kozhikode, to the central part of the state in Palghat and Thrissur (Trichur), Alappuzha (Alleppey) and Kottayam, to the south in the environs of Thiruvananthapuram), which consisted of regular visits to community centers and village libraries (where people often congregate), meetings with neighborhood and women's groups, visits to micro-production units, community meetings (I attended two out of four village assemblies), local cultural events (e.g., street theater, local plays), and marches and demonstrations. In addition to spending time in communities, in Kerala my primary modes of transportation were buses and rickshaws and I took to the habit of asking rickshaw drivers their views on the CPI(M) and the decentralization campaign. While I spent more time in communities in which the CPI(M) is dominant, I also made great effort to spend time in communities (and meet with neighborhood groups) in which political contestation is high (i.e., communities in which neither the CPI(M) nor Congress Party[2] win consistently) and communities in which the opposition is dominant. It was through many informal conversations in various venues that I came to appreciate the embeddedness of these parties in their societies.

In addition to participant observation, a significant portion of my research was through in-depth interviews of party leaders, activists, rank-and-file members, and non-party subalterns and activists, as well as independent intellectuals. I conducted formal interviews with many top-level leaders (central committee and state committee members), provincial leaders, district and branch leaders, as well as non-party activists. In Kerala I conducted 75 formal interviews in 2000 and 2002. Many of these interviews were with more than one person. For example, when I interviewed a number of elected officials from the same area I usually interviewed them together and have counted the interview as one interview. In South Africa I conducted 91 formal interviews between 2001 and 2003. In both Kerala and South Africa I conducted numerous informal interviews (conversations at events, meetings, and political schools) with ordinary rank-and-file members and "fellow travelers." To protect their confidentiality, I have given all of my informants and interviewees pseudonyms. I refer to people by their real names only when I discuss their official functions, not personal communications with me. My interviews with collectivities (e.g., elected representatives of a council) are referred to by the institution or structure they represent (i.e., I do not name specific individuals but cite, e.g., "Interview with Kalliaseri Panchayat Representatives").

In addition to participant observation and interviews, I also collected a great deal of historical documents in archives and libraries in both places. In South Africa I visited the William Cullen Archive at the University of Witwatersrand (housing a wide range of party-related documents), the Mayibuye Center for Historical Papers at the University of Western Cape (where the ANC's and SACP's documents from exile are housed), the Manuscripts and Archive Department at the University of Cape Town (where the comprehensive Jack and Ray Simons' papers are stored), the National Archives of South Africa in Pretoria (where the apartheid state's records are held), and the SACP Chris Hani Memorial Library at its head office in Johannesburg as well as the SACP provincial offices in KwaZulu Natal and Gauteng. In Kerala, I visited the Kerala State Archives in Thiruvananthapuram, the extensive historical documents collection at the Center for Development Studies (Ulloor), the library at the University of Kerala, the CPI(M) archives at the AKG Center for Research and Study, the CPI Library in Thiruvananthapuram, the C. Achyutha Menon Center Library, and the State Planning Board.

In addition to the primary data I have made extensive use of the plethora of secondary sources on the two societies. Indeed, in many respects this study was made possible, to make a play on Sir Isaac Newton's famous phrase, by standing on the shoulders of the commitments, testimony, and analyses of the many activists, academics, and writers who came before me.[3] Through the variety of primary and secondary sources I have been able to piece together the ideology, politics, and practices of the Communist Parties in Kerala and South Africa in the late twentieth century and offer an explanation for their divergence.

Notes

Chapter 1   Introduction: Hegemonic and Counter-Hegemonic Generative Politics

1. I use participatory democracy to refer to the republican political tradition of citizen participation in deliberation, decision making, and implementation. Representative democracy, by contrast, refers to the liberal political tradition of representative government based on regular and fair electoral competition.

2. I refer to Western scholarship rather than U.S. because it can also be traced through post–World War II European thinkers. There are, however, notable exceptions to this broad characterization (e.g., Tarrow, 1989).

3. For Kerala see V.M. Fic (1970); T.K. Oommen (1985); K.N. Panikkar (1992); T.M. Thomas Isaac (1982, 1997, 2000); T. Nossiter (1982, 1988); P. Heller (1999); R. Herring (1983); R. Jeffrey (1992); and R. Franke (1993). For South Africa see G. Mbeki (1963); R. Bernstein (1999); J. Slovo (1976, 1991); Simons and Simons (1983); C. Bundy (1979, 1991); S. Clingman (1998); P. Delius (1993); and T. Lodge (1983, 2002).

4. A note about terminology is in order as the word faction is highly contentious, denoting firmly entrenched power politics. I have chosen to use faction (rather than tendency or group), because it also denotes real links to specific interests. I want to stress that I use faction to categorize different groups with specific ideological visions about the primary agents of change. In both parties, what began as ideological cleavages evolved into factions as different groups got access to power.

5. In Kerala the working class includes both urban and rural workers as agricultural laborers are highly organized and constitute a large portion of the working class. In South Africa the working class refers to urban (industrial) laborers; rural laborers have been sorely neglected by the party.

6. The CPI(M) does not have a developed statist faction, though it certainly displays elements of one. The reason for its relative absence is related to the 1964 split with the CPI, which was partially due to tensions around parliamentarianism and the relation to the state. The CPI has a predominant statist faction.

7. Peter Evans (1995) argues that such an alliance between local capital and the state can facilitate national development in the form of industrialization.

8. A note on "participation" is warranted since it has become a catch-all phrase used by activists, politicians, and academics of all political hues. For example, some scholars refer to participation to simply mean a person was present at a particular activity. This use of participation says nothing of the capacity to affect the outcome of the activity. Drawing on Pateman's categories, I use participation to refer to participation *in* decision making,

which requires opportunities for people to influence decisions affecting their lives as well as to have the power to enact the decisions they have made (Pateman, 1999: 67–70).

9. Participation can also, however, lead to cynicism and disaffection.

10. While the grassroots faction looks to a broader constituency, it still sees the working class as a strategically placed actor that plays a fundamental role in transformation.

11. Claus Offe problematizes this periodization as he rightly shows the earlier links to the 1960s U.S. civil rights, antiwar, and student movements and the 1950s European non-institutional movement politics (e.g., movements focusing on military integration and rearmament) (Offe, 1990: 232). For my purposes, the exact lineage of the movements is less important than the character of their relationship to the Old Left and political parties. Here Offe concurs that what makes these movements "new" is their autonomy from established political parties (Offe, 1990: 232).

12. Offe explains that the new movements concentrate their conflict on subjectivity and existential issues, which contrasts with the earlier axes of sociopolitical conflict of freedom versus privilege of the liberal-bourgeois movements and the social justice and economic security versus private property and economic power of the social democratic movements (Offe, 1990: 233–34).

13. Social movements often define their goals "as alternatives to the political process, political parties, the state, and the capture of state power" (Routledge, 2002: 272).

14. Looking at the Italian party-movement nexus Tarrow suggests that "parties are more usefully seen as offstage, but creative prompters in the origins, dynamics, and the ultimate institutionalization of the new movements" (Tarrow, 1990: 254).

15. For example, in his classic study on the political role of urban communities, Castells (1983) argues that while political parties connect social movements to society, the sine qua non condition of social movements' success is that "they must be organizationally and ideologically autonomous of any political party" (322). See also Offe for a discussion of the dilemmas social movements face with regard to institutionalization and formal political parties (1990: 240–45). For a critique of the dominant literature on parties see Kitschelt (1989, 1990).

16. This *volte-face* was a response to the failures of communist governments, widespread depoliticization of the "masses," the abandonment of socialist visions in the 1990s, and the precarious position of the organized working class due to changes in the economy. In addition, learning from social movements, many political parties incorporated broader issues of gender, race, ethnicity, and ecology into their ideological and programmatic frameworks. Implicit in this process of renewal is the recognition that the notion of a universal class that performs a liberating mission through state power is obsolete (Offe, 1990: 234).

17. For example, Giddens argues that both the peace and ecological movements lack a "structure of objectives" and "find it easier to state what they are against than what they are for" (1986: 13–16).

18. New social movement theorists have also tended to emphasize the confrontational forms of action used by social movements (Tarrow, 1990: 263).

19. The concept of repertoire of contention is developed by Tilly (1978, 1986). Tarrow develops the idea further and defines three main protest repertoires: conventional, confrontational, and violent (1989, chapter five).

20. Archon Fung and Erik Olin Wright (2003) touch on this dilemma as well. In the epilogue Fung and Wright theorize "empowered participatory governance" (EPG) and the different nature of power, which they divide into adversarial and collaborative. In their work they are interested to develop a theoretical model of EPG and the necessary

institutional arrangements. They are, therefore, more concerned with questions of deliberation and participation and only raise questions of the nature of politics in their epilogue. For my purposes, the nature of the politics (i.e., protest or generative) is at the center.

21. The roots of my concepts "protest" and "generative" politics can be found in Hannah Arendt's "liberation" and "revolution" (Arendt, 1963). Liberation refers to a process of struggle to transcend an existing system of oppression and exploitation, while revolution is fundamentally about constructing something new.

22. I want to make clear that generative politics is distinct from parliamentary politics. Offe juxtaposes the political discourse of movement politics, which are "negative demands on isolated and disjointed issues" to the discourse of parliamentary politics that are "agenda-generated rather than event-generated" and "consists of competing proposals rather than the expression of protest and rejection" (Offe, 1990: 244).

23. I am specifically referring to capitalist hegemony (the rule of capital). By contrast, the content and practice of socialist hegemony is defined by subaltern classes.

24. Wright and Burawoy explain that "to say that civil society is 'dominant' is therefore to say that the basic direction of economic activity and of state policies are determined by collective actions organized through such associations within civil society" (2004: 7).

25. For example, Routledge theorizes the importance of "constructive resistance" for social movements in which they construct alternative development practices that are also alternatives to the role of the state. Such views romanticize local-level initiatives, exaggerate the inherent capacities of civil society, and are difficult to sustain without state support.

Part I   Ideology and Practice of Socialist Democracy

1. I use neoliberal to refer to late twentieth-century capitalism with its emphasis on less state involvement in both the economic domain and in providing public goods to the citizenry, and more "free market" autonomy to penetrate economies in countries around the world.

Chapter 2   Communist Renewal and Ideological Convergence

1. Both parties held National Congresses in the early 1990s (the SACP held its 8th National Congress in 1991; the CPI(M) held its 14th Congress in 1992), at which fundamental questions about socialism, Marxism, and democracy were asked.

2. I do not use democratic socialism or radical social democracy as both parties insist that democratic socialism is, for them, tainted with the Eurocommunist experience and social democracy refers to the Scandinavian experience in which parliamentary (not participatory) democracy is the primary means.

3. The SACP held Congresses in 1991, 1995, 1998, and 2002 as well as three important strategy conferences in 1993, 1999, and 2000. The CPI(M) held Congresses in 1992, 1995, 1998, and 2002 as well as two important conferences in Kerala in 1994 and 2000.

4. The CPI(M)'s commitment to encouraging democratic debate was strengthened in response to the CPC's repression of the student movement in 1989. The events at Tiananmen Square sparked widespread debate within the CPI(M), though in public the party came out in support of the CPC (Interview with Ashok, June 16, 2002).

5. Whether this commitment to multiparty parliamentary system is a principled commitment is left for interpretation. For example, the party states that

> democracy and democratic rights would be inseparable elements of the socialist juridical, political, and social order. [...] Under Socialism, the right to dissent, freedom of expression and plurality of opinion will flourish with the aim of strengthening Socialism. The question of whether other political parties exist or a multi-party system will prevail, depends crucially on the role that these parties have played during the process of revolution and socialist transformation. (CPI(M), 1992: 148)

   At the same time, in a 1998 Congress Resolution the party argues that it must "strengthen parliamentary democracy by proportional representation with a partial list system for elections." (CPI(M), 1998: 419)

6. Notwithstanding its own internal organizational transgressions, the party had from the 1920s committed itself to political and economic democracy in society.

7. The ANC adopted a similar analysis at its 1969 Morogoro conference.

8. Such a commitment to a multiparty system was not automatically accepted within the ranks of the SACP and was embedded within a more radical conception of democracy. At an SACP-COSATU meeting in March 1990, a caution against ruling out the short-term necessity for a single-party system as well as the dangers in idealizing a multiparty system was articulated. It was argued at this meeting that

> while a one-party system cannot be ruled out in principle—particular conditions may make it necessary—nevertheless in general the multi-party system provides one of the favorable conditions for democratic participation. Yet, second, a multi-party parliamentary political system is not, on its own, sufficient, it has to be supplemented by strong institutions and mass, independent organizations—women, students, trade unions, civics and so forth—which can participate in the decision-making process. (SACP, 1990b: 13–14)

9. The RDP was a common Alliance program for economic reconstruction and development of South African society. It was formulated by left intellectuals, COSATU, the SACP, and ANC.

10. See, for example Schulz (1981) and Little (1981). Both scholars demonstrate that political participation in the Soviet Union was often higher than in liberal democracies and that the governments in these states were often responsive to the demands of the citizenry.

11. Evans juxtaposes a developmental state to a predatory state. Predatory states "extract at the expense of society, undercutting development even in the narrow sense of capital accumulation." Predatory states lack the ability to prevent individuals from pursuing their own goals and thus individual maximization comes before collective goals. Ties to society become ties to individuals "not connections between constituencies and the state as an organization" (Evans, 1995: 12).

12. The term bourgeois is not really applicable for Kerala as there was not a developed indigenous bourgeoisie at this time, but it is often used to describe the wealthy and conservative non-landlord class.

13. In the 1989 Program struggle was outlined as follows:

> In the period after the seizure of power by the democratic forces, the working class will need to continue to struggle against capitalism. It will need to strengthen its organizations and build the basis of working class and popular power in the economy, in all sectors of the state and in the communities where the people live. A deliberate effort will have to be made to prevent attempts by the bourgeoisie and aspirant capitalist elements [...] to dominate state power. (SACP, 1989a: 39)

14. NEDLAC formed in 1995 by an Act of Parliament (35 of 1994) as a statutory body with considerable power and membership from representatives of business, labor, community and development organizations, and government. It is a consultative forum for labor legislation and social and economic policies (Gostner and Joffe, 2000: 78). The power of labor and community organizations, however, is contingent on broader power relations and organizational capacities.

15. The SACP and CPI(M) were also sidestepping the old debate between "revolutionary" versus "reformist" strategies to socialism (SACP, 1999: 4–6; CPI(M), 1990: 311). Reformists believe that working through an affirmative state can ameliorate severe economic inequality, eliminate poverty, and offset market irrationalities (such as the negative externalities in public goods, labor reproduction, and the environment). Moreover, reformists argue that wholesale rupture with capitalism will not necessarily produce the desired alternative, but more likely will result in societies with new forms of inequality and economic irrationalities. The revolutionary camp argues that reformist efforts at change are merely cosmetic and do not challenge the destructive properties of capitalism. Instead, they argue that a completely new society that does not produce inequality and economic irrationality could be built through smashing the old system (Wright and Burawoy, 2004: 1–2). The CPI(M) and SACP were moving beyond this state-centered approach to transformation and developed a society-centered vision of social change that sought to increase the capacity of civil society in relation to the state and economy.

16. The party was adopting Samir Amin's notion of delinking in which popular national demands are placed before market demands and the market is engaged on terms beneficial to national development (Amin, 1990 [1985]).

17. This understanding of socialism posits socialism as a negation of capitalism (i.e., the private ownership of the means of production).

18. Indicating awareness of the need to elaborate viable alternatives, SACP leader Rob Davies argued:

> If socialists and communists are to regain more of the initiative in the national economic debate, we need to produce more substantive answers about what it is that distinguishes the vision of socialism we are defending from that which failed in Eastern Europe. [...] The kind of policy which emerges in the stage of national democratic construction will significantly affect the prospects of a socialist project in the future. (Davies, 1991: 38)

19. See, e.g., Malinga (1990), Ramaphosa (1993), Marais (1994 and 1996), Cronin (1995), Gomomo (1995), Erwin (1989, 1994, and 1996), Nondwangu (1996), Nzimande (1996 and 1998), Satgar and Mantashe (1996), Dexter (1996), SACP (1997), Satgar (1997), Tripartite Alliance (1997 and 1997b), Carrim and Kondlo (1999), Netshitenzhe (2000), and Pape (2001). In addition the SACP and COSATU held a "Socialist Conference" in November 1994 to further clarify their thinking.

20. For example, it was argued that "a coherent transformation will require state ownership; policies that influence private investment; changed rights of access to and use of natural resources (e.g. land, water, minerals, forests, marine resources) and a range of regulatory and supervisory dispensations" (Tripartite Alliance, 1997: 17).

21. In 1995 the SACP argued that the following state interventions were necessary to transform market power relations: develop active labor market, state subsidies (e.g., housing subsidies), progressive government tendering policies compelling companies to implement worker training, encourage community banks, use public sector corporations to democratize the markets, mobilize worker provident and pension funds, democratize relevant financial institutions, establish consumer negotiating forums (e.g., rent

boards), mobilize mass opinion to influence the market (product specific boycotts), and the regulation of markets (SACP, 1995: 17).

Chapter 3   The Counter-Hegemonic Politics of the CPI(M)

1. Interview with Ravi, April 19, 2002.
2. Between 1971 and 1980 there were 309 strikes with 136,386 workers involved resulting in a total of 1,332,562 "man-days" lost. This compares with 1980–1990 where there were only 133 strikes with 78,845 workers involved and a total of 1,180,325 man-days lost. This trend continued into the 1990s. Between 1990 and 1996 there were only 44 strikes with 56,738 workers involved and a total of 908,231 man-days lost. These figures represent annual averages (GOK, Labour Department, *Administration Report of Labour Department* quoted in Heller, 2000: 76).
3. Since 1957 the Communist Party has been in and out of government, with the 1957–1959 Ministry being the only time it held state power alone. The rest of its tenure in government has been in CPI(M)-led coalitions. The years it has held state power are 1957–1959 (ministry dissolved by Central government); 1967–1969 (ministry internally dissolved); 1979–1981 (ministry dissolved); 1987–1991 (held full term); 1996–2001 (held full term); 2006 to present.
4. Over half of the population is in either mass or class organizations (e.g., trade unions, peasant associations, employee's organizations, student, youth, and women's organizations).
5. Interview with Vishnu, January 7, 2002.
6. Interview with Arjuna, July 7, 2000.
7. Decentralization was not a new theme for the party. In 1957 the party attempted to legislate provisions for decentralization.
8. This attempt at decentralization was limited because of national legislation (e.g., limited funds could be devolved). In 1993 new national legislation was adopted, which allowed for significant decentralization in terms of finances, power, and authority to local government.
9. Interviews with Raj, January 12, 2002; Mohan, May 12, 2002; Ved, January 29, 2002; Ashok, June 16, 2002; Devan, February 4, 2002.
10. The KSSP is a volunteer-based mass movement that has played an important role in promoting democratic decentralization and ecological thinking into the CPI(M).
11. While the literacy campaign was very successful, there were weaknesses. For example, the initial literacy classes were not followed by refresher classes and after achieving near total literacy there was a slide backward by a few percentage points.
12. In early 1991 Kerala's literacy rate was 94 percent for men and 87 percent for women with the overall rate at 90.6 percent. In 1995 the literacy rate was 93 percent (GOK, 1998a). Percentages for 1991 were taken from the 1991 Indian Census (Bose, 1991: 69).
13. Interview with Devan, February 4, 2002.
14. Approximately 200 of the 900 grama panchayats developed comprehensive village resource maps and many other villages developed less comprehensive village resource maps; interview with Ashok, June 16, 2002.
15. Interview with Ramesh, March 20, 2002.
16. Interview with Ashok, June 16, 2002.
17. In 1994 Kerala's population density was 786 people per km². This number comes into sharp relief when compared to India as a whole, which has a population density 279 people per km² (GOK, 1994 and UNDP, 1997).

18. Interview with Apu, April 16, 2002.
19. Panchayat is the term for rural municipality.
20. Interview with Savathree, January 15, 2002.
21. Interview with Raj, January 12, 2002.
22. In the 1940s Gandhi had been a champion of decentralization through a federation of villages meeting local needs through local production. The party's vision differed as it emphasized district councils, while Gandhi emphasized village structures.
23. Interview with Savathree, January 15, 2002.
24. There were three main areas of change: (1) increased financial capacity of lower-level panchayats by imposing revenue-sharing schemes and giving local governments the power to tax; (2) mandated one-third reservation of elected representatives for women, Scheduled Castes, and Scheduled Tribes in proportion to their population in the area; and, (3) establishment of a direct participatory institution, Grama Sabhas (village councils or people's assemblies).
25. Interview with Savathree, January 15, 2002.
26. There were a series of other laws complementing these efforts such as laws ensuring transparency of administration and access to information as well as government orders concerning accounting systems, reporting procedures, and powers of officials.
27. Interview with Vishnu, January 7, 2002.
28. Interview with Ravi, April 19, 2002.
29. With 95 percent electoral support in Kalliasseri, 13 of the 14 elected representatives are CPI(M). Throughout the 1990s all but one panchayat elected representatives were CPI(M). The one elected representative that was not CPI(M) was CPI. Thus, the area is considered totally "red."
30. For example, one of the leading party activists in the region, Nambiar, was panchayat president and sympathetic to decentralization. Together with a leading KSSP activist from the region, T. Gangadharan (T.G.), the conditions proved ideal for incubating the novel political project.
31. Interview with Shiva, April 18, 2002.
32. Interview with Shiva, April 18, 2002.
33. Interview with Kalliasseri Panchayat elected representatives, April 19, 2002.
34. The population and land size were attained from the panchayat office (April 19, 2002). The density on the land was calculated by dividing the population (30,000) by the size of the area (60.7 km²).
35. 100 cents equals 1 acre; 1 cent land equals .01 acre.
36. Interview with Kalliasseri Panchayat elected representatives, April 19, 2002.
37. Interview with production unit, April 19, 2002.
38. There are 14 wards in the panchayat.
39. Interview with Shiva, April 18, 2002.
40. Interview with Shiva, April 18, 2002.
41. Interview with Vishnu, January 7, 2002.
42. Interview with Kalliasseri Panchayat elected representatives, April 19, 2002.
43. Interview with Nilesh, April 19, 2002.
44. Interview with Kalliasseri Panchayat elected representatives, April 19, 2002.
45. Interview with Shiva, April 18, 2002.
46. Interview with Vishnu, January 7, 2002.
47. See Putnam (1993) for discussion of democratic promoting civil society.
48. Interview with Meera, January 14, 2002.
49. E.M.S. Namboodiripad was the first chief minister of the state in 1957–1959 and was the party's leading intellectual and most popular leader.

50. Interview with Vishnu, January 7, 2002.
51. Interview with Meera, January 14, 2002.
52. Interview with Nilesh, April 19, 2002.
53. This information is based on my fieldwork in villages in Mararikulam, Kannur, and the environs of Thiruvanathapuram. It is also drawn from documents generated by the decentralization campaign and from the May 2000 conference and October 2005 conference.
54. Discussion with members from Karakulam Grama Panchayat, June 6, 2002.
55. Interview with Ramesh, March 20, 2002.
56. Interview with Vishnu, January 7, 2002.
57. Interview with Mohan, March 13, 2002; interview with Ashok, January 18, 2002.
58. Interview with Arjuna, July 7, 2000.
59. Before 1996 local governments received around Rs. 200 million from the state's annual plan budget. In 1997–1998, Rs. 10,250 million were devolved to local government and in 1998–1999 to Rs. 11,780 million was devolved from the state's annual plan budget (Isaac and Franke, 2001: 17; Isaac and Heller, 2003: 82).
60. Interview with Vishnu, January 7, 2002.
61. The councils for each tier of government are directly elected through a "first-past-the-post" constituency system.
62. Interview with Kanjikuzhi Grama Panchayat elected representatives, April 16, 2002.
63. Interview with Arjuna, March 25, 2002.
64. Visit to village in Kanjikuzhi Panchayat, April 17, 2002.
65. The production units were kept below the stipulated membership number that would require them to register with the Ministry of Cooperatives. The Ministry is fraught with bureaucratic and hierarchical structures that have come to hinder cooperative development. Keeping the production units out of the Ministry helped ensure they would not become party-political structures.
66. Interview with Vishnu, January 7, 2002.
67. This data is based on 47 visits to micro-production units across the state in 2002.
68. Interview with Sita, April 20, 2002.
69. Interviews with Kanjikuzhi Grama Panchayat and Kanjikuzhi Block Panchayat, April 16, 2002.
70. The importance of markets was raised by party activists and government officials throughout the state.
71. The selection of beneficiaries exemplifies the commitment to transparency. The selection of beneficiaries was historically a notorious area for patronage politics and corruption, but under the Campaign this trend was challenged. Panchayats were required to publicize and prominently display criteria, prioritization, and selection of beneficiaries and to publicly present the beneficiary lists and criteria for selection to the Grama Sabhas.
72. Visit to village in Allaphuza District, March 2002.
73. In the first couple years Grama Sabhas were held twice a year, but in subsequent years the number of legally mandated Grama Sabhas was increased to four per year each with a specific objective. For example, at the first Grama Sabha of the year citizens identify and prioritize problems and form sectoral development seminars. At later Grama Sabhas, development plans are presented and discussed and beneficiaries selected.
74. I attended 42 neighborhood group meetings in Kannur, Allaphuzha, and Thiruvananthapuram districts. I also discussed the role of neighborhood groups in my interviews with panchayat-elected representatives and government officials as well as informal discussions with members of neighborhood groups.

75. Interview with Surekha, January 15, 2002.
76. Interview with Mohan, March 13, 2002.
77. Interview with Ramesh, March 20, 2002.
78. Interview with Devan, February 4, 2002.
79. I attended two Grama Sabhas and numerous community meetings, neighborhood group meetings, and women's group meetings during 2002.
80. To ensure meetings were not dominated by local political elites there were strict guidelines limiting the time for speeches. In addition, thousands of facilitators were trained to run small group meetings that kept discussions focused, but gave ordinary citizens a chance to speak freely.
81. These efforts of popular communication were part of the counter-hegemonic generative politics. They represent efforts to construct alternative visions on the terrain of civil society. Indeed, the CPI(M) sought alternative forms of media to rebut the dominant ideology found in mass media (what the party refers to as "bourgeois media"). During my research I witnessed a number of examples of these alternative forms of media.
82. Interview with Ramesh, July 2, 2002.
83. Interview with Subhash, April 14, 2002.
84. Development seminars had an average of 231 delegates of which 13.8 percent were officials, 10.5 percent were Scheduled Castes and Scheduled Tribes, and 22.1 percent were women (Isaac and Heller, 2003: 92).
85. The details of these different phases were covered in a number of conference papers presented at the International Conference on Democratic Decentralization, Thiruvananthapuram, May 20–25, 2000.
86. Interview with Ishaan, January 8, 2002.
87. All elected representatives were expected to participate in the training programs for the state, district, or local key resource persons.
88. Interview with Yuvi, April 17, 2002.
89. Interview with Mohan, May 12, 2002.
90. While I have focused on the Campaign's role in nurturing and facilitating citizen participation in development, there were also tangible effects. By 1999, 98,494 houses had been erected, 240,307 sanitary latrines built, 50,162 wells dug, 17,489 public taps provided, 16,563 ponds cleaned, and over 8,000 kilometers of roads constructed. In addition to these achievements, 2,800,179 individuals received agricultural support in the form of seedlings and fertilizers (the figures are from the State Planning Board cited in Isaac and Heller, 2003: 100).
91. M.A. Baby, *Seminar Address*, "Seminar on Decentralization, Social Security, and Sustainable Development," Mararikulam, May 11–13, 2002.
92. Interview with Ved, January 23, 2002.
93. Interview with Vishnu, January 7, 2002.
94. Countering international trends to call such groups micro-finance self-help groups, activists in Kerala called them women's neighborhood groups (Interview with Vishnu, January 7, 2002).
95. Interview with Surekha, January 15, 2002; interview with Rekha, April 16, 2002.
96. Discussions with field officers and party activists in Mararikulam in March and April 2002.
97. For example, Kanjikuzhi panchayat (which is in Mararikulam) has twice been awarded "best panchayat in the state" and three other panchayats have been awarded the best in the district.
98. The women's group idea in Mararikulam originated from experiments in Alappuzha Municipality in 1993.

99. In addition to the 1,500 Kudumbashree groups, there are 500 self-help groups organized by the church, voluntary organizations, and caste groups and 300 SGSY self-help groups formed by the Rural Development Department.
100. Interview with Apu, April 16, 2002.
101. I visited approximately 20 groups in this area of the state in 2000 and 2002 and attended a mass meeting in which approximately 5,000 women were present in March 2002.
102. I witnessed many of these activities during March and April 2002 when I spent time in the region.
103. Kanjikuzhi Women's Group meeting, March 28, 2002.
104. This data is from a questionnaire administered in 2001 by Binitha V. Thampi in Mararikulam. The original data was written up in a collaborative conference paper "Women's Neighborhood Groups: Towards a New Perspective" by Thomas Isaac, Michelle Williams, Pinaki Chakraborthy, and Binitha V. Thampi; May 2002.
105. Interview with Subhash, April 14, 2002.
106. Interview with women from a Kanjikuzhi Kudumbasree Self Help Group, March 28, 2002.

Chapter 4 The Hegemonic Politics of the SACP

1. This periodization does not deny the turbulent and sad phase of the 1930s. For my purpose I have chosen to periodize the 1920s through the 1950s based on similar practices of mass mobilizing and participatory organizing in which it helped forge a vibrant civil society as it organized labor into trade unions and residents into community groups.
2. The CPSA was banned in 1950. Communists, therefore, worked in the various Congress Alliance affiliates and trade unions.
3. The Freedom Charter was adopted in 1955 and became the ANC's official program. It became the common platform for the SACP and ANC.
4. One of the results of this tension between military and political activity was the formation of a six-member Politico-Military Strategy Commission (Oliver Tambo, Joe Modise, Joe Slovo, Moses Mabhida, Joe Gqabi, and Thabo Mbeki). All of the members except Joe Gqabi had been on the study visit to Vietnam.
5. The *Green Book*, largely drafted by Slovo and named after the color of its cover, was a seminal document that criticized the ANC/SACP's strategy for parallelism between the political and military approaches, with priority given to the military (Karis and Gerhart, 1997: 303–04).
6. These details are from interviews I conducted with five different activists involved at the time. All five activists discussed similar types of propaganda activity.
7. The confrontations of the 1970s resulted in state-led political (e.g. Tricameral parliament) and labor (e.g. Wiehan Commission) reforms in the early 1980s. The Tricameral parliament attempted to co-opt the Indian and Colored communities by giving them their own parliament operating alongside the white parliament. Africans were given a limited form of local government with the Black Local Authorities and independence to the Bantustans.
8. In the late 1980s it also launched a covert operation, Operation Vula, which was meant to keep underground armed structures alive. There is little known about Operation Vula, though recent scholarship has begun to uncover its past (see Conny Braam, 2004; Mac Maharaj, 2007).
9. Interview with Mark, September 11, 2001.

10. Interviews with Senso, October 7, 2001; Edward, September 14, 2001; and Judith, July 12, 2001.
11. Interview with Judith, July 12, 2001.
12. The Sunset Clauses were the brainchild of SACP leader Joe Slovo. Many claim the Sunset Clauses were paramount in breaking the deadlock in the negotiations without permanently hindering qualitative democratic advance. Others claim that by ensuring a drawn-out transformation of the civil service, the Sunset Clauses put the potential for radical transformation on hold.
13. Interview with John, February 9, 2001.
14. Interview with Bambata, April 1, 2001.
15. Interview with Ram, October 16, 2001.
16. NEDLAC formed in February 1995 through the integration of the National Manpower Commission (NMC) and the National Economic Forum (NEF). NEDLAC is a statutory body with considerable power and stability and recognizes membership from representatives of business, labor, community and development organizations, and government (Gostner and Joffe, 2000: 78). The Act requires consultation of all proposed labor legislation and social and economic policies, which allows considerable formal space for labor and community to shape policy. The ability of labor and community representatives to shape policy, however, is contingent on power relations and organizational capacities.
17. Meeting in Pimville, Soweto, July 2002.
18. Interviews with Oscar, October 2005; Janet, June 1, 2006; Karen, April 10, 2001.
19. Interview with Bambata, April 1, 2001.
20. The allocation of funds is determined by the number of people living in rural areas and school-aged children in the province (e.g., KwaZulu Natal received the largest grant (R23 billion) because of its high number of rural residents while the Northern Cape's small rural population lent it an allocation of R2.7 billion) (Lodge, 2002: 35). The central government's allocation is the primary source of funding.
21. Paradoxically, while regional government is responsible for majority of services it has limited discretion in determining policy, but it does have latitude to interpret and implement laws (Lodge, 2002: 32, 37).
22. Between 1996 and 1998 personnel expenditure rose from 46.6 percent to 50.1 percent of total expenditure despite the decline in the size of public service by 13 percent due to "right sizing." The provincial expenditure rose in the same period from 53 percent to 59 percent of the provincial budgets (Baskin, 2000: 164).
23. Chapter seven, section 152 of the Constitution, 1996.
24. The one exception to this was the 2001 Gauteng Provincial Congress and the 2003 Gauteng SACP Conference (discussed later).
25. Interviews with Bambata, March 28, 2001; Petros, October 5, 2001; Lucas, February 25, 2001.
26. Interview with Lungile, October 7, 2001.
27. Interview with Frank, September 5, 2001.
28. Interview with Frank, September 5, 2001.
29. In fact, I found only three documents on the campaign written in 1992 and 1993 assessing the failure of the campaign and drawing lessons for future campaigns.
30. Interview with Devi, July 24, 2001.
31. The three secretaries were Paul Mashitile (acting secretary), Jabu Moleketi, and Trevor Fowler.
32. In both the 2002 and 2007 Congresses many of these leaders have been marginalized from the party.

33. Interviews with Frank, June 11, 2001; Bob, August 4, 2001; Ram, October 16, 2001.

34. Interview with Mark, September 11, 2001. This view was expressed on numerous occasions, especially by members from the statist faction.

35. Jabu Moleketi was the Gauteng SACP provincial secretary (at the time it was called Transvaal region) for two terms until 1999. He was Gauteng provincial MEC of finance from 1994 to 2004. After the 2004 national elections he was promoted to the post of deputy minister of finance under Trevor Manuel. He is no longer an active member of the party.

36. Interview with Judith July 12, 2001.

37. It can be seen even earlier. For example, as early as the mid-1980s certain prominent ANC leaders (most notably President Thabo Mbeki) accepted the need for privatization of certain state-owned enterprises. Some scholars argue that the semisecret negotiations between the ANC and South African business that began in 1985 led the ANC to be increasingly oriented toward negotiations and accommodation with capital (Eidelberg, 2000: 133).

38. The ANC's first serious attempt to develop economic policy was the 1990 "Discussion Document on Economic Policy" issued by its new Department of Economic Policy (DEP). The document was strongly influenced by COSATU's Economic Trends Group (Marais, 2001: 124).

39. In 1991 Mandela told business people in Pittsburgh, United States of America, that

    the private sector must and will play the central and decisive role in the struggle to achieve many of [the transformation] objectives...let me assure you that the ANC is not an enemy of private enterprise...we are aware that the investor will not invest unless he or she is assured of the security of their investment....The rates of economic growth we seek cannot be achieved without important inflows of foreign capital. We are determined to create the necessary climate which the foreign investor will find attractive. (Mandela, "Continuation Lecture," University of Pittsburgh, December 6, 1991, quoted in Gelb, 1999: 13)

40. Marais explains that the "'growth through redistribution' approach was severely censured by mainstream economists and the media. Attacks ranged from consternation about the 'socialist' undertones of the [1990] document to complaints about its alleged overtones of macro-economic populism" (Marais, 2001: 125–26).

41. The document consistently refers to the importance of people's participation in every stage: "This must not be a process of telling people what the new government's RDP will do for them, but of encouraging people to play an active role in implementing their own RDP with government assistance" (ANC, 1994: 147).

42. P.G. Eidelberg explains the importance of the RDP to the SACP as it corresponded with "a general anti-capitalist mass mobilization, which would permit even individual social-ist projects to be built *ad hoc* already during the national democratic, post-apartheid phase of the revolution" (Eidelberg, 2000: 143).

43. Stephen Gelb, who was involved in drafting GEAR, explains that the "immediate aim of the GEAR strategy was to signal to potential investors the government's (and especially the ANC's) commitment to the prevailing orthodoxy" (Gelb, 1999: 16). Similarly, Marais notes that the ANC-led government's economic policy was "geared to service the respective prerogatives of domestic and international capital and the aspirations of the emerging black bourgeoisie—at the expense of the impoverished majority's hopes for a less iniquitous social and economic order" (Marais, 2001: 123–24).

44. While SACP members Langa Zita, Dale McKinley, and Vishwas Satgar (1996) responded immediately with a critique of GEAR, it took the SACP leadership a year before it presented an official critique (Nzimande and Cronin, 1997).

45. Interview with Devi, August 28, 2001.
46. Interview with Lucas, April 10, 2001.
47. Tabling the issue through NEDLAC marks a shift for the party. Up to this point, the SACP had not been a participant of NEDLAC as it was skeptical of corporatist arrangements and criticized its failure to provide meaningful access to policy making for the trade union and community constituencies (Eidelberg, 2000: 152). To participate the party works through the community and development constituency.
48. March and rally July 21, 2001. I attended a similar march in August 2001.
49. While it worked within these institutions the party was also ambivalent: it worked to influence ANC policy, but it also remained ideologically at variance with much of ANC thinking.
50. Squatter settlement in Inanda, October 7, 2001.
51. During the weeks leading up to and during the strike the South African newspapers were full of articles detailing the confrontation and exclaiming the imminent break in the Alliance.
52. Cooperatives are part of building a counter-hegemonic generative project as they attempt to establish a new moral and intellectual order based on social needs (Burawoy, 2003: 15).
53. I attended this conference and was able to speak with a number of people from across the country about local efforts to build cooperatives (SACP and COSATU National School on Cooperatives, September 12–14, 2001).
54. It was set up in a top-down manner with little mass involvement and never really took off.
55. There are even signs to suggest that the national-level SACP has played a destructive role in the National Cooperative Alliance of South Africa (NCASA).
56. The opposition was mounted by a group within the trade union faction. I attended this Congress.
57. I attended these forums during 2001 and 2003.
58. I attended meetings of three different branches involved in cooperative development. I also visited a number of cooperatives in Emfuleni, Ekhurhurleni, and Midrand in 2001 and 2003.
59. I attended the political school, October 2001.
60. I attended this conference, July 20, 2003.
61. I attended eight workshops with the cooperatives in 2001 and 2003. I also attended meetings between the cooperative board and the municipal council's Local Economic Development Department in 2001.
62. I attended two groundwork phase conferences held by the LED department in 2002 and 2003.
63. Interview with Jeffrey, July 10, 2003.
64. Interview with Lungile, October 7, 2001.
65. Interview with Shabalala, October 19, 2001.
66. Interview with Pietermaritzberg District Executive Members, Pietermaritzberg, October 3, 2001.
67. I visited a number of these and all of them were built by local contractors and were designed in environmentally sensitive ways to maximize the use of natural lighting, ventilation, etc.
68. I visited these cooperatives and food garden ventures in July 2003.
69. The activists came up with a code of conduct that included not emphasizing party affiliation in their work. The team agreed not to wear SACP t-shirts or bring in SACP politics into the work, but rather focuses on development issues.

70. I have borrowed this analogy from Eduardo Galeano's vignette "Ten Years Ago I Attended the Dress Rehearsal of this Play" characterizing the Argentine 1976 political tragedy (Galeano, 1983: 16).

Part II Party, Class, and State in Historical Context

1. Drawing on Peter Evans, Gay Seidman characterizes the South African economy as "associated-dependent development" by which is meant an economy in which industrial production expands, but the economy remains dependent on international markets and imported capital and technology (Seidman, 1994: 44; Evans, 1979).
2. Between 1969 and 1976 underemployment increased to 22 percent while output grew at 3.9 percent a year (Maree, 1978: 23).

Chapter 5 Party Capacities in Historical Perspective

1. The Communist Party has a federal structure with the state committee responsible for developments within the state. The national-level structure deals with national and international issues, and questions that require an all-India perspective. Overall, however, the state structures have a great deal of autonomy.
2. For an account of early agrarian conditions in Malabar and the emergence of resistance see K.N. Panikkar (1992).
3. Coir is the husk of the coconut used to make rugs and mats. Toddy is the sap of the coconut distilled to make a mildly alcoholic drink.
4. Before 1956 Kerala was divided into three regions. Travancore and Cochin were under princely state rule; Malabar was part of the Madras presidency under British colonial rule. After Independence, Nehru's government initially shied away from tackling the edifice of princely rule. Under severe pressure from the Communist Party (and others) the national government eventually dissolved princely states and incorporated the former princely regions into India (CPI, 1956b: 684–86). The Communist Party led the Unite Kerala campaign, which united the three regions of Kerala into one state based on the common Malayalam language.
5. The uprisings were named after the two villages, Punnapra and Vayalar, where they took place and are the first urban working-class uprisings in Indian history (Heller, 1999: 173).
6. Kerala is unique in India for its religious diversity: Hindus make up slightly less than 60 percent of the population, while Muslims and Christians each claim approximately 20 percent of the population. Despite its religious diversity, Kerala has seen relatively little communal violence with three major world religions living peacefully together for centuries.
7. The CPI was pro-Moscow, while the CPI(M) took an independent international approach and maintained fraternal relations with both the CPSU and CPC, but did not ally with either.
8. These cleavages were explicitly laid out by E.M.S. Namboodiripad in "Draft Resolution on the Party Programme and the Current Political Situation in the Country" (April 1961).
9. Interview with Jayendra, June 7, 2002.
10. Interview with Vinold, April 16, 2002.
11. While in government, the CPI(M) also reconstituted the District Development Councils and set up a state planning board as well as initiated a Civil Supplies Popular Committee to procure and distribute food (Nossiter, 1982: 248).

12. They began with silent picketing in front of houses of guilty landlords and then moved to the direct occupation of land (Herring, 1983: 203).

13. Interview with Ravi, April 19, 2002.

14. Interview with Vinod, April 16, 2002.

15. The 1974 Act provided agricultural laborers security of employment, fixation of wages and hours, creation of a welfare fund, a pension scheme, and the establishment of machinery for settling disputes.

16. In 1991 Kerala child labor was less than 0.6 percent compared to the national average of 5.4 percent (GOI, 2002).

17. For example, in the recent growth from 717,645 in 1998 to 796,073 in 2001 West Bengal and Kerala accounted for 68.91 percent of the growth (CPI(M), 2002b: 32).

18. Kerala has the highest percentage among all the states of working-class members. The other leading state, West Bengal, has only 51.6 percent from working-class, poor peasant, and agricultural laborer sectors.

19. To be elected a delegate to a National Congress is an indication of leadership. This comparison is complicated by the fact that the numbers for delegates to the Congress are from the all-India party. The data are not disaggregated by state. Given the high percentage of working-class members in Kerala it is quite likely that a large percentage of the 218 working-class delegates were from Kerala.

20. By late 2002, the membership grew to approximately 360,000.

21. This ratio was derived by dividing the population (32 million) by 301,562 members. Taking the 2002 membership number of 360,000 there is approximately one party member for every 88 people.

22. Members elected to government positions (e.g., parliament, legislative assembly, etc.) give their salaries to the party and the party in turn provides a salary to the member.

23. The 17-member Polit Bureau is constituted from the central committee members. From the Polit Bureau a seven-member secretariat is formed. The number of the Central Committee and Polit Bureau members increase as the party grows. For example, at the 16th Congress in 1998, 66 members were elected to the Central Committee while by 2002 it grew to 79 members (CPI(M), 2002b: 42).

24. The party collected Rupees 42,768,439. for the Academy. Most of the funds were collected by door-to-door canvassing. The Academy is on 36 acres of land near Thiruvananthapuram, the state capital.

25. The director of the EMS Academy is T.M. Thomas Isaac, one of the party's leading intellectuals and activists. Isaac has been instrumental in the shift to counter-hegemonic generative politics of the 1990s.

26. Interview with Savathree, January 15, 2002.

27. In 1942 the party started a weekly newspaper, *Deshabhimani*. By 1945 it was being published daily and has never ceased publication.

28. Interview with Ayob, April 19, 2002.

29. Both the *People's Democracy* and *The Marxist* are national publications.

30. Interview with Sita, April 20, 2002.

31. Interview with Sharmila, March 12, 2002.

32. The original name of the party was the Communist Party of South Africa. In 1950 the CPSA was dissolved in response to the apartheid regime's Suppression of Communism Act. In 1953 the South African Communist Party (SACP) was reconstituted clandestinely.

33. In 1922, white workers went on strike in response to efforts by employers to replace white workers with cheaper black skilled workers. Prime Minister Smuts responded with the strong arm of the state; it took the defense force a week to quell the violence in which hundreds died. The event is popularly called the Rand Revolt (Moodie, 1975).

34. Party leader S.P. Bunting was expelled. Years later (long after Bunting had died) the SACP overturned his and many other expulsions in an effort to rehabilitate the party.

35. For example, Gana Makabeni of the African Clothing Workers Union and T.W. Thibedi of the Native Laundry Workers were expelled (Kiloh and Sibeko, 2000: xxxiii).

36. Kiloh and Sibeko estimate the numbers to have dropped from 4,000 to 851 members (Kiloh and Sibeko, 2000: xxxiv). Most estimates, however, are between 150 and 300.

37. Vanguard Booksellers was founded by party members (Julius and Tilly First and Fanny Klenerman), but when Klenerman later broke from the party she retained control of the bookshop (Bernstein, 1999: 118).

38. People's Bookshop was owned by the Communist Party (registered in the name of the Central Committee). When the Suppression of Communism Act came in 1950 the bookshop was disposed of in order to keep it out of the Liquidator's hand. Due to confusion within the party, the stock of Marxist and Left books stored in a storage garage was eventually destroyed (Bernstein, 1999: 119–20).

39. The Central Committee decided to dissolve the party formally on the last day of the parliamentary debate on the Act. Member of Parliament and CPSA member Sam Kahn announced to Parliament the dissolution of the Communist Party of South Africa moments before the Act became law (Bernstein, 1999: 125).

40. The formation of the new party emerged out of an ad hoc committee elected to draft a reply to the government Liquidator's formal notice of an official list of "communists." Party members collectively decided to draft a joint reply repudiating the Act. The committee consisted of Moses Kotane, Yusaf Dadoo, Michael Harmel, Bram Fischer, Vernon Berrange, and Rusty Bernstein (Bernstein, 1999: 127). Shortly after the letter was sent, the committee organized a clandestine conference in which a new leadership was elected and basic principles of organization (e.g., code of silence about the party's existence) were settled. Moses Kotane and Yusaf Dadoo were elected unanimously to secretary and chair, respectively (Bernstein, 1999: 131).

41. A number of communists were integrally involved in drafting the Freedom Charter. For example, party activist and intellectual Rusty Bernstein played a crucial role in collating and synthesizing the aspirations expressed in the thousands of written comments collected from subaltern classes (Bernstein, 1999: 154–55).

42. On March 21, 1960, the Sharpville township police opened fire on a peaceful demonstration killing 69 protestors (shooting many in the back as they were running away). The massacre triggered cycles of protest and repression around the country, ultimately leading to the banning of the ANC and Pan Africanist Congress.

43. The Rivonia Trial sent Nelson Mandela, Walter Sisulu, and many other leaders to prison.

44. At various times the movement had training camps in Tanzania, Angola, Zambia, and Mozambique. People were also sent to the Soviet Union and Eastern Europe for training.

45. The growth in the union movement reflected the growth in the manufacturing industry and the corresponding increase in the African working class. Between 1960 and 1980 Africans in manufacturing work increased from 308,332 to 780,904 (Kiloh and Sibeko, 2000: 68).

46. The confrontations of the 1970s led the state to adopt political (e.g., Tricameral parliament) and labor (e.g., Wiehan) reforms in the early 1980s. The Tricameral parliament attempted to co-opt the Indian and Colored communities by giving them their own parliament, which operated alongside the white parliament. Africans were given a limited form of local government with the Black Local Authorities and independence to the Bantustans.

47. The two major groups in the union movement were the community-based trade unions (which were active in community struggles and close to SACTU, the SACP, and ANC) and the progressive unions that stayed clear of political affiliation such as FOSATU (Kiloh and Sibeko, 2000: 83).

48. In 1985 the SACP deliberated on the ANC's talks with members of the South African ruling elite and began discussing the possibility of a negotiated settlement.

49. The exact number of members during exile is uncertain due to clandestine conditions. For my purposes, the exact numbers are not important. Rather what is important is the dramatic increase in membership.

50. It should be noted, however, that while most people joined the SACP after 1990 the majority of these new members had been active in the liberation struggle, but were not officially in the SACP.

51. Interview with Petros, October 5, 2001.

52. Chris Hani was tragically murdered by right-wing extremists outside his home in Johannesburg. Hani rivaled Nelson Mandela in popularity (he received the second most votes after Mandela at the ANC's national conference) and many saw him as a potential future leader of the country.

53. Joe Slovo died of cancer.

54. For example, Chris Hani served on the ANC National Executive Committee since 1974 and Joe Slovo worked with the ANC since the 1950s. Before 1969 the ANC had a policy to not allow whites to join the ANC. This was changed at the Morogoro Conference when whites were allowed to join the ANC, but not allowed to serve in the top leadership. At the 1985 Kabwe Conference, the ANC amended this policy as well.

55. Membership is open to all South Africans who accept the Program and policies of the Party, "undertake to carry out its decisions and to be active in an SACP structure," and pay dues (SACP Constitution, 1999). At the 2002 Congress there was a proposed amendment to the Constitution reintroducing a 6- to 12-month probation period for all new members. The amendment was not implemented, but the fact that it was raised for the first time indicates concern with open membership.

56. There are a number of signed-up members in the SACP who are in arrears and, therefore, are not included in the membership tally. For example, in May 2003 in Gauteng province there were 1,507 paid-up members, but 7,502 signed-up members.

57. The total number of voting delegates was 899: 32 Central Committee members, 76 Provincial Executive Committee members, 40 District Secretaries, and 750 branch delegates (SACP, 2002a: 11).

58. This number was calculated by taking the population (44 million) divided by the 2003 membership number of 25,998.

59. These numbers were for 2003. The party's Constitution specifically states that either the provincial secretary or deputy secretary shall be a full-time paid employee of the party (SACP Constitution, 1999, section 14.4).

60. It should be noted that highly paid leadership is not unique to the SACP, but rather is the trend in the labor movement and political structures in general. It would seem that leaders are demanding salaries they could command in other lines of work. For example, the general secretary earns equivalent to a highly paid member of parliament.

61. There are 25 elected central committee members and five elected office bearers (General Secretary, Chairperson, Deputy Secretary, Deputy Chairperson, and Treasurer). In addition to the 30 members, there are five co-opted members to the central committee. All provincial secretaries and chairpersons are ex-officio members of the central committee. The central committee includes one-third women.

62. The Polit Bureau's equivalent in Kerala is the state secretariat, which meets daily and the state committee (i.e., the state-level central committee) meets fortnightly.

63. The provincial executive committee consists of 15 members in addition to the 5 elected office bearers. It meets at least once every two months, while the provincial working committee meets weekly or fortnightly.

64. In addition to the five office bearers a district executive committee consists of a minimum of four and maximum of seven elected members.

65. *Umsebenzi online* is a forum for the general secretary to communicate.

66. I was unable to find details about circulation and readership for any of the publications.

67. In 2003 the SACP launched its Youth League.

68. COSATU claims a membership from its affiliates of approximately 1.2 million while the ANC's membership hovers at 600,000 (though many are inactive).

69. Both CNETU (in the 1940s) and SACTU (1955 through 1990) were both more interdependent with the party.

Chapter 6   Organizational Faultlines

1. This was Lenin's view of the party outlined in *What Is to Be Done?* (1902). In Lenin's later writings on trade unions he refined his view and gave more weight to the importance of spontaneous consciousness of the masses.

2. In recent years there has been two other factions—in the traditional sense of the world—in the Kerala party, linked to two leaders' power struggles.

3. Interview with Gupta, June 10, 2002.

4. The large-scale migration of educated Malayalis (especially nurses) to the Gulf States, Bombay, Delhi, and the United States alleviated the chronic unemployment and helped cushion the state from the effects of low economic growth. By 1987 over 682,000 Malayalis had migrated (Franke and Chasin, 1994: 69).

5. The growth in labor productivity has been higher for Kerala than the rest of India (Khera, 1991; Arun, 1992). Heller explains that "between 1976 and 1987, labor productivity growth in Kerala increased annually by 6.9 percent, compared to 3.9 percent for India" (Heller, 1999: 211).

6. For example, by the mid-1990s a few key leaders in the State Secretariat (the state-level equivalent to the Polit Bureau) were won over and supported the grassroots faction's initiatives.

7. Interview with Arjuna, March 25, 2002.

8. This information is from interviews with KSSP members in Thiruvananthapuram, Trichur, Alleppey, and Kannur in 2002. I also discussed these issues with the director and deputy director of the Integrated Rural Technology Center (IRTC), Palghat, June 2000.

9. While the KSSP is organizationally autonomous there is a great deal of overlap in membership with the CPI(M) at every level of both organizations. One KSSP leader and long-time party member explained to me that there has been a great deal of allure around the party in the past and most KSSP members wanted to join the party (though this sentiment has tapered off in recent years) (Interview with Arjuna, April 24, 2002). Ideologically they also share a great deal as the KSSP describes itself as a combination of Marxian and Gandhian ideas (though its vision of local development is more participatory and radical than Gandhi's and its Marxism is grounded in an appreciation of the resource-limited environment).

10. Visit to IRTC, June 2000.

11. The expulsions were politically motivated. Party members are supposed to inform the party if they are involved in any projects that accept overseas funding. KSSP and another research institution received project funding from Danish and Swiss governments, and this was used to expel a few grassroots faction leaders. There was no charge of misuse of funds or corruption, just failure to inform the party of foreign donor funding. The irony in one of the cases is the party member was deployed by the party to run the organization, which later led to his expulsion.

12. It is estimated that the units grew "from 241 in 40 units in November 1986 to 267 in 45 units in November 1987. By the time of the 7th Congress, in April 1989, the party boasted of 340 members distributed in 48 units that were located in eight regions: London, Lusaka, Angola, Swaziland, Mozambique, Dar es Salaam, Zimbabwe and Botswana" (Maloka, 2002: 56). Maloka estimates the party in exile at 494 in 1989. These numbers are significantly lower than the 2000 to 3000 members often cited. Conditions of clandestinity make it difficult to determine actual numbers. Maloka estimates the underground numbers at 99 members in 35 units (Maloka, 2002: 57).

13. In exile, a dissident group questioning the relation between the party and the ANC were expelled from the ANC (with the party's support), and is recorded in the annals of history as the "Gang of Eight" (Shubin, 1999: 135).

14. Interview with Lucas, July 18, 2001; Interview with Mark, September 11, 2001.

15. Both trade union and statist factions see development occurring through industrialization. For example, in its 1995 *Strategy and Tactics* document the party argued that economic development would come through "massive inward industrialization based on urban and rural infrastructural development" (SACP, 1995: 6).

16. While Tambo was not a party member, he was sympathetic to and closely allied with the party and had deep personal relations with many party leaders.

17. An activist I spoke to described the original relationship as the ANC governing, the SACP the brains, and COSATU the muscle.

18. While the federation had its ambivalences, the majority of trade union workers supported the ANC-led Alliance. A 1991 survey found 94 percent COSATU shopstewards intended to vote for the ANC and only 3 percent would vote SACP (Pityana and Orkin, 1992: 1–2, 58–59). Another survey in April 1994 found that 81 percent COSATU union members supported the Alliance (Ginsburg and Webster, 1995: 85; Levy, 1995: 50; Torres, 1995: 78).

19. Both allies, however, were problematic. The ANC was increasingly moving toward a pro-capitalist orientation, especially in terms of its macroeconomic policy. As a working-class organization COSATU's primary preoccupation is with working-class demands and corporatist bargaining structures. Thus, ideologically the SACP was at variance with both its Alliance partners.

20. The relation between the two was confirmed in 1990 with the decision to dissolve SACTU (the exiled union federation that formed in 1955 in close alliance with the SACP) and transfer assets to COSATU.

Chapter 7   Party and Class under Electoral Politics

1. I am not arguing that electoral systems have definitive effects on political parties. For example, while I claim that low contestation reduces leverage of subaltern classes it does not follow that this inevitably leads a party away from representing the interest of subaltern classes. The CPI(M) in West Bengal is an example of a dominant political party in an electoral system with low contestation that continues to represent the interest of subalterns.

2. While I am making an argument about the interconnection between competitive electoral fields and responsiveness to the base, I am not arguing that this is always the case. I can imagine a situation in which a competitive electoral field does not enhance subaltern leverage (such as the United States where the working class is weak and does not have significant leverage in the electoral field).

3. Interview with Ved, January 29, 2002.

4. Crore is a numerical term used in India; one crore equals 10 million.

5. Remittances from overseas Keralites in the late 1990s played an important role in the economy with some estimates at 13 percent of the domestic income (see Prakash, 1999a).

6. The average annual growth rate was 3.48 percent, which compares unfavorably against the national average annual growth rate of over 6 percent since the 1980s (World Bank, 2004).

7. Approximately 10 percent of Kerala's workforce (1.8 million people in 2004) is abroad, which is roughly the same percentage of the organized sector in Kerala (Harilal, 2005: 100–01).

8. Interview with Ashok, June 16, 2002.

9. Interview with Meera, January 14, 2002.

10. A 1996 survey of 16 states found "that 45 percent of Keralites think elected officials care what ordinary people think, 41 percent think elections make a difference in government actions, 54 percent trust state government, 58 trust local government, and 20 percent express 'a great deal of interest' in politics" (Isaac and Franke, 2001: 37).

11. Interview with Vishnu, January 7, 2002.

12. Before 1980 the CPI(M) joined coalitions based on an anti-Congress coalition, which brought it into coalition arrangements with conservative parties, some even more conservative than Congress. This was in contrast to the CPI(M) in West Bengal, which formed a strictly United *Left* Front of Marxist parties (Left Front presumes a measure of like-mindedness whereas a united front does not presume any like-mindedness (Nossiter, 1988: 87)). After 1980, the CPI(M) shifted its approach and since that time has only joined coalitions with progressive parties.

13. This has become so much a part of the political culture that many people say it is the nature of politics in Kerala. Many Malayalis on both sides of the political fence see the fluctuation between Fronts as a source of pride and feel that it kept the parties in check.

14. South African political parties electorally compete through a system of proportional representation in which lists of candidates are presented to the electorate. The national assembly has 400 seats and the 9 provinces are allocated seats according to the share of the population.

15. In the three post-apartheid national elections (1994, 1999, and 2004), the ANC's electoral support has grown from 62.65 percent (252 seats) in 1994 to 66.35 percent (266 seats) in 1999 and still further to 69.68 percent (279 seats) in 2004 (Independent Electoral Commission, 2004 quoted in Southall and Daniel, 2005: 38.). While the ANC won majority in 2004, disaggregating the numbers shows that only 57 percent (15,833,554) of all estimated eligible voters (27,438,897) cast ballots (6.76 million did not register and 5.06 million registered but did not vote). Thus, 70 percent of votes cast translate into only 40 percent of the entire eligible voting population (Southall and Daniel, 2005: 40). Nevertheless, for the foreseeable future there is not a viable opposition party that could seriously challenge the ANC's electoral dominance.

16. Between 1985 and 1993 the net *outflow* of capital averaged 2.3 percent of GDP; this turned around between 1994 and 1996, which saw net *inflow* of capital average 2.6 percent of GDP (Marais, 2001: 109).

17. The manufacturing sector was bedridden with low local demand and a failure to penetrate export markets. Between 1960 and 1988 manufactured products' share of total exports fell from 31 percent to 12 percent and growth in manufacturing output dropped from 9.9 percent to –1.2 percent (Macro-Economic Research Group, 1993: 241, table 7.4; Marais, 2001: 103; Black, 1991). Manufacturing accounted for 23.4 percent of GDP in 1983, 21 percent in 1993, and 19.4 percent in 2002 (World Bank, 2004a).

18. In 1991 the mining sector accounted for 65.6 percent of export earnings, yet shed 30 percent of its workforce between 1987 and 1995 with employment declining from 753,460 to 512,722. Employment levels in gold and coal (the two largest sectors) fell by 35 percent and 47 percent, respectively, while platinum increased by 7 percent (Mineral Bureau figures cited in ILO, 1996: 277 quoted in Marais, 2001: 103–04)

19. Three major financial institutions actively sought to influence the debate through scenario planning projects. Thus, under the leadership of Clem Sunter (Anglo-American), Bob Tucker (Nedcor/Old Mutual), and Lawrence Schlemmer (Sanlam) the policy debate was subtly directed to suit capital's interests.

20. In 1993 Nedcor and Old Mutual published *Prospects for Successful Transition* in which "a black/white coalition government [...] would achieve considerable redistribution through high and sustained growth in a market-oriented economy, and which would respect the macrobalances so essential to sound economic growth" (cited in Bond, 2000: 59).

21. Alec Erwin became the Minister of Trade and Industry.

22. The six members were: Provincial and Local Government Minister Sydney Mufamadi, Public Enterprises Minister Jeff Radebe, Public Services and Administration Minister Geraldine Fraser-Moleketi, Defence Minister Charles Nqakula, Water Affairs and Forestry Minister Ronnie Kasrils, and the Minister without Portfolio in the Office of the Presidency Essop Pahad. The three not to be reelected to the Central Committee were Jeff Radebe, Geraldine Fraser-Moleketi, and Essop Pahad.

23. One of the effects of the nature of the Alliances is that it has made political positions (appointed and elected members of parliament, ministers, etc.) accountable to only the ANC. Positions are not SACP positions, but rather are given to individuals who are SACP members. This has further emasculated the SACP and diminished its ability to push its perspectives through state channels.

24. Interview with Ram, October 16, 2001.

25. Why the SACP did not think about the long-term implications of these decisions seems curious, especially given the efforts by certain members of COSATU to form a Workers' Party with the SACP.

26. For example, the SACP provided the ANC direct links with the Soviet Union where activists were trained and from whom a great deal of financial and military support was given during exile.

27. The ANC Political-Military Strategy Commission's *Green Book* states the ANC's long-term commitment to a socialist South Africa (1979).

28. Interview with Judith, September 29, 2001.

29. Interview with Nzipo, January 3, 2004.

30. At the SACP's 10th Congress in 1998 both Nelson Mandela and Thabo Mbeki scolded the SACP for its confrontational stand toward GEAR. This public and harsh admonishment by the top two leaders of the ANC signaled a new low point in the relationship between the SACP and ANC.

31. Interview with Frank, September 5, 2001.

Methodological Appendix

1. While I took Malayalam language classes, I only became proficient enough to buy vegetables from the local produce stand. I, therefore, hired a research assistant to accompany
   me into the field. My research assistant turned out to be a wonderful compliment as her
   disarmingly charming personality warmed many skeptics to us. I also took Zulu tutorials
   at UC Berkeley, and while Zulu is easier to learn than Malayalam, here too, my communication abilities were very rudimentary. The majority of South Africans, however, speak
   English fluently, which is especially true of members of the Communist Party. For the
   most part, English is the language of most communication in both parties.
2. The Congress Party is the other main party in Kerala.
3. In describing the impact of his *Principia Mathematica* (1687) Sir Isaac Newton wrote "If I
   have seen further it is by standing on the shoulders of Giants." I have borrowed the phrase
   in order to convey the sentiment that my study has been made possible by the hard work
   and indefatigable commitments of many (past and present) activists and thinkers who
   continue to struggle to create a more just and equitable world.

Selected Bibliography

Primary Sources

Kerala Primary Documents

CPI. 1953. "Programme of the Communist Party of India." In *Documents of the Communist Movement of India (DCMI)*, vol. VII (1952–1956). Calcutta: National Book Agency Private Limited: 283–300.

———. 1956a. "Resolution and Report on the 20th Party Congress of the CPSU." In *DCMI*, vol. VII (1952–1956): 658–83.

———. 1956b. "Report to the Fourth Party Congress." In *DCMI*, vol. VII (1952–1956): 539–655.

———. 1964a. "Programme of the Communist Party of India." In *DCMI*, vol. XB (1964 Part II): 11–76.

———. 1964b. "Fight against Revisionism Political-Organizational Report." In *DCMI*, vol. XB (1964 Part II): 77–179.

———. 1964c. "On the Tasks of the Party in the Present Situation." In *DCMI*, vol. XB (1964 Part II): 180–89.

———. 1964d. "Address of Welcome to Delegates of Seventh Congress of Communist Party of India." In *DCMI*, vol. XB (1964 Part II).

———. 1964e. "Resolution on the Kerala Election." In *DCMI*, vol. XB (1964 Part II): 231–34.

———. 1967. "The New Situation and the New Tactics." Central Committee Resolution.

———. 1968. "Constitution of the CPI(M)."

———. 1978. "Salkia Plenum Report: Report on Organization," December 27–31, 1978. In *DCMI*, vol. XVIII (1978–1979): 295–355.

———. 1981. "Central Committee Resolution on Kerala." In *DCMI*, vol. XIX (1980–1981): 385–89.

———. 1989. "Political Resolution." Adopted by 13th Congress, Trivandrum, December 27, 1988–January 1, 1989. In *DCMI*, vol. XXII (1987–1988): 509–81.

———. 1989a. "Political-Organizational Report." Adopted by 13th Congress, Trivandrum, December 27, 1988–January 1, 1989. In *DCMI*, vol. XXII (1987–1988): 582–699.

———. 1990. "On Certain Political-Ideological Issues Related to Developments in Some Socialist Countries." Central Committee Resolution, May 28–31.

———. 1992. "Resolution on Certain Ideological Issues." Congress Resolution, Madras, January 3–9, 1992. In *DCMI*, vol. XXIV (1992–1993): 112–50.

CPI. 1992a. "Political Review Report." Congress Resolution, Chennai, January 3–9, 1992. In *DCMI*, vol. XXIV (1992–1993): 64–111.

———. 1992b. "Report on Organization and Tasks." Congress Resolution, Madras, January 3–9, 1992. In *DCMI*, vol. XXIV (1992–1993): 151–213.

———. 1992c. "Political Report." Adopted by Central Committee, March 19–22, 1992. In *DCMI*, vol. XXIV (1992–1993): 316–48.

———. 1992d. "Current Crisis and our Tasks." Adopted by Central Committee, December 23–24, 1992. In *DCMI*, vol. XXIV (1992–1993): 527–38.

———. 1994a. "Note on Political Developments." Adopted by Central Committee, April 12–15, 1994. In *DCMI*, vol. XXV (1994–1996): 50–65.

———. 1995. "Political Resolution." Adopted by 15th Congress, Chandigarh, April 3–8, 1995. In *DCMI*, vol. XXV (1994–1996): 235–96.

———. 1995a. "Political-Organizational Report." Adopted by 15th Congress, Chandigarh, April 3–8, 1995. In *DCMI*, vol. XXV (1994–1996): 297–439.

———. 1995b. "Report on 15th Kerala State Congress," February.

———. 1998. *Documents of the Communist Movement in India (DCMI)*, vol. I–XXVI (1921–1998). Delhi: National Book Agency.

———. 1998a. "Political Resolution." Adopted by the 16th Congress, Calcutta, October 5–11, 1998. In *DCMI*, vol. XXVI (1997–1998): 371–422.

———. 1998b. "Political-Organizational Report." Adopted by 16th Congress, Calcutta, October 5–11, 1998. In *DCMI*, vol. XXVI (1997–1998): 423–603.

———. 2001. "Review of the May 2001 Assembly Elections." Adopted by the Central Committee, August 11–12, 2001.

———. 2002a. "Report on Organization." Congress Report, 17th Congress, Hyderabad, March 19–24.

———. 2002b. "Political-Organizational Report." Congress Report, 17th Congress, Hyderabad, March 19–24.

———. 2002c. "Report of the Credentials Committee." Congress Report, 17th Congress, Hyderabad, March 19–24.

Government of India (GOI). 1991. Census of India, *Kerala: Workers and Their Distribution*.

———. 2002. *State Profiles*.

Government of Kerala (GOK). *Handbook on Co-operative Movement in Kerala*. Registrar of Co-operative Societies. (Annual).

———. 1973. *Report of the Study Group on Mechanization in Coir Industry in Kerala*. State Planning Board.

———. 1989a. *Eighth Five Year Plan: Report on the Task Force on Agricultural Employment*. State Planning Board.

———. 1991b. *Report of the Task Force for the Review of Implementation of Plan Schemes under the Industries Sector*. State Planning Board.

———. 1993. *Statistics for Planning*. Department of Economics and Statistics.

———. 1994. *Economic Review*. Planning and Economic Affairs Department.

———. 1996. *Ninth Five Year Plan (1997–2002)*; *Task Force on Modern Small Scale Industries*. State Planning Board.

———. 1996a. *Economic Review*. Planning and Economic Affairs Department.

———. 1996b. *Social Security Initiatives in Kerala: Report of the Expert Committee*. State Planning Board.

———. 1998a. *Economic Review 1997*. Planning and Economic Affairs Department.

———. 2000. *Economic Review*. Planning and Economic Affairs Department.

———. 2003. *State of the Economy*.

———. 2004. *Economic Review*. Planning and Economic Affairs Department. www.kerala.gov.in/dept_planning/ecnomicrvw_04.htm.

———. 2004a. *Industrial Policy 2003*. Department of Industries. www.keralaindustry.org/indpolicy.htm.

Kalliasseri Panchayat. 1995. *Kalliasseri Report*.

South Africa Primary Documents

ANC. 1955. *The Freedom Charter*.

———. 1969. "Morogoro Consultative Conference Documents."

———. 1997 [1979]. *Green Book*. Politico-Military Strategy Commission Report. In *From Protest to Challenge: Nadir and Resurgence, 1964–1979*, ed. Karis and Gerhardt. Vol. 5. Bloomington: Indiana University Press.

ANC and SACP. 1986. "Ungovernability and People's Power." Political Commission Discussion Document. Mayibuye Center for Historical Papers: ANC and SACP Archive; July 2.

ANC. 1992. "Negotiations: A Strategic Perspective." Adopted by the NEC, November 25.

———. 1994. *Reconstruction and Development Programme*. Johannesburg: Umanyano Publications.

Alliance. 1993a. "Strategic Objectives of the National Liberation Struggle." Alliance Discussion Paper. *The African Communist*, 133/2.

COSATU. 1996. "Discussion Document." Johannesburg: COSATU.

Department of Finance. 1996. *Growth Employment and Redistribution Strategy*. Pretoria: Department of Finance.

Financial Sector Campaign Coalition. 2003. "Draft Annual Report of the Financial Sector Campaign Coalition: From 21 August 2002 to 30 June 2003."

Macro-Economic Research Group (MERG). 1993. *Making Democracy Work*. Oxford and Cape Town: Center for Development Studies.

Parliament of South Africa. 1994. National Economic, Development and Labour Council Act 35 of 1994.

SACP Program. 1963 [1962]. *The Road to South African Freedom: Program of the SACP*. *The African Communist*, 1: 24–70.

SACP. 1970. "Augmented Meeting of the Central Committee." Inner-Party Bulletin, No. 1, July, 1970. UCT Simons Collection: BC1081, file 018.11.

———. 1972. "Report on Organization." William Cullen Archives: K-G, A2675, File III, Folder 695.

———. 1984. "Party Organization." UCT Simons Collection: BC1081, file 014.5; November.

———. 1985. "Report of the Industrial Sub-Committee to the CC." UCT Simons Collection: BC1081, file 014.5; November.

———. 1985a. "The South African Communist Party Holds Its Congress." *The African Communist*, 101/2.

———. 1986a. "65 Years in the Frontline of Struggle." Mayibuye Center for Historical Papers: ANC and SACP Archive.

———. 1987. "On the Trade Union Movement in South Africa: Its Role in the Struggle for National Democracy and Socialism." Mayibuye Center for Historical Papers: ANC and SACP Archive.

———. 1989a. *The Path to Power: Program of the SACP* .*The African Communist*, 118/3.

———. 1989b. "Capitalism vs. Socialism." SACP Editorial. *The African Communist*, 119/4.

SACP. 1990. "Advance and Avoid the Traps!" Central Committee Statement. *The African Communist*, 120/1.

———. 1990a. "The Class Struggle Is Alive and Kicking." SACP Editorial. *The African Communist*, 120/1.

———. 1990b. "Editorial." *The African Communist*, 122/3.

———. 1990c. "Internal Party Bulletin." UCT Simons Collection: BC1081, file 018.11; February.

———. 1990d. "An Economic Policy Framework." UCT Simons Collection: BC1081, file 07.6; March 27.

———. 1990e. "Party Briefing Document." UCT Simons Collection: BC1081, file 012; November.

———. 1990f. "Public Launch of the Legal SACP." Central Committee Report. UCT Simons Collection: BC1081, files 08.2.

———. 1991a. "Political Report," 8th Congress of SACP; December.

———. 1991b. "The Many Caps Debate." ILG Discussion Document. Manuscript in UCT Simons Collection: BC1081, file 07.5.

———. 1992. *Building Workers' Power for Democratic Change*, Manifesto of the SACP. Johannesburg: Umsebenzi Publications.

———. 1992a. "How to Take the Triple H Campaign: Discussion Document for Central Committee of the SACP."

———. 1992b. "Draft Document Presented at the SACP Consultative Conference; June 20."

———. 1992c. "Broad Negotiations Perspective." Polit Bureau Discussion Document.

———. 1993. "The Role of the SACP in the Transition to Democracy and Socialism." Central Committee Discussion Paper for SACP Strategy Conference, May 1993. *The African Communist*, 133/2.

———. 1993a. "SACP Triple-H Campaign: Proposals for Resuscitation."

———. 1994a. "Towards a Massive ANC Election Victory." SACP Editorial. *The African Communist*, 136/1.

———. 1994b. "The Present Political Situation." Central Committee Discussion Document. *The African Communist*, 137/2.

———. 1994c. "Defending and Deepening a Clear Left Strategic Perspective on the RDP." Prepared for the Socialist Conference on Reconstruction and Development, November 5–6, 1994. *The African Communist*, 138/3.

———. 1995. *Socialism Is the Future, Build It Now: Strategic Perspectives*. Strategy and Tactics adopted at 10th National Congress; April 6–8.

———. 1995a. "Consolidating Our Strategic Unity—the SACP's 9th Congress." SACP Editorial. *The African Communist*, 141/2.

———. 1996. "Challenging the Neo-Liberal Agenda in South Africa." Discussion Paper. UCT Simons Collection: BC1081, file 07.6.

———. 1997. "Economic Policy in the Alliance." *The African Communist*, 147/3.

———. 1998. *Build People's Power—Build Socialism Now!* Program of the SACP.

———. 1998a. "A Socialist Approach to the Consolidation and Deepening of the NDR." *The African Communist*, 149/2.

———. 1999. "Discussion Documents." SACP Strategy Conference, September 3–5.

———. 1999a. "Constitution."

———. 2002. *Program of Action*.

———. 2002a. "Program and Rules of the 11th Congress." Rustengberg; July 24–28.

———. 2002b. *Bua Komanisi*, 2/4, November.

———. 2002c. "Political Report to the 11th Congress." Rustengberg; July 24–28.

———. 2002d. "State of the Organization Report to the 11th Congress." Rustengberg; July 24–28.

———. 2003. *Bua Komanisi*, 3/1, July.

———. 2003a. *Bua Komanisi*, 3/3, September.

———. 2004b. *Program of Action*.

———. "Educating for Democracy and Socialism!" Undated manuscript.

———. "The Creation of Underground Units." Undated manuscript from early 1980s. UCT Simons Collection: BC1081, file 011.2.

———. "Combat Underground: Strategy and Tactics of Revolutionary Struggle for Seizure of Power." Undated manuscript from 1980s. Mayibuye Center for Historical Papers: ANC and SACP archive.

SACP and ANC. "Guidelines for the Expansion of Our Internal Organization." Undated manuscript from 1970s. Mayibuye Center for Historical Papers: ANC and SACP Archives.

———. 1986. "Speeches by Alfred Nzo (Secretary General of ANC) and Joe Slovo (chairman of SACP): SACP's 65th Anniversary." London, July 30.

SACP Gauteng Province. 2001. *Building a People's Economy*. Document Adopted by Guateng Provincial Congress, July. Johannesburg.

———. 2001a. *Relation between Theory and Practice*.

———. 2003. *Socialism and Local Economic Development*. Paper prepared for Conference on Socialism and Local Economic Development, July.

SACP Western Cape Region. 1993. "Information Package on Health, Hunger, and Housing." September.

———. 1997. "Engaging with GEAR: a contribution from the Western Cape SACP." Unpublished manuscript, February 1997; UCT Simons Collection: BC1081, file 09.1.

SANCO. 1994. "Making People-Driven Development Work," Report of the Commission on Development Finance. *The African Communist*, 137/2.

Statistics South Africa. 2001. *Census*.

Tripartite Alliance. 1993. *Reconstruction and Development Programme, Fourth Draft. The African Communist*, 3.

———. 1994. "Broad Strategic Tasks Facing the ANC after April 28." Discussion paper presented at the ANC National Conference on Reconstruction and Strategy, Johannesburg, January 21–23. *The African Communist*, 136/1.

———. 1995. "The Need for an Effective ANC-Led Political Center." *The African Communist*, 142/3.

———. 1997. "The Role of the State." Summit Document. *The African Communist*, 148/4.

———. 1997a. "Assessment of the Current Phase of Transformation." Summit Document. *African Communist*, 148/4.

———. 1997b. "Key policy intervention." Summit Document. *The African Communist*, 148/4.

Secondary Sources

Altman, Miriam. 2005. "The State of Employment." In *State of the Nation: South Africa 2004–2005*, ed. John Daniel, Roger Southall, and Jessica Lutchman. Cape Town: Human Sciences Research Council.

Amin, Samir. 1990 [1985]. *Delinking: Towards a Polycentric World*. London: Zed Books.

———. 1990a. "The Future of Socialism." In *The Future of Socialism: Perspectives from the Left*, ed. William K. Tabb. New York: Monthly Review Press.

Arendt, Hannah. 1951. "Totalitarianism" Part III. In *The Origins of Totalitarianism*. Hartcourt: Brace and Company.

———. 1985 [1963]. *On Revolution*. New York: Penguin Books.

Arun, T.G. 1992. "Growth and Structural Changes in the Manufacturing Industries in Kerala, 1976–1987." M.Phil, Dissertation. Center for Development Studies, Thiruvananthapuram.

Baiocchi, Gianpaolo. 2003. "Participation, Activism, and Politics: The Porto Alegre Experiment." In *Deepening Democracy: Institutional Innovations in Empowered Participatory Governance*, ed. Archon Fung and Erik Olin Wright. London and New York: Verso Press.

———. 2005. *Militants and Citizens: The Politics of Participatory Democracy in Porto Alegre*. Stanford: Stanford University Press.

Barrell, Howard. 1990. *MK: The ANC's Armed Struggle*. Johannesburg: Penguin Books.

Baskin, Jeremy. 1991. *Striking Back: A History of COSATU*. Johannesburg: Ravan Press.

———. 1996. *Against the Current: Labour and Economic Policy in South Africa*. Johannesburg: Ravan Press.

———. 2000. "Public Service Bargaining: An Assessment of the Three-Year Wage Agreement." In *Public Service Labour Relations in a Democratic South Africa*, ed. Glenn Adler. Johannesburg: Witwatersrand University Press.

Basu, Jyoti. 1998. "Introductory Note." In *Documents of the Communist Party of India*, vol. XIV (1970). Calcutta: National Book Agency Private Limited.

Bernstein, Hilda. 1994. *The Rift: The Exile Experience of South Africans*. London: Jonathan Cape.

Bernstein, Rusty. 1999. *Memory against Forgetting: Memoirs from a Life in South African Politics, 1938–1964*. London and New York: Viking Penguin Books.

Black, A. 1991. "Manufacturing Development and the Economic Crisis: A Reversion to Primary Production?" In *South Africa's Economic Crisis*, ed. Stephen Gelb. Cape Town and London: David Philip and Zed Books.

Blackburn, Robin. 1991. "Fin de Siècle: Socialism after the Crash." In *After the Fall: The Failure of Communism and the Future of Socialism,* ed. Robin Blackburn. London: Verso Press.

Block, Fred. 1980. "Eurocommunism and the Stalemate of European Communism." In *The Politics of Eurocommunism: Socialism in Transition*, ed. Carl Boggs and David Plotke. Boston, MA: South End Press.

Boggs, Carl and David Plotke, ed. 1980. *The Politics of Eurocommunism: Socialism in Transition*. Boston, MA: South End Press.

Bond, Patrick. 2000. *Elite Transition: From Apartheid to Neoliberalism in South Africa*. London and Pietermartizburg: Pluto Press and University of Natal Press.

Bonner, Philip. 1983. "The Transvaal Native Congress 1917–1920: The Radicalisation of the Black Petty Bourgeoisie on the Rand." In *Industrialization and Social Change in South Africa: African Class Formation, Culture, and Consciousness 1870–1930*, ed. Shula Marks and Richard Rathbone. London and New York.

Bose, Ashish. 1991. *Population of India: 1991 Census Results and Methodology*. New Delhi: B.R. Publishing Co.

Braam, Conny. 2004. *Operation Vula*. Johannesburg: Jacana Books.

Brooks, Alan. 1967. *From Class Struggle to National Liberation: The Communist Party in South Africa, 1940 to 1950*. Dissertation, University of Sussex.

Bruce, Iain. 2004. *The Porto Alegre Alternative: Direct Democracy in Action*. London: Pluto Press.

Bundy, Colin. 1988 [1979]. *The Rise and Fall of the South African Peasantry*. London: James Currey.

————. 1991. *The History of South African Communist Party*. Cape Town: University of Cape Town Press.

Bunting, Brian. 1971. "South Africa's 'Outward' Policy." William Cullen Archives, K-G, A2675, III, 695; July.

Burawoy, Michael. 2003. "For a Sociological Marxism: The Complementary Convergence of Antonio Gramsci and Karl Polanyi." *Politics and Society*, 31/1 (March): 1–69.

Carrim, Yunus. 2001. "From Transition to Transformation: Challenges of the New Local Government System." *The African Communist*, 156/1.

Carrim, Yunus and Ncumisa Kondlo. 1999. "Public-Private Partnerships: The Challenges for Local Government." *The African Communist*, 151/2.

Castells, Manuel. 1983. *The City and the Grassroots: A Cross-Cultural Theory of Urban Social Movements*. Berkeley: University of California Press.

————. 1989. *The Informational City: Information Technology, Economy Restructuring, and the Urban-Regional Process*. Oxford: Blackwell.

Chase-Dunn, Christopher. 1990. "Socialism and Capitalism on a World Scale." In *The Future of Socialism: Perspectives from the Left*, ed. William K. Tabb. New York: Monthly Review Press.

Chang, Ha-Joon. 2002. *Kicking Away the Ladder: Development Strategy in Historical Perspective*. London: Anthem Press.

————. 2004 [2003]. *Globalization, Economic Development and the Role of the State*. London: Zed Books.

Claudin, Fernando. 1975 [1970]. *The Communist Movement: From Comintern to Cominform, Vol. I and II*. New York: Monthly Review Press.

Clingman, Stephen. 1998. *Afrikaner Revolutionary: Bram Fischer*. Amherst: University of Michigan Press.

Cohen, Joshua and Joel Rogers. 1986 [1983]. *On Democracy: Toward a Transformation of American Society*. New York: Penguin Books.

————. 1995. *Associations and Democracy*. London: Verso.

Collier, Ruth Berins and David Collier. 1991. *Shaping the Political Arena*. New Jersey: Princeton University Press.

Courtois, Stephane, et al. 1999. *The Black Book of Communism: Crimes, Terror, Repression*. Cambridge, MA: Harvard University Press.

Cronin, Jeremy. 1990. "Building the Legal Mass Party." *South African Labour Bulletin*, 15/3.

————. 1992. "The Boat, the Tap, and the Leipzig Way: A Critique of Some Strategic Assumptions in Our Ranks." Draft paper for the Consultative Conference, June.

————. 1994. "Bolshevism and Socialist Transition." *The African Communist*, 136/1.

————. 1994a. "Sell-Out, or the Culminating Moment? Trying to Make Sense of the Transition." Paper presented to University of Witwatersrand History Workshop, Johannesburg, July.

————. 1995. "Challenging the Neo-Liberal Agenda in South Africa." *The African Communist*, 139/140/1.

————. 1995a. "The RDP Needs Class Struggle." *The African Communist*, 142/4.

Cunningham, Frank. 2002. *Theories of Democracy: A Critical Introduction*. London: Routledge.

Daniel, John, Adam Habib, and Roger Southall, eds. 2003. *State of the Nation: South Africa 2003–2004*. Cape Town: HSRC Press.

Daniel, John, Roger Southall, and Jessica Lutchman, eds. 2005. *State of the Nation: South Africa 2004–2005*. Cape Town: HSRC Press.

Das, Jayadeva D. 1983. *Working Class Politics in Kerala: A Study of Coir Workers*. Kariavattom: T.C. Lilly Grace.

Datt, Guarav and Martin Ravallion. 1996. "Why Have Some Indian States Done Better than Others at Reducing Poverty?" Policy Research working paper no.1594, World Bank, Washington, D.C.

Davies, Robert. 1988. "Nationalization, Socialization and the Freedom Charter." In *After Apartheid: Renewal of the South African Economy*, ed. J. Suckling and L. White. London: James Curry.

———. 1991. "Rethinking Socialist Economics for South Africa." *The African Communist*, 125/2.

———. 1997. "Engaging with the GEAR." SACP discussion document, March.

Davies, Robert, Dan O'Meara, and Sipho Dlamini. 1984. *The Struggle for South Africa: A Reference Guide to Movements, Organizations, and Institutions*, volume 1. London: Zed Books.

Delius, Peter. 1993. "Migrant Organization, the Communist Party, and the ANC and the Sekhukhuneland Revolt, 1940–1958." In *Apartheid's Genesis, 1935–1962*, ed. Phillip Bonner, Peter Delius, and Deborah Posel. Johannesburg: University of the Witwatersrand Press.

———. 1996. *A Lion amongst the Cattle*. Portsmouth, NH: Heinemann Press.

Desai, Manali. 1999. *Nationalism, Class Conflict, and Socialist Hegemony: Towards an Explanation of "Development Exceptionalism" in Kerala, India 1934–1941*. Ph.D. dissertation thesis submitted at UCLA.

De Sousa Santos, Boaventura. 2006. *The Rise of the Global Left: The World Social Forum and Beyond*. London: Zed Books.

———. 2007. "The World Social Forum and the Global Left." Draft paper presented at the *Politics and Society* mini-conference, New York, August 9.

Dexter, Philip. 1996. "Marxism and the National Question in a Democratic South Africa." *The African Communist*, 145/3.

Dreze, Jean and Amartya Sen. 2002. *India Development and Participation*. New Delhi: Oxford University Press.

Dubow, Saul. 2000. *The African National Congress*. Johannesburg: Jonathan Ball Publishers.

Duverger, Maurice. 1974. *Modern Democracies: Economic Power versus Political Power*. Illinois: Dryden Press.

Eidelberg, P.G. 2000. "The Tripartite Alliance on the Eve of a New Millennium: COSATU, the ANC, and the SACP." In *Trade Unions and Democratization in South Africa, 1985–1997*, ed. Glenn Adler and Eddie Webster. Johannesburg: University of Witwatersrand Press.

Escobar, Arturo. 1992. "Culture, Economics, and Politics in Latin American Social Movements Theory and Practice." In *The Making of Social Movements in Latin America: Identity, Strategy, and Democracy*, ed. Arturo Escobar and Sonia E. Alvarez. Colorado: Westview Press.

Esping-Anderson, Gustov. 1990. *The Three Worlds of Welfare Capitalism*. Princeton: Princeton University Press.

Erwin, Alec. 1989. "Thoughts on a Planned Economy." *Work in Progress*, 61 (September–October).

———. 1994. "The RDP: A View from the Tripartite Alliance." *South African Labour Bulletin*, 18/1 (January–February).

———. 1996. "Building the New South Africa's Economy." *The African Communist*, 145/3.

Evans, Peter. 1979. *Dependent Development: The Alliance of Multinational State and Local Capital in Brazil*. Princeton: Princeton University Press.

———. 1995. *Embedded Autonomy: States and Industrial Transformation*. Princeton: Princeton University Press.

———. 1997. "The Eclipse of the State? Reflections on Stateness in an Era of Globalization." *World Politics*, 50 (October): 62–87.

Everatt, David. 1991. "Alliance Politics of a Special Type: The Roots of the ANC/SACP Alliance, 1950–1954." *Journal of Southern African Studies*, 18/1 (March).

Eyal, Gill. 2002. "Eastern Europe as Laboratory for Economic Knowledge: The Transnational Roots of Neoliberalism." *American Journal of Sociology*, 108/2 (September).

Fic, V.M. 1970. *Kerala, Yenan of India: Rise of Communist Power, 1937–1969*. Bombay: Nachiketa Publications.

Fine, Robert and Dennis Davis. 1991. *Beyond Apartheid: Labour and Liberation in South Africa*. Johannesburg: Ravan Press.

First, Ruth. 1972. "Protest and Politics in the Shadow of Apartheid." *New Middle East*, July.

Fisher, William and Thomas Ponniah. 2003. *Another World Is Possible*. London and New York: Zed Books.

Fligstein, Neil. 2001. "Social Skill and the Theory of Fields." *Sociological Theory*, 19/2 (July): 105–25.

Foucault, Michel. 1995 [1977]. *Discipline and Punish: The Birth of the Prison*. New York: Vintage Books.

Franke, Richard. 1993. *Life Is a Little Better: Redistribution as a Development Strategy in Nadur Village, Kerala*. Boulder, CO: Westview.

Franke, Richard and Barbara Chasin. 1994. *Kerala: Radical Reform as Development in an Indian State*. Food First Development Report, no.6. San Francisco.

Frankel, Francine. 1978. *India's Political Economy: 1947–1977*. Princeton: Princeton University Press.

Friedman, Steven. 1987. *Building Tomorrow Today: African Workers in Trade Unions 1970–1984*. Johannesburg: Ravan Press.

Fung, Archon and Erik Olin Wright. 2003. *Deepening Democracy: Institutional Innovations in Empowered Participatory Governance*. London and New York: Verso Press.

———. 2003a. "Thinking about Empowered Participatory Governance." In *Deepening Democracy: Institutional Innovations in Empowered Participatory Governance*, ed. Archon Fung and Erik Olin Wright. London and New York: Verso Press.

———. 2003b. "Countervailing Power in Empowered Participatory Governance." In *Deepening Democracy: Institutional Innovations in Empowered Participatory Governance*, ed. Archon Fung and Erik Olin Wright. London and New York: Verso Press.

Galeano, Eduardo. 1983. *Days and Nights of Love and War*. New York and London: Monthly Review Press.

Garner, Ash, Roberta and Mayer Zald. 1987. "Social Movement Organizations: Growth, Decay, and Change." In *Social Movements in an Organizational Society*, ed. Mayer Zald and John McCarthy. New Jersey: Transaction Books.

Gelb, Stephen, ed. 1991. *South Africa's Economic Crisis*. Cape Town and London: David Philip and Zed Books.

———. 1994. "Development Process for South Africa." Paper presented to WIDER Workshop on Medium Term Development Strategy, Phase II, Helsinki, April 15–17.

———. 1999. "The Politics of Macroeconomic Policy Reform in South Africa." Symposium, History Workshop of the University of the Witwatersrand, Johannesburg, September 18.

———. 2005. "An Overview of the South African Economy." In *State of the Nation: South Africa 2004–2005*, ed. John Daniel, Roger Southall, and Jessica Lutchman. Cape Town: Human Sciences Research Council.

George, Jose. 1984. *Politicisation of Agricultural Workers in Kerala: A Study of Kuttanad.* New Dehli: K.P. Bagchi.

George, K.K. 1999. *Limits to Kerala Model of Development.* Thiruvananthapuram: Center for Development Studies.

————. 2005. "Introduction." In *Kerala's Economy: Trajectories, Challenges, and Implications,* ed. D. Rajasenan and Gerard de Groot, 1–11. Cochin: Cochin University: 1–11.

Gevisser, Mark. 1996. *Portraits of Power: Profiles in a Changing South Africa.* Johannesburg: David Philip Publishers.

Giddens, Anthony, "Modernity, Ecology and Social Transformation." Unpublished manuscript (1986).

Ginsburg, D. and Eddie Webster. 1995. *Taking Democracy Seriously: Worker Expectations and Parliamentary Democracy in South Africa.* Durban: Indicator Press.

Goldfrank, Ben. 2003. "Making Participation Work in Porto Alegre." In *Radicals in Power: The Workers' Party (PT) and Experiments in Urban Democracy in Brazil,* ed. Gianpaolo Baiocchi. New York: Zed Books: 27–52.

Goldfrank, Ben and Aaron Schneider. 2003. "Restraining the Revolution or Deepening Democracy? The Workers' Party in Rio Grande do Sul." In *Radicals in Power: The Workers' Party (PT) and Experiments in Urban Democracy in Brazil,* ed. Gianpaolo Baiocchi. New York: Zed Books: 155–75.

Gomomo, John. 1995. "Privatization and the Reorganization of State Assets." *The African Communist,* 141/2.

Gopalan, A.K. 1959. *Kerala: Past and Present.* London: Lawrence and Wishart.

————. 1973. *In the Cause of the People: Reminiscences.* Bombay: Orient Longman.

Gorz, Andre. 1994. *Capitalism, Socialism, Ecology.* London: Verso Press.

Gostner, Karl and Avril Joffe. 2000. "Negotiating the Future: Labour's Role in NEDLAC." In *Engaging the State and Business: The Labour Movement and Co-Determination in Contemporary South Africa,* ed. Glenn Adler. Johannesburg: Witwatersrand University Press.

Götz, Graeme A. 2000. "Shoot Anything that Flies, Claim Anything that Falls: Labour and the Changing Definition of the Reconstruction and Development Program." In *Trade Unions and Democratization in South Africa, 1985–1997,* ed. Glenn Adler and Eddie Webster. Johannesburg: University of Witwatersrand.

Gouldner, Alvin. 1955. "Metaphysical Pathos and the Theory of Bureaucracy." *American Political Science Review,* 49: 496–507.

————. 1970. *The Coming Crisis of Western Sociology.* New York: Basic Books.

Gramsci, Antonio. 1992 [1971]. *Selections from the Prison Notebooks,* ed. Quintin Hoare and Geoffrey Nowell Smith. New York: International Publishers.

————. 1977. *Selections from Political Writings, 1910–1920,* ed. Quintin Hoare. London: The Camelot Press, Ltd.

Gusfield, Joseph. 1968. "Social Movements: The Study." In *International Encyclopedia of the Social Sciences,* vol.14, David Sills (ed.). New York: MacMillan.

Habermas, Jurgen. (1991) "What Does Socialism Mean Today? The Revolutions or Recuperation and the Need for New Thinking." In *After the Fall: The Failure of Communism and the Future of Socialism,* ed. Robin Blackburn. London: Verso Press.

Habib, Adam and Rupter Taylor. 2000. "Political Alliances and Parliamentary Opposition in Post-apartheid South Africa." *Opposition in South Africa's New Democracy* from Kariega Game Reserve, Eastern Cape, June 28–30. Johannesburg: KAS.

Harilal, K.N. 2005. "Migration and Development." In *Kerala Economy: Trajectories, Challenges, and Implications,* ed. D. Rajasenan and Gerard de Groot. Cochin: Cochin University of Science and Technology Press.

Hart, Gillian. 2002. *Disabling Globalization: Places of Power in Post-Apartheid South Africa.* Berkeley: University of California Press.

Held, David. 1996 [1987]. *Models of Democracy* (second edition). Stanford: Stanford University Press.

Heller, Patrick. 1995. "Social Capital as Product of Class Mobilization and State Intervention: Industrial Workers in Kerala, India." *World Development*, 24/6: 1055–71.

———. 1999. *The Labor of Development: Workers and the Transformation of Capitalism in Kerala, India.* Ithaca: Cornell University Press.

———. 2000. "Social Capital and the Developmental State: Industrial Workers in Kerala." In *Kerala the Development Experience: Reflections on Sustainability and Replicability*, ed. Govindan Parayil. London: Zed Books.

———. 2001. "Moving the State: The Politics of Democratic Decentralization in Kerala, South Africa, and Porto Alegre." *Politics and Society*, 29/1: 131–63.

Herring, Ronald. 1983. *Land to the Tiller: The Political Economy of Agrarian Reform in South Asia.* New Haven: Yale University Press.

Hindson, Doug. 1987. "Overview: Trade Unions and Politics." In *The Independent Trade Unions, 1974–84*, ed. Johann Maree. Johannesburg: Ravan Press.

Hobsbawm, Eric. 1991. "Out of the Ashes." In *After the Fall: The Failure of Communism and the Future of Socialism*, ed. Robin Blackburn. London: Verso Press.

Holloway, John. 2002. *Change the World without Taking Power: The Meaning of Revolution Today.* London: Pluto Press.

Houston, G.R. Humphries, and I Liebenberg. 2001. *Public Participation in Democratic Governance in South Africa.* Cape Town: Jacaranda Printers.

Hudson, Peter. 1986. "The Freedom Charter and Socialist Strategy in South Africa." *Politikon*, 13/1 (June).

IDASA. 2006. *The Role of Ward Committees in Enhancing Public Participation in Rustenburg Municipality: A Critical Evaluation.* Cape Town.

Institute for Industrial Education. 1974. *The Durban Strikes 1973: Human Beings with Souls.* Durban and Johannesburg: Institute for Industrial Education and Ravan Press.

Isaac, T.M. Thomas. 1982. "Class Struggle and Structural Changes in the Coir Mat and Matting Industry in Kerala." *Economic and Political Weekly*, 17/31: PE13–29.

———. 1994. "The Left Movement in Kerala: Lessons of the Past and Challenges of the Present." In *International Congress on Kerala Studies Documents*, vol. I, August 27–29.

———. 1997. "People's Plan Campaign: An Interim Assessment and Response to a Critique." In *The People's Plan: A Debate on Kerala's Decentralized Planning Experiment*, ed. N.P. Chekutty. Kozhikode: Calicut Press.

———. 1998. "Decentralization, Democracy, and Development: A Case Study of the People's Campaign for Decentralized Planning in Kerala." Unpublished paper, Kerala State Planning Board.

———. 2000. "Campaign for Democratic Decentralization in Kerala: An Assessment from the Perspective of Empowered Deliberative Democracy." Unpublished manuscript.

Isaac, T.M. Thomas and Patrick Heller. 2003. "Democracy and Development: Decentralized Planning in Kerala." In *Deepening Democracy: Institutional Innovations in Empowered Participatory Governance*, ed. Archon Fung and Erik Olin Wright. London and New York: Verso Press.

Isaac, T.M. Thomas and Richard Franke. 2001 [2000]. *Local Democracy and Development: People's Campaign for Decentralized Planning in Kerala.* New Delhi: Leftword Press.

Isaac, Thomas, Richard Franke, and Pyaralal Raghavan. 1998. *Democracy at Work in an Indian Industrial Cooperative.* Ithaca: Cornell University Press.

Isaac, Thomas, Michelle Williams, Pinaki Chakraborthy, and Binitha V. Thampi. 2002. "Women's Neighborhood Groups: Towards a New Perspective." Mararikulam Conference on Sustainable Development, May 9–12.

Jeffrey, Robin. 1992. *Politics, Women, and Well-Being*. London and New Delhi: Oxford University Press.

Jenkins, J. Craig. 1977. "Radical Transformations of Organizational Goals." *Administrative Sciences Quarterly*, 22: 568–86.

Johns, Sheridan III. 1972. *From Protest to Challenge: A Documentary History of African Politics in South Africa, 1882–1964: Protest and Hope, 1882–1934*, vol. 1. Stanford: Hoover Institution Press.

Jordan, Pallo. 1992. "The Challenges that Face South African Socialists." *New Nation*, January 23.

Joseph, K.P. 1999. "Poor Management of State Finances in Kerala." In *Kerala's Economic Development: Issues and Problems*, ed. B.A. Prakash. New Delhi: Sage Publications.

Kannan, K.P. 1990. "Kerala's Economy at the Crossroads?" *Economic and Political Weekly*, 25 (N35–3): 1951–56.

———. 1995. "Declining Incidence of Rural Poverty in Kerala." *Economic and Political Weekly* (October 14–21): 2651–62.

Kaplan, D. 1991. "The South African Capital Goods Sector and the Economic Crisis." In *South Africa's Economic Crisis*, ed. Stephen Gelb. Cape Town and London: David Philips and Zed Books.

Karis, Thomas. 1973. *From Protest to Challenge: A Documentary History of African Politics in South Africa, 1882–1964: Hope and Challenge: 1935–1952*, vol. 2. Stanford: Hoover Institution Press.

Karis, Thomas and Gail M. Gerhard. 1977. *From Protest to Challenge: A Documentary History of African Politics in South Africa, 1882–1964: Challenge and Violence, 1953–1964*, vol. 3. Stanford: Hoover Institution Press.

———. 1977a. *From Protest to Challenge: A Documentary History of African Politics in South Africa, 1882–1964: Political Profiles, 1882–1964*, vol. 4. Stanford: Hoover Institution Press.

———. 1997. *From Protest to Challenge: A Documentary History of African Politics in South Africa, 1882–1979: Nadir and Resurgence, 1964–1979*, vol.5. Stanford: Hoover Institution Press.

Kasrils, Ronnie. 1998 [1993]. *Armed and Dangerous*. Johannesburg: Jonathan Ball Publishers.

Khera, R.N. 1991. "Growth of the Registered Manufacturing Sector at the State Level." *Journal of Income and Wealth*, 13/1: 114–22.

Kiloh, Margaret and Archie Sibeko. 2000. *A Fighting Union: An Oral History of the South African Railway and Harbour Workers Union, 1936–1998*. Johannesburg: Ravan Press.

Kitschelt, Herbert. 1984. *Der Ökologische Diskurs*. Frankfurt: Campus.

———. 1989. *The Logics of Party Formation: Structure and Strategy of Belgian and West German Ecology Parties*. Ithaca, NY: Cornell University Press.

———. 1990. "New Social Movements and the Decline of Party Organization." In *Challenging the Political Order: New Social and Political Movements in Western Democracies*, ed. Russel J. Dalton and Manfred Kuechler. New York: Oxford University Press.

Klein, Naomi. 2004. "Reclaiming the Commons." In *A Movement of Movements*, ed. T. Mertes. London: Verso Press: 219–29.

Kohli, Atul. 1990. *Democracy and Its Discontent: India's Growing Crisis of Governability*. Cambridge: Cambridge University Press.

———. 2004. *State-Directed Development: Political Power and Industrialization in the Global Periphery*. New York: Cambridge University Press.

Kurian, N.J. and Joseph Abraham. 1999. "The Financial Crisis: An Analysis." In *Kerala's Economic Development: Issues and Problems*, ed. B.A. Prakash. New Delhi: Sage Publications.

Lambert, Robert. 1993. "Trade Unionism, Race, Class and Nationalism in the 1950s Resistance Movement." In *Apartheid's Genesis, 1935–1962*, ed. Phillip Bonner, Peter Delius, and Deborah Posel. Johannesburg: Wits University Press.

Lenin, Vladimir Illich Ulyanov. 1977 [1902]. *What Is to Be Done?*. In *Lenin Selected Works, vol. I*. Moscow: Progress Publishers.

———. 1977 [1905]. *Two Tactics of Social Democracy in the Democratic Revolution*. In *Lenin Selected Works, vol. I*. Moscow: Progress Publishers.

———. 1977 [1917]. *State and Revolution*. In *Lenin Selected Works, vol. II*. Moscow: Progress Publishers.

LeRoux et. al. 1993. *The Mont Fleur Scenarios*. Cape Town: University of Western Cape.

Lerumo, A. (Michael Harmel). 1987 [1971]. *Fifty Fighting Years: The SACP, 1921–1971*. London: Inkululeko Publications.

Levin, Richard. 1995. "The Agrarian Question in South Africa: Toward a Socialist Perspective." Prepared for the Spring Party School of the SACP; SACP Chris Hani Memorial Library; September.

Levy, Andrew, ed. 1995. *Annual Report on Labor Relations in South Africa, 1995–1996*. Johannesburg: Andrew Levy and Associates.

Lipset, Seymour. 1959. "Some Social Requisites of Democracy: Economic Development and Political Legitimacy." *American Political Science Review*, 53.

———. 1963. *Political Man: The Social Bases of Politics*. New York: Anchor Books.

———. 1968 [1950]. *Agrarian Socialism*. Berkeley: UC Press.

———. 1999 [1961]. "Introduction." In *Political Parties*, ed. Robert Michels. New Brunswick, NJ and London: Transaction Publishers: 15–39.

Lipset, S., Martin Trow, and James Coleman. 1956. *Union Democracy*. New York: Anchor Books.

Little, Richard. 1981. "Bureaucracy and Participation in the Soviet Union." In *Political Participation in Communist Systems*, ed. Schulz, Donald and Jan Adams. New York: Pergamon Press.

Lodge, Tom. 1983. *Black Politics in South Africa Since 1945*. London: Longman Publishers.

———. 2003 [2002]. *Politics in South Africa: From Mandela to Mbeki*. Cape Town: David Philip and Oxford: James Currey.

Luckhardt, K. and B. Wall. 1980. *Organize or Starve! The History of the South African Congress of Trade Unions*. London: Lawrence and Wishart.

Macun, Ian. 2000. "Growth, Structure, and Power in the South African Union Movement." In *Trade Unions and Democratization in South Africa, 1985–1997*, ed. Glenn Adler and Eddie Webster. Johannesburg: University of Witwatersrand.

Maharaj, Mac. 2007. *Shades of Difference: Mac Maharaj and the Struggle for South Africa*. New York: Viking.

Malinga, Phineas. 1990. "Nationalization or Free Enterprise?" *The African Communist*, 123/4.

Maloka, Eddy. 2002. *South African Communist Party: 1963–1990*. Johannesburg: Africa Institute.

Mandela, Nelson. 1993. "Will the ANC Sell-Out Workers?" Speech at COSATU Special Congress. *The African Communist*, 134/3.

Manor, James. 1999. *The Political Economy of Decentralization*. Washington, DC: The World Bank.

Marais, Hein. 1994. "Radical as Reality." *The African Communist*, 138/3.

———. 1996. "All Geared Up." *The African Communist*, 145/3.

———. 2001 [1998]. *South Africa Limits to Change: The Political Economy of Transformation.* Cape Town: University of Cape Town Press.

Marcuse, Herbert. 1958. *Soviet Marxism: A Critical Analysis*. New York: Columbia University Press.

Maree, Johann. 1978. "The Dimensions and Causes of Unemployment in South Africa." *South African Labor Bulletin*, 4/3: 15–50.

———. 1987. "Overview: Emergence of the Independent Trade Union Movement." In *The Independent Trade Unions, 1974–84*, ed. Johann Maree. Johannesburg: Ravan Press.

Marks, Shula and R. Rathbone ed. 1983. *Industrialisation and Social Change in South Africa: African Class Formation, Culture and Consciousness 1870–1930*. London and New York.

Mbeki, Govan. 1984 [1963]. *The Peasants' Revolt*. London: International Defence and Aid Fund for Southern Africa. .

McAdam, Doug, Sydney Tarrow, and Charles Tilly. 2001. *Dynamics of Contention*. Cambridge: Cambridge University Press.

McCarthy, John D. and Mayer N. Zald. 1977. "Resource Mobilization and Social Movements: A Partial Theory." *American Journal of Sociology*, 82: 1212–41.

McKinley, Dale. 1997. *The ANC and the Liberation Struggle: A Critical Political Biography*. London: Pluto Press.

Menon, Dilip M. 1994. *Caste, Nationalism, and Communism in South India: Malabar 1990–1948*. Cambridge: Cambridge University Press.

Menon, Sreedhara. 1997. *Kerala and Freedom Struggle*. Kottayam: D.C. Books.

Meredith, Martin. 2002. *Fischer's Choice: A Life of Bram Fischer*. Johannesburg and Cape Town: Jonathan Ball Publishers.

Mertes, Tom. 2004. *A Movement of Movements: Is Another World Really Possible?* London: Verso.

Michels, Robert. 1999 [1910]. *Political Parties: A Sociological Study of the Oligarchical Tendencies of Modern Democracy*. New Brunswick, NJ and London: Transaction Publishers.

Mill, John Stuart. 1950 [1881]. *Philosophy of Scientific Method*, ed. Ernest Nagel. New York: Hafner.

Milliband, Ralph. 1991 "Reflections on the Crisis of Communist Regimes." In *After the Fall: The Failure of Communism and the Future of Socialism*, ed. Robin Blackburn. London: Verso Press.

Moleketi, Jabu. 1993. "Is a Retreat from National Democratic Revolution to National Bourgeois Revolution Imminent?" *The African Communist*, 133/2.

Moodie, Dunbar. 1975. *The Rise of Afrikanerdom: Power, Apartheid, and the Afrikaner Civil Religion*. Berkeley: University of California Press.

Moore, Barrington. 1966. *Social Origins of Dictatorship and Democracy: Lord and Peasant in the Making of the Modern World*. New York: Beacon Press.

Muraleedharan, S. 2005. "Industrial Growth in Kerala." In *Kerala Economy: Trajectories, Challenges, and Implications*, ed. D. Rajasenan and Gerard de Groot. Cochin: Cochin University of Science and Technology Press.

Naidoo, Vino. 2005. "The State of the Public Service." In *State of the Nation: South Africa 2004–2005*, ed. John Daniel, Roger Southall, and Jessica Lutchman. Cape Town: Human Sciences Research Council.

Nair, K. Ramachandran. 1973. *Industrial Relations in Kerala*. New Delhi: Sterling.

Namboodiripad, EMS. 1957. "First Communist Government Formed in India in Kerala: Statement of Policy." In *Documents of the Communist Movement in India*, vol. VIII (1957–1961). Calcutta: National Book Agency Private Limited (April 5): 56–69.

———. 1991. "For Full Powers and Responsibilities." *Deshabhimani*, March.

———. 1994. "International Congress on Kerala Studies: Presidential Address." In *Kerala Studies Congress Documents, vol. I*, August 27–29.

Narayana, D. 1990. "Agricultural Economy of Kerala in the Post-Seventies: Stagnation or Cycles?." Working Paper no. 235, Center for Development Studies, Trivandrum.

Netshitenzhe, Joel. 2000. "The National Democratic Revolution and Class Struggle." *The African Communist*, 154/2.

Nondwangu, Silumko. 1996. "An Alternative Macro-Economic Strategy?" *The African Communist*, 145/3.

Nossiter, Thomas. 1982. *Communism in Kerala: A Study in Political Adaptation*. Berkeley: University of California Press.

———. 1988. *Marxist State Governments in India*. London: Pinter Publishers.

Nqakula, Charles. 1994. "Forward with a People-Driven RDP." *The African Communist*, 138/3.

Nyawuza. 1985. "New Marxist' Tendencies and the Battle of Ideas in South Africa." *The African Communist*, 103/4.

Nzimande, Blade. 1993. "SACP: Contribution towards an Election Manifesto." Draft discussion document. Manuscript in UCT Simons Collection: BC1081, file 07.5.

———. 1995. "The Character of Our Party: Building the SACP in the Present Period." *The African Communist*, 139/140 (1).

———. 1996. "The Role of the Working Class in Consolidating and Deepening the National Democratic Revolution." *The African Communist*, 145/3.

———. 1998. "The Role of the SACP in the Alliance: Our Vision of Socialism." *The African Communist*, 150/4.

Nzimande, Blade and Jeremy Cronin. 1997. "We Need Transformation not a Balancing Act: Looking Critically at the ANC Discussion Document." *The African Communist*, 146/2: 62–70.

Offe, Claus. 1984. *Contradictions of the Welfare State*. Cambridge: MIT Press.

———. 1985. "New Social Movements: Changing Boundaries of the Political." *Social Research*, 52: 817–68.

———. 1990. "Reflections on the Institutional Self-Transformation of Movement Politics: A Tentative Stage Model." In *Challenging the Political Order: New Social and Political Movements in Western Democracies*, ed. Russel J. Dalton and Manfred Kuechler. New York: Oxford University Press.

Oommen, T.K. 1985. *From Mobilization to Institutionalization: The Dynamic of the Agrarian Movement in Twentieth Century Kerala*. New Delhi: Sangam Books.

———. 1992. "The Acute Unemployment Problem in Kerala: Some Explanatory Hypotheses." *IASSI Quarterly*, 10/3: 231–55.

Padayachee, Vishnu. 1994a. "Can the RDP Survive the IMF?" *Southern Africa Report*, 9/5.

———. 1994b. "Dealing with the IMF: Dangers and Opportunities." *South African Labour Bulletin*, 18/1, January/February.

———. 1994c. "Debt, Development, and Democracy: The IMF in Post-Apartheid South Africa." *Review of African Political Economy*, 21/62.

Panikkar, K.N. 1992. *Against Lord and State: Religion and Peasant Uprisings in Malabar: 1836–1921*. Delhi: Oxford University Press.

Panitch, Leo. 2001. *Renewing Socialism: Democracy, Strategy, and Imagination*. Boulder, CO: Westview Press.

Pape, John. 2001. "The Myth of 'South Fundamentals': South Africa and Global Economic Crises." *The African Communist*, 156/1.

Parmeswaran, M.P. 2000. "What Does the Kerala Model Signify? Towards the Possible 'Fourth World.'" In *Kerala the Development Experience: Reflections on Sustainability and Replicability*, ed. Govindan Parayil. London: Zed Books.

Pateman, Carole. 1999 [1970]. *Participation and Democratic Theory*. Cambridge: Cambridge University Press.

Pierson, Christopher. 1995. *Socialism after Communism: The New Market Socialism*. Cambridge: Polity Press.

Pityana, Sipho Mila and Mark Orkin. 1992. *Beyond the Factory Floor: A Survey of COSATU Shop-Stewards*. Johannesburg: Ravan Press.

Piven, Francis Fox and Richard Cloward. 1977. *Poor People's Movements*. New York: Vintage.

Posel, Deborah. 1991. *The Making of Apartheid 1948–1961: Conflict and Compromise*. Oxford and New York: Oxford University Press.

————. 2001 [1993]. "Influx Control and Urban Labour Markets in the 1950s." In *Apartheid's Genesis, 1935–1962*, ed. Phillip Bonner, Peter Delius, and Deborah Posel. Johannesburg: Wits University Press.

Poulantzas, N. 1975. *Classes in Contemporary Capitalism*. London: New Left Books.

————. 1980 [1978]. *State, Power, Socialism*. London: Verso.

Prakash, B.A., ed. 1999. *Kerala's Economic Development: Issues and Problems*. New Delhi: Sage Publications.

————. 1999a. "The Economic Impact of Migration to the Gulf." In *Kerala's Economic Development: Issues and Problems*, ed. B.A. Prakash. New Delhi: Sage Publications.

————. 1999b. "Economic Reforms and the Performance of Kerala's Economy." In *Kerala's Economic Development: Issues and Problems*, ed. B.A. Prakash. New Delhi: Sage Publications.

Przeworski, Adam. 1985. *Capitalism and Social Democracy: Studies in Marxism and Social Theory*. Cambridge: Cambridge University Press.

Przeworski, Adam, Michael E. Alvarez, Jose Antonio Cheibub, and Fernando Limongi. 2000. *Democracy and Development: Political Institutions and Well-Being in the World, 1950–1990*. Cambridge: Cambridge University Press.

Putnam, Robert. 1993. *Making Democracy Work: Civic Traditions in Modern Italy*. New Jersey: Princeton University Press.

Rabinowitch, Alexander. 1978 [1976]. *The Bolsheviks Come to Power: The Revolution of 1917 in Petrograd*. New York: W.W. Norton and Company.

Ramachandran, V.K. 1996. "On Kerala's Development Achievements." In *Indian Development*, ed. Jean Dreze and Amartya Sen. Delhi: Oxford University Press.

Ramaphosa, Cyril. 1993. "The Role of Trade Unions in Transition." *The African Communist*, 133/2.

Ray, Raka. 1999. *Fields of Protest: Women's Movements in India*. Minneapolis: University of Minnesota Press.

Roberts, Benjamin. 2005. "'Empty Stomachs, Empty Pockets': Poverty and Inequality in Post-Apartheid South Africa." In *State of the Nation: South Africa 2004–2005*, ed. John Daniel et al. Cape Town: Human Sciences Research Council.

Roberts, Kenneth. 1998. *Deepening Democracy? The Modern Left and Social Movements in Chile and Peru*. Stanford, CA: Stanford University Press.

Routledge, Paul. 2002. "Resisting and Reshaping the Modern: Social Movements and the Development Process." In *Geographies of Global Change*, ed. Michael Watts et al. Oxford: Blackwell: 263–79.

Rueschemeyer, Dietrich, Evelyne Huber Stephens, and John D. Stephens. 1992. *Capitalist Development and Democracy*. Chicago: University of Chicago Press.

Rumney, Reg. 2005. "Who Owns South Africa: An Analysis of State and Private Ownership Patterns." In *State of the Nation: South Africa 2004–2005*, ed. John Daniel et al. Cape Town: Human Sciences Research Council.

SAIRR. 1992. "Race Relations Survey 1991/92." Johannesburg.

Sandbrook, Richard, Marc Edelman, Patrick Heller, and Judith Teichman. 2007. *Social Democracy in the Global Periphery*. Cambridge: Cambridge University Press.

Sapire, Hilary. 1993. "African Political Organizations in Brakpan in the 1950s." In *Apartheid's Genesis, 1935–1962*, ed. Phillip Bonner, Peter Delius, and Deborah Posel. Johannesburg: Witwatersrand University Press.

———. 1988. *African Urbanization and Struggles against Municipal Control in Brakpan, 1920–1958*. Ph.D. Dissertation, University of the Witwatersrand, South Africa.

Sartori, Giovanni. 1976. *Parties and Party Systems: A Framework for Analysis*. Cambridge: Cambridge University Press.

Satgar, Vishwas. 1997. "Workplace Forums and Autonomous Self-Management." *African Communist*, 147/3: 63–74.

———. 2000. "The LRA of 1995 and Workplace Forums: Legislative Provisions, Origins, and Transformative Possibilities." In *Engaging the State and Business: The Labour Movement and Co-Determination in Contemporary South Africa*, ed. Glenn Adler. Johannesburg: Witwatersrand University Press.

———. 2001. "Critical Literature Review and Discussion Paper: Worker Owned Co-Operatives, Development, and Neo-Liberal Economic Adjustment." *African Communist*, 156/1: 60–77.

———. 2002. "Thabo Mbeki and the South African Communist Party." In *Thabo Mbeki's World: The Politics and Ideology of the South African President*, ed. Sean Jacobs and Richard Calland. London: Zed Books and Pietermaritzburg: University of Natal Press.

Satgar, Vishwas and Gwede Mantashe. 1996. "The Labor Market and Job Creation." *African Communist*, 144/2: 11–19.

Sathyamurthy, T.V. 1985. *India since Independence: Studies in the Development of the Power of the State, Vol 1, Center-State Relations: The Case of Kerala*. Ajanta Publications.

Saul, John S. and Stephen Gelb. 1981. *The Crisis in South Africa: Class Defense, Class Revolution*. New York and London: Monthly Review Press.

Schorske, Carl. 1955. *German Social Democracy, 1905–1917*. Cambridge: Harvard University Press.

Schulz, D. 1981. "Political Participation in Communist Systems: The Conceptual Frontier." In *Political Participation in Communist Systems*, ed. Schulz, Donald and Jan Adams. New York: Pergamon Press.

Schumpeter, Joseph A. 1975 [1942]. *Capitalism, Socialism, and Democracy*. New York: Harper Colophon Books.

Seekings, Jeremy. 2000. *The UDF: A History of the United Democratic Front in South Africa, 1983–1991*. Cape Town: David Philip.

Seema, T.N. and Vanitha Mukherjee. 2000. "Gender Governance and Citizenship in Decentralized Planning." Paper presented at the International Conference on Democratic Decentralization; Thiruvananthapuram (May 23–27).

Seidman, Gay. 1994. *Manufacturing Militance: Workers Movements in Brazil and South Africa*. Berkeley: University of California Press.

Selznick, Phillip. 1952. *Organizational Weapon*. Santa Monica: Rand Corporation.

Shubin, Vladimir. 1999. *ANC: A View from Moscow*. Bellville: Mayibuye Books.

Simons, Jack and Ray Simons. 1983. *Class and Colour in South Africa 1850–1950*. International Defence and Aid Fund.

Skocpol, Theda. 1979. *State and Social Revolutions: A Comparative Analysis of France, Russia, and China*. Cambridge: Cambridge University Press.

———. ed. 1984. *Vision and Method in Historical Sociology*. Cambridge: Cambridge University Press.

Slovo, Joe. 1976. "South Africa: No Middle Road." In *Southern Africa: The New Politics of Revolution,* ed. Basil Davidson, Joe Slovo, and Anthony R. Wilkinson. New York and Middlesex, England: Pelican Books.

———. 1989. *The South African Working Class and the National Democratic Revolution.* SACP Publication.

———. 1990. "Has Socialism Failed?" *The African Communist,* 121/2.

———. 1991. "Socialist Aspirations and Socialist Realities." *The African Communist,* 124/1.

———. 1993. "The Negotiations Victory: A Political Overview." *The African Communist,* 4.

———. 1997. *Slovo: The Unfinished Autobiography of ANC leader Joe Slovo,* ed. Philip van Niekerk. Cape Town: Ocean Press.

Smith, S.A. 1983. *Red Petrograd: Revolution in the Factories, 1917–1918.* Cambridge: Cambridge University Press.

Southall, Roger. 2005. "Black Empowerment and Corporate Capital." In *State of the Nation: South Africa 2004–2005,* ed. John Daniel et al. Cape Town: Human Sciences Research Council.

Southall, Roger and John Daniel. 2005. "The State of Parties Post-Election 2004: ANC Dominance and Opposition Enfeeblement." In *State of the Nation: South Africa 2004–2005,* ed. John Daniel et al. Cape Town: Human Sciences Research Council.

Stepan-Norris, Judith and Maurice Zeitlin. 2003. *Left Out: Reds and America's Industrial Unions.* Cambridge: Cambridge University Press.

Strange, Susan. 2000 [1996]. *The Retreat of the State: The Diffusion of Power in the World-Economy.* Cambridge: Cambridge University Press.

Subrahmanian, K.K. 2005. "Growth Performance." In *Kerala Economy: Trajectories, Challenges, and Implications,* ed. D. Rajasenan and Gerard de Groot. Cochin: Cochin University of Science and Technology Press.

Surjeet, Harkishan Singh. 1997. "Forward." In *Documents of the Communist Movement in India,* vol. VIII (1957–1961). Calcutta: National Book Agency Private Limited: ix–xv.

———. 1997a. "Forward." In *Documents of the Communist Movement in India,* vol. XA (1964 Part I). Calcutta: National Book Agency Private Limited: xi–xiv.

———. 1998. "Forward." In *Documents of the Communist Movement in India,* vol. XXIV (1992–1993). Delhi: National Book Agency.

Suttner, Raymond. 2001. *Inside Apartheid's Prison.* Melbourne and New York: Ocean Press.

Suttner, Raymond and Cronin, Jeremy. 1986. *Thirty Years of the Freedom Charter.* Johannesburg: Ravan Press.

Talmon, J.L. 1952. *The Origins of Totalitarian Democracy.* London: Secker and Warburg.

Tambo, Oliver. 1985. "An Interview with Comrade Oliver Tambo—President of the ANC." Mayibuye Center for Historical Papers: ANC and SACP archive.

Tarrow, Sidney. 1967. *Peasant Communism in Southern Italy.* New Haven: Yale University Press.

———. 1989. *Democracy and Disorder: Social Conflict, Protest and Politics in Italy, 1965–1975.* Oxford: Oxford University Press.

———. 1990. "The Phantom at the Opera: Political Parties and Social Movements of the 1960s and 1970s in Italy." In *Challenging the Political Order: New Social and Political Movements in Western Democracies,* ed. Russell J. Dalton and Manfred Kuechler. New York: Oxford University Press.

Thampi, M.M. 1999. "Economic Liberalization and Industrial Development in Kerala: Challenges to New Investments." In *Kerala's Economic Development: Issues and Problems,* ed. B.A. Prakash. New Delhi: Sage Publications.

Tharamangalam, Joseph. 1981. *Agrarian Class Conflict: The Political Mobilization of Agricultural Laborers in Kuttanad, South India*. Vancouver and London: University of British Columbia Press.

Tilly, Charles. 1978. *From Mobilization to Revolution*. Reading: Addison-Wesley.

———. 1986. *The Contentious French*. Cambridge, MA: Harvard University Press.

———. 1997. "Social Movements as Political Struggle." Draft article for the Encyclopedia of American Social Movements, July.

Tocqueville, Alexis de. 2001. *Democracy in America*. New York and London: Signet Classic.

Tornquist, Olle. 1991. "Communists and Democracy: Two Indian Cases and One Debate." *Bulletin of Concerned Asian Scholars*, 23/2: 63–76.

———. 2000. "The New Popular Politics of Development: Kerala's Experience." In *Kerala the Development Experience: Reflections on Sustainability and Replicability*, ed. Govindan Parayil. London: Zed Books.

Torres, L. 1995. *South African Workers Speak*. Oslo: FAFO.

Touraine, Alain. 1981. *The Voice and the Eye: An Analysis of Social Movements*. Cambridge: Cambridge University Press.

Tshwete, Steve. 1988. "Politics and the Army." Paper presented to the Department of Political Education Workshop, Lusaka, February 23–28. Mayibuye Historical Papers.

Turok, Ben. 1993. "South Africa's Skyscraper Economy: Growth or Development?" In *Development and Reconstruction in South Africa: A Reader*. Johannesburg: Institute for African Alternatives.

———. 1993a. "The Meaning of Power." *Development and Reconstruction in South Africa: A Reader*. Johannesburg: Institute for African Alternatives.

———. 1993b. "Democracy, State and Civil Society." In *Development and Reconstruction in South Africa: A Reader*. Johannesburg: Institute for African Alternatives.

United Nations. 2004. *World Development Report*.

United Nations Development Program (UNDP). 1997. *Human Development Report*.

——— (UNDP). 2000. *Human Development Report*.

——— (UNDP). 2004. *Human Development Report*.

van Niekerk, Philip. 1997. "White Hero of Black Revolution Faces Up to His Final Struggle." In *Slovo: The Unfinished Autobiography of ANC Leader Joe Slovo*. Cape Town: Ocean Press.

Varshney, Ashutosh. 1998 [1994]. *Democracy, Development and the Countryside: Urban-Rural Struggles in India*. Cambridge: Cambridge University Press.

Veron, Rene. 2000. "Sustainability and the 'New' Kerala Model." In *Kerala the Development Experience: Reflections on Sustainability and Replicability*, ed. Govindan Parayil. London: Zed Books.

Von Holdt, Karl. 2003. *Transition from Below: Forging Trade Unionism and Workplace Change in South Africa*. Scottsville: University of Natal Press.

Voss, Kim and Rachel Sherman. 2000. "Breaking the Iron Law of Oligarchy: Union Revitalization in the American Labor Movement." *American Journal of Sociology*, 106/2: 303–49.

Wallerstein, Immanuel. 1990. "Anti-Systemic Movements: History and Dilemmas." In *Transforming the Revolution: Social Movements and the World-System*, ed. Amin, Samir, Giovanni Arrighi, Andre Gunder Frank, Immanuel Wallerstein. New York: Monthly Review Press.

Webster, Eddie. 2000. "The Alliance under Stress: Governing in a Globalizing World." In *Opposition in South Africa's New Democracy*. Kariega Game Reserve, Eastern Cape, June 28–30. Johannesburg: KAS.

Webster, Eddie and Ian Macun. 2000. "A Trend toward Co-Determination?: Case Studies of South African Enterprises." In *Engaging the State and Business: The Labour Movement and Co-Determination in Contemporary South Africa*, ed. Glenn Adler. Johannesburg: Witwatersrand University Press.

Weiner, Myron. 1991. *The Child and the State in India*. Princeton, NJ: Princeton University Press.

Wolpe, Harold. 1972. "Capitalism and Cheap Labour-Power in South Africa: From Segregation to Apartheid." *Economy and Society*, 1/4.

———. 1988. *Race, Class, and the Apartheid State*. London: James Currey.

World Bank, Development Data Group. 2003. *ICT at a Glance: India*. October 3.

———. 2003a. *ICT at a Glance: South Africa*. October 3.

World Bank, Country Profiles. 2004. *India at a Glance*. Development Economics Central Database, September 15.

———. 2004a. *South Africa at a Glance*. Development Economics Central Database, September 15.

———. 2007. Country Profiles: India. April 23.

World Economic Forum. 2003. *Global Competitiveness Report 2002–2003*.

———. 2003a. *Global Information Technology Report 2002–2003*.

Wright, Erik Olin and Michael Burawoy. 2004. "Taking Seriously the Social in Socialism." Unpublished draft chapter.

Wright, Erik Olin. 2006. "Compass Points: Towards a Socialist Alternative." *New Left Review*, 41 (September and October).

Younis, Mona. 2000. *Liberation and Democratization: The South African and Palestinian National Movements*. Minneapolis: University of Minnesota Press.

Zachariah, Mathew and R. Sooryamoorthy. 1994. *Science in Participatory Development: The Achievements and Dilemmas of a Development Movement: The Case of Kerala*. London: Zed Books.

Zald, Mayer N. and John D. McCarthy, eds. 1987. *Social Movements in an Organizational Society*. New Brunswick and Oxford: Transaction Books.

Zita, Langa. 1993. "Moving beyond the Social Contract." *The African Communist*, 133/2.

Zita, Langa, Dale McKinley, and Vishwas Satgar. 1996. "A Critique of Government's Macro-Economic Strategy: Growth, Employment and Redistribution." *Debate*, 1.

Index